Literature, Criticism, and Style

A Practical Guide to Advanced Level English Literature

Steven Croft and Helen Cross

OXFORD UNIVERSITY PRESS

Oxford University Press, Great Clarendon Street, Oxford OX2 6DP

Oxford   New York
Athens   Auckland   Bangkok   Bogota   Buenos Aires
Calcutta   Cape Town   Chennai   Dar es Salaam
Delhi   Florence   Hong Kong   Istanbul   Karachi
Kuala Lumpur   Madrid   Melbourne
Mexico City   Mumbai   Nairobi   Paris   São Paulo   Singapore
Taipei   Tokyo   Toronto   Warsaw

and associated companies in
Berlin   Ibadan

Oxford is a trademark of Oxford University Press

© Steven Croft and Helen Cross 1997
First published 1997
Reprinted 1997, 1998

ISBN 0 19 831172 9 (School edition)
ISBN 0 19 831443 4 (Bookshop edition)

Printed in Great Britain

Cover image by Gary Thompson
Illustrative montages by Gary Thompson pp. 1, 5, 38, 63, 96, 117, 127, 139,
146, 154, 159, 184, 194, 204, 211, 221, 233, 241, 246, 252; line work heads
by John Dunne pp. 5, 32, 38, 51, 63, 86, 96, 111, 117, 127, 139, 154, 159,
184, 194, 246
Handwriting by Kathy Baxendale pp. 143, 144, 191, 192, 238, 239

Contents

Acknowledgements

• •

The authors and publisher are grateful for permission to reprint the following copyright material:

Peter Ackroyd: extract from *Hawksmoor* (Hamish Hamilton, 1985), Copyright © Peter Ackroyd, 1985, reprinted by permission of Penguin Books Ltd.
Margaret Atwood: extracts from *The Handmaid's Tale* (Cape, 1986), Copyright © 1986 O. W. Toad Limited, reprinted by permission of Curtis Brown and McClelland and Stewart, The Canadian Publishers Inc.
Iain Banks: extract from *The Crow Road* (Abacus, 1995), reprinted by permission of Little Brown.
Max Beerbohm: 'The mote in the middle distance' from *A Christmas Garland* reprinted by permission of Sir Rupert Hart-Davis on behalf of Mrs E. Reichman.
Alison Brackenbury: 'School Dinners' from *Christmas Roses and Other Poems* (1988) reprinted by permission of the publishers, Carcanet Press Ltd.
Ray Bradbury: 'The Pedestrian' from *The Golden Apples of the Sun* (Granada, 1978) reprinted by permission of the Peters Fraser & Dunlop Group Ltd.
Angela Carter: extract from 'The Snow Pavilion' first published in *New Stories 4.* (Hutchinson, 1979), Copyright © Angela Carter 1979, reprinted by permission of the Estate of Angela Carter c/o Rogers, Coleridge & White, 20 Powis Mews, London W11.
Geoffrey Chaucer: extracts from the Riverside edition of *The Complete Works*, Copyright © 1987 by Houghton Mifflin Company.
Wendy Cope: 'Engineers' Corner' from *Making Cocoa for Kingsley Amis* by Wendy Cope (1986), reprinted by permission of the publishers, Faber & Faber Ltd.
Richard Curtis: 'Sons and Aztecs' from *Not 1982* by Richard Curtis, reprinted by permission of The Peters Fraser & Dunlop Group Ltd.
Elizabeth Daryush: 'Anger lay by me all night long' from *Collected Poems* edited by D. Davie (1976), reprinted by permission of the publishers, Carcanet Press Ltd.
Margaret Drabble: extract from 'Hassan's Tower' in *Winter's Tales* (Macmillan, 1966), reprinted by permission of the Peters Fraser & Dunlop Group Ltd.
Gavin Ewart: 'Ending' from *No Fool Like an Old Fool* (Gollancz Poets, 1976), reprinted by permission of Margo Ewart.
U. A. Fanthorpe: 'Waiting Gentlewoman' from *Selected Poems*, Copyright © U. A. Fanthorpe 1986, reprinted by permission of Peterloo Poets.
E. M. Forster: extracts from *A Room with a View* reprinted by permission of King's College, Cambridge, and The Society of Authors as the literary representative of the E. M. Forster Estate.
Brian Friel: extract from *Making History* (1989), reprinted by permission of the publishers, Faber & Faber Ltd.
John Galsworthy: extract from *Strife* reprinted by permission of The Society of Authors as the literary representative of the Estate of John Galsworthy.
Jane Gardam: 'Stone Trees' from *Pangs of Love* by Jane Gardam (Abacus), reprinted by permission of David Higham Associates.
Grahame Greene: 'I Spy' from *Twenty-One Stories* by Grahame Greene (Heinemann, 1954), reprinted by permission of David Higham Associates.
Thomas Hardy: 'The Voice' from *The Complete Poems* (1976) and extract from 'The Tradition of Eighteen Hundred and Four, Christmas 1882' from *Wessex Tales* (1966), reprinted by permission of Papermac, Macmillan Publishers Ltd.
Seamus Heaney: 'Mother of the Groom' from *Wintering Out* by Seamus Heaney reprinted by permission of the publishers, Faber & Faber Ltd.
John Hersey: extract from *Hiroshima* (Hamish Hamilton, 1966, Penguin revised edition, 1968), Copyright © 1966 by John Hersey, Copyright renewed 1973 by John Hersey, Copyright © John Hersey 1985, reprinted by permission of Penguin Books Ltd.

Susan Hill: extracts from 'Missy' and 'Halloran's Child' taken from *A Bit of Singing and Dancing* by Susan Hill (Hamish Hamilton), Copyright © Susan Hill, 1971, 1972, 1973, reprinted by permission of Richard Scott Simon Ltd.
A. E. Housman: 'Eight O'Clock' from *Last Poems* reprinted by permission of The Society of Authors as the literary representative of the Estate of A. E. Housman.
Ted Hughes: 'Wind', 'Swifts', and 'Second Glance at a Jaguar' all from *New Selected Poems 1957–1994*, and extract from *Poetry in the Making* by Ted Hughes, reprinted by permission of the publishers, Faber & Faber Ltd.
Brian Keenan: extract from *An Evil Cradling* (Hutchinson, 1992), reprinted by permission of Brian Keenan, c/o Elaine Steele.
Philip Larkin: 'Naturally the Foundation Will Pay Your Expenses' from *Collected Poems* (1988), reprinted by permission of the publishers, Faber & Faber Ltd.
D. H. Lawrence: extract from *The Rainbow* (Penguin, 1949), reprinted by permission of Laurence Pollinger Ltd and the Estate of Frieda Lawrence Ravagli.
Penelope Lively: extract from *City of the Mind* (Penguin, 1992), Copyright © Penelope Lively 1992, reprinted by permission of Penguin Books Ltd.
Louis Macneice: 'Prayer Before Birth' from *Collected Poems* (Faber & Faber), reprinted by permission of David Higham Associates.
Norman Nicholson: 'To a Child Before Birth' from *Collected Poems* (Faber & Faber), reprinted by permission of David Higham Associates.
John Pilger: extract from 'Video Nasties' in *Distant Voices* by John Pilger (Vintage, 1992), reprinted by permission of David Higham Associates.
Sylvia Plath: 'Frog Autumn' from *Collected Poems* (1981), reprinted by permission of the publishers, Faber & Faber Ltd.
Willy Russell: extract from Educating Rita (Methuen) Copyright © 1985 by Willy Russell, reprinted by permission of Reed Books.
Anthony Trollope: extract from his *Autobiography* (OUP, 1980), reprinted by permission of Oxford University Press.
Elizabeth Walter: extract from 'Dual Control' in *Dead Women and Other Haunting Experiences* by Elizabeth Walter (Collins Harvill, 1975), reprinted by permission of the Harvill Press, London.
Tennessee Williams: extracts from *A Streetcar Named Desire* (New Directions), Copyright © 1947,1953 by Tennessee Williams, renewed 1975, 1981 The University of the South, reprinted by permission of Casarotto Ramsay Ltd on behalf of The University of the South, Sewanee, Tennessee and New Directions Publishing Corp. All rights whatsoever in this play are strictly reserved and application for performance etc. must be made before rehearsal to Casarotto Ramsay Ltd., National House, 60-66 Wardour Street, London W1V 4ND. No performance may be given unless a licence has been obtained.

We are also grateful to the following students for allowing us to use their responses as examples: Suzanne Hobson, Julia Landon, Louise Marshall, James Parkinson, Richard J. Smith and Ian Swainson; and to the following for permission to reproduce material from examination papers and specimen papers: The Associated Examining Board (AEB), Edexcel Foundation, London Examinations (formerly ULEAC), Northern Examinations and Assessment Board (NEAB), University of Cambridge Local Examination Syndicate (UCLES). Any example answers to examination questions or hints on answers used in this book are the sole responsibility of the authors and have not been provided or approved by the examining boards.

We have tried to trace and contact all copyright holders before publication. If notified the publishers will be pleased to rectify any errors or omissions at the earliest opportunity.

Section I
Encountering Literature

1 An Introduction to A-level Literature Study

Reasons for choosing to study English Literature at A-level or AS-level can vary tremendously. Some sixth-form students choose the subject because they have always loved English and want to go on to study it at Higher Education level. Others choose it simply because they enjoyed English at GCSE level and achieved a reasonable result.

However, English is also a popular choice with 'mature' students. Very often the circumstances under which these students study are rather different to those of the school-based student. They might be studying the course over one year by attending an evening class at the local college or they might be attending workshop sessions at a college, or studying at home on a distance learning or correspondence basis.

Whatever your individual circumstances, though, the work that you will need to complete and the demands of assessment will be exactly the same. Obviously, everyone is an individual and one of the great strengths of English is that it encourages and requires the development of that individuality through studies that are stimulating, challenging, and enjoyable. This 'enjoyment' factor should not be dismissed lightly. Of course it does not mean that you will 'like' every text that you read. After all, it is possible to enjoy studying a text purely because of the academic challenges it presents. Enjoyment is important for another reason – students who enjoy their studies tend to be the ones whose motivation is highest and who ultimately achieve the best results.

Your past experience of studying English will probably have shown that it is rather different to other subjects. Unlike most other subjects, English Literature does not consist of a body of knowledge that you can 'learn' in the conventional sense. Instead, you need to develop your own ideas and responses to the texts that you study and to base these responses firmly on evidence that you have gathered from your own readings of these. The development of these informed, independent opinions and judgements will underpin everything that you do in your study of literature at A-level or AS-level.

Reading, talking, and writing

Your studies will involve a good deal of reading with your set texts forming the heart of this. However, the most successful students are those whose reading takes them beyond the texts that they must study. Such students read widely around the texts and the subject, building up a knowledge and understanding of literature that is not restricted simply to set texts. This background reading is the key element in developing an appreciation of literature and often is the difference between those students who achieve the higher grades and those who do not.

Discussion is also an important way in which to develop and test out your ideas about literature. Although your teacher or lecturer will give you guidance, they will not tell you what to think. They will encourage you to weigh various views and interpretations against each other and to formulate your own ideas. Talking to others about your ideas is an important (and enjoyable) way of doing this, so you will probably find yourself involved in a good deal of discussion work, in class, small groups, or with a partner.

If you are studying literature through a distance learning or correspondence course you are at a disadvantage here in not having the same opportunity to exchange ideas with others on a regular basis. It may be a good idea to find yourself a 'mentor' who can help you by talking through the work with you.

As far as 'writing' goes the course will involve writing about a whole variety of texts in many different forms. There will be essays on the set texts, 'unseen' pieces to be tackled, coursework pieces to complete, and notes of different kinds to be made.

Certainly this book will provide a full complement of spoken and written activities and will introduce you to a wide range of texts to help prepare you for your final assessment.

Assessment objectives

At the very core of every A- and AS-level English Literature syllabus are the Assessment Objectives. As they are common to all English Literature syllabuses, it is well worth becoming familiar with them and thinking very carefully about how they will underpin your studies. Here they are:

Candidates should be able to:

- respond with knowledge and understanding to literary texts of different types and periods
- communicate clearly the knowledge, understanding, and insight appropriate to literary study, using appropriate terminology and accurate written expression
- show detailed understanding of the ways in which writers' choices of form, structure, and language shape meanings
- articulate informed, independent opinions and judgements, showing understanding of different interpretations of literary texts by different readers
- show understanding of the contexts in which literary texts are written and understood
- show understanding of the contexts and cultural and historical influences upon literary texts
- explore and comment on relationships and comparisons between literary texts

It is worth noting that although these objectives are common to all Exam Boards, individual Boards are free to add to them if they wish. So do consult the syllabus for your course to ensure that you are clear about its specific objectives. If you are studying a syllabus that has added to these objectives it will not mean that you will have to do extra work. Any additional objectives really just make more explicit the things that all students will be assessed in.

Summary   The work that you do will require you to:
- analyse texts
- explore and express your views on them
- work independently
- take a major responsibility for your learning
- develop informed personal responses to the material you study

Aims of the book

With the Assessment Objectives in mind, *Literature, Criticism, and Style* has been devised to guide you through your A-level course.

Section I introduces the main types of writing that you are likely to study during your course. It offers approaches and strategies for tackling each genre and each unit culminates in a Special Feature, looking at the work of an important writer in that genre.

Section II looks particularly at the skills required in writing about texts. Its aim is to help you write confidently and effectively about set texts and unseens. It also gives insights into how writers themselves draft.

Section III addresses the skills you will need towards the end of your course as you approach the exam. It looks at individual papers as well as how to tackle coursework and revision. The Chronology and Glossary should help to put your study of literature into perspective and to sum up the terms of literary criticism.

Above all we hope that you will enjoy your study of Literature at A-level and that this book will add to that enjoyment and contribute to your success.

2 Poetry

Objectives	• To identify ways in which you can approach the reading of poetry
	• To explore ways of writing about poetry
	• To consider some of the features to look for in analysing poems
	• To prepare for studying set poetry texts
	• To prepare for an 'unseen' examination in poetry

What is poetry?

The question of what exactly poetry is – what marks it out as being different from prose, is a question that poets, writers, philosophers, and critics have, over the centuries, tried to answer. In fact, there are almost as many 'definitions' of poetry as there are poets. Here are some of them:

❝ Poetry is the spontaneous overflow of powerful feelings: it takes its origin from emotion recollected in tranquillity. ❞ *(William Wordsworth)*

❝ Poetry is the sound of human speech at those times when it comes closest to the speech of angels and the speech of animals. ❞ *(John Wain)*

❝ Poetry: the best words in the best order. ❞ *(Samuel Taylor Coleridge)*

❝ Poetry is not a turning loose of emotion, but an escape from emotion; it is not the expression of personality, but an escape from personality. ❞ *(T. S. Eliot)*

You will have noticed how these 'definitions' present quite different views of what poetry actually is. Think about each of these views and what these writers, drawn from different centuries, are saying about the nature of poetry. Through your study of English you will have come into contact with a variety of poetry, perhaps ranging from the works of Chaucer and Shakespeare to those of twentieth-century writers. Are these views borne out by your experiences of poetry so far?

Activity

> 1 Think about your own view of poetry for a moment. Without discussing it with others, write a short paragraph describing what you think poetry is.
> 2 Now compare your view with a partner and discuss how similar, or different, your views are.

Reading poetry

The study of poetry is a central element in all A-level English Literature syllabuses. Whether you are preparing for the 'unseen' paper, studying a poetry set text, or writing on poetry for coursework, all involve the detailed study of various poems. Even though the outcome of your work might be presented in different forms, the skills, techniques, and approaches that you need to use are essentially the same.

It is true that the poetry elements of A-level English Literature present particular challenges. For a number of reasons, some poetry is only fully accessible to us today if we carry out a certain amount of research such as looking up difficult words, phrases, and references. However, 'responding to poetry' cannot be 'taught' (or learned, for that matter) in the same way that some subjects can. It is no good looking for some kind of 'secret formula' that you can apply to any poem. Although most poetry is written to be read by others, and in that sense carries a 'public' voice, it can also be an intensely individual medium of communication and the responses it can evoke can be equally intense and individual. Much poetry works in a very personal way and your response to a particular poem might not be the same as another person's. Words and images carry with them connotations that might trigger different responses in the minds of different people. So while it is often possible to say what a poem 'is about' in general terms, the only really genuine response is that 'personal response' that an individual reader feels.

This does not mean that 'anything goes', of course. For example, comments like 'I haven't a clue about this' or 'This means nothing to me' may be personal responses but they are not much good in terms of a 'literary' response. At A-level you will be required to give what the objectives describe as 'informed, independent opinions and judgements' and to 'respond with knowledge and understanding to literary texts' of various kinds.

In this section we will look at some of the things that you can do to find your way into and through a poem. Here are some general strategies for improving your understanding of poetry.

- Read voraciously – become as familiar as possible with as wide a range of poetry as possible.
- Think about how language is used and make a note of any interesting features, lines, images, etc. that you come across in your reading of poetry.
- Think about the ideas contained in the poems you read.
- Read other people's responses to poetry – not as a substitute for forming your own views but as a 'broadening' influence. (These responses could be found in various study guides, articles in literary journals, or reviews in newspapers or critical works.) They might suggest things that had not occurred to you or they might stimulate your own thoughts if you disagree with their view.
- Read poems aloud – either in company or alone. Very often reading a poem aloud helps deepen understanding and it certainly gives you a greater insight into features such as tone and rhythm.
- Adopt a questioning attitude. Whenever you read a poem ask yourself questions about it. The three key questions to ask are: 'What is this poem about?'; 'How is it written?'; 'Why has the poet chosen to write the poem in this particular way?'
- If you are studying the work of an individual poet, reading their work beyond the set poems will help you to understand the particular poems you are working on.

Activity | Think of other strategies that you could use to help make your study of poetry more effective. It might be helpful to discuss your ideas with a partner and make a list of them.

Having said that there is no set formula that can be applied to poetry to produce the required response, there are certain features of poetry that you will need to be aware of in order to begin to appreciate how a poem 'works', i.e. what the poet does to achieve the desired effect on the reader. Different critical books may refer to them in slightly different terms but basically these are the key elements that combine to create the overall effect of a poem. You will, no doubt, be familiar with some or all of these already.

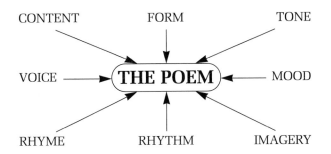

Activity | Consider each of these aspects of poetry. Discuss your ideas in a small group and write brief notes explaining what each means.

Using these aspects of poetry to answer questions on the poems you study is really just a more detailed way of asking those three basic questions that we have already mentioned: 'What is this poem about?'; 'How is it written?'; 'Why has the poet chosen to write it in this particular way?' Answering these three questions will take you to the heart of almost any poem.

However, although we may look at elements such as content, form, and imagery in order to study their particular contributions to a poem, in reality they are completely interrelated and interdependent. The overall effect (and effectiveness) of a poem is dependent on all the individual elements within it working in unity (or acting in discord with one another if that produces the effect that the poet wants).

Content and poetic voice

In simple terms the **content** of a poem is what it is all about – the ideas, themes, and storyline that it contains.

It is useful to begin a consideration of a poem by getting a general outline of what it is about. This is sometimes referred to as the **surface meaning** of the poem. Establishing this surface meaning will give you a framework on which to build the more detailed and complex ideas that form as your analysis of the poem develops. Sometimes it is possible to respond to a poem without fully understanding every word or phrase and sometimes meaning 'evolves' as you continue to study a poem. However, having an initial idea or impression of what a poem is about, can be an important first step towards a fuller and more assured understanding.

When considering the content of a poem it is also important to identify the **poetic voice** of the poem. In other words decide who the 'speaker' of the poem is. In many cases the poetic voice may well be the poet's, but it may be that the words of the poem are 'spoken' through a character that the poet has created or a narrator figure other than the poet. This happens in *The Canterbury Tales*, where usually a particular character is telling the tale. Chaucer (the writer) often then interrupts his character (his fictitious narrator) to address the reader.

Identifying the 'speaker' also helps to determine a number of other aspects of the poem such as tone, mood, and the overall intention behind the poem. The poetic voice could be the poet's genuine voice expressing a heartfelt emotion or it could be the voice of a narrator expressing a view or feeling that the poet may or may not share.

Activity Now have a look at this poem by Philip Larkin. How does an awareness of the poetic voice here help you form an impression of what the poet is saying?

Naturally the Foundation Will Pay Your Expenses *title, expectations*

tone →

Hurrying to catch my Comet *Plane*
  One dark November day, *feeling/sense*
Which soon would snatch me from it *metaphorical language*
  To the sunshine of Bombay,
I pondered pages Berkeley *US*
  Not three weeks since had heard,
Perceiving Chatto darkly
  Through the mirror of the Third.

condescending Crowds, colourless and careworn,
  Had made my taxi late,
Yet not till I was airborne
  Did I recall the date –
That day when Queen and Minister
  And Band of Guards and all *Oxymoron*
Still act their solemn-sinister *Remembrance Day 11th Nov.*
  Wreath-rubbish in Whitehall. *War Dead*

It used to make me throw up,
  These mawkish nursery games: *contradictory*
O when will England grow up? *Personification.*
  – But I outsoar the Thames,
And dwindle off down Auster
  To greet Professor Lal
(He once met Morgan Forster),
  My contact and my pal.

Philip Larkin

Naturally the Foundation Will Pay Your Expenses is written in the first person and so the 'voice' could be that of the poet himself speaking. However, to appreciate Larkin's intentions here it is necessary to recognize that the 'speaker' of the poem is a narrator figure. The views that he expresses are not necessarily those of Larkin himself. In fact, the 'speaker' here is an English academic who jets around the world giving his paper to major universities. Larkin is present here too but his attitudes and ideas lie behind the words spoken by his character. He satirizes his character in order to cast a critical light on the persona he has created and the views that are expressed through him.

Activity

> **1** Now read the following poems through carefully.
> **2** Before you discuss your ideas with anyone write down your first thoughts on what each poem is about and on the poetic voice which each presents. Spend about ten minutes setting your ideas down.
> **3** Now join two or three other students in a small group. Each read their notes out to the others as a starting point for discussion on the content and poetic voice of the poems.
> **4** Review your notes and make any changes or additions that you wish in the light of the discussion. Do you find any aspect of these poems difficult to explain? If so, can you say why?

Mother of the Groom

What she remembers
Is his glistening back
In the bath, his small boots
In the ring of boots at her feet.

Hands in her voided lap,
She hears a daughter welcomed.
It's as if he kicked when lifted
And slipped her soapy hold.

Once soap would ease off
The wedding ring
That's bedded forever now
In her clapping hand.

Seamus Heaney

School Dinners

Why do I dream now, of people from school?
I am not old. They are not dead.
Yet warm before waking they surface, thin,
or in Janice's case, still fat.
                              She dyed her hair
in red rat's tails; thought brash. She hitched her skirt,
her wide thighs wobbled. She was kind as silk.
One day, chattering, tipped salad cream
over her favourite pudding;
                              did remember
to ask the boy's address, but found it false.
They left the seaside camp. She had a daughter,

who now, I think, must be the age
of Janice in my dream; when giggling still
she reached out for the cheap gold-coloured jug.

Eight people made that table. Who do I still know?
No one who could tell me how she lives,
cooking great Sunday dinners? married? happy?
My ignorance stays perfect as the moon
dropped, like a coin through a barley field,
drowned, in all the blue waste of the sky.

Sitting by my daughter in a car
borne smooth and cool, through tunnelled trees
it strikes me, quick as shivering, that when
they must end, yet I will see them there
small and clear, in the battered jug,
their mistakes; their tails of red hair.

Alison Brackenbury

Tone and mood

The effect that a poem has on the reader is very closely determined by the tone and mood that it creates. As we have already discussed, a poem contains a 'voice' and like any voice it can project a certain **tone** that gives the listener (or reader) certain messages. Obviously there are many different kinds of tone. The tone might be angry or reflective, melancholy or joyful, bitter or ironic. Just as the tone of voice in which someone speaks tells us a great deal about the way they feel, so the tone of the 'poetic voice' tells us a great deal about how the poet or the narrator of the poem feels.

The **mood**, on the other hand, although very closely connected with the tone, is not quite the same thing. When we refer to the mood of a poem we are really talking about the **atmosphere** that the poem creates. Very often tone and mood in a poem are closely linked and a certain tone produces a certain mood. For example, if the poet uses a melancholy tone it is unlikely that the mood of the poem will be bright and lively. Sometimes, though, the poet may quite deliberately use a tone that does not match the mood the poem creates in order to achieve a particular effect – underlining a certain irony, for example. The overall impact of a poem stems not only from the literal meaning of the words but from the tone and mood that they create. One of the most effective ways of recognizing the tone of a poem is to hear the poem read aloud.

Try reading poems out loud for yourself, experimenting with different ways of reading each particular poem. The more practice you get at reading poems aloud and the more you are able to hear others read them, the better able you will be 'hear' poems in your mind when you read them to yourself. The tone of a poem can be communicated to the reader or listener in many ways and it is through being sensitive to the poet's tone that we can begin to understand the intention that lies behind the words.

Here are three well-known poems for you to consider.

Upon Westminster Bridge,

Sept. 3, 1802
Earth has not anything to show more fair:
Dull would he be of soul who could pass by
A sight so touching in its majesty:
This City now doth, like a garment, wear
The beauty of the morning: silent, bare,
Ships, towers, domes, theatres, and temples lie
Open unto the fields, and to the sky;
All bright and glittering in the smokeless air.
Never did sun more beautifully steep
In his first splendour, valley, rock or hill;
Ne'er saw I, never felt, a calm so deep!
The river glideth at his own sweet will:
Dear God! the very houses seem asleep;
And all that mighty heart is lying still!

William Wordsworth

Engineers' Corner

Why isn't there an Engineers' Corner in Westminster
Abbey? In Britain we've always made more fuss of a
ballad than a blueprint... How many schoolchildren
dream of becoming great engineers?
Advertisement placed in *The Times* by the Engineering Council.

We make more fuss of ballads than of blueprints –
That's why so many poets end up rich,
While engineers scrape by in cheerless garrets.
Who needs a bridge or dam? Who needs a ditch?

Whereas the person who can write a sonnet
Has got it made. It's always been the way,
For everybody knows that we need poems
And everybody reads them every day.

Yes, life is hard if you choose engineering –
You're sure to need another job as well;
You'll have to plan your projects in the evenings
Instead of going out. It must be hell.

While well-heeled poets ride around in Daimlers,
You'll burn the midnight oil to earn a crust,
With no hope of a statue in the Abbey,
With no hope, even, of a modest bust.

No wonder small boys dream of writing couplets
And spurn the bike, the lorry and the train.
There's far too much encouragement for poets –
That's why this country's going down the drain.

Wendy Cope

Frog Autumn

Summer grows old, cold-blooded mother.
The insects are scant, skinny.
In these palustral homes we only
Croak and wither.

Mornings dissipate in somnolence.
The sun brightens tardily
Among the pithless reeds. Flies fail us.
The fen sickens.

Frost drops even the spider. Clearly
The genius of plenitude
Houses himself elsewhere. Our folk thin
Lamentably.

Sylvia Plath

Activity

> 1 Read each of the poems through to yourself, deciding what sort of tone of voice you would use for each.
> 2 In a small group, take turns to read each poem out loud. If possible, use a cassette recorder to tape these readings.
> 3 Discuss the readings and make brief notes on the kind of tone that you think is most appropriate for each poem. Describe the kind of mood that is created in each.
> 4 Discuss the methods used by these poets to create a specific tone and mood.

Summary

Here are some ideas of how tone and mood can be created:
- through the loudness or softness of the voice speaking the poem
- through the rhythm that is created
- through the poet's choice of words
- through the emphasis placed on particular words or phrases
- through the breaks and pauses that the poet places in the poem (often the things which go unsaid can tell you a great deal)

Imagery

Essentially the true 'meaning' of a poem lies in the total effect that it has upon the reader. Very often that effect will stimulate a response which is not just a reaction to what the poet has to say, but which draws on the reader's own intellectual and emotional experience. Imagery can be of central importance in creating this response within the reader.

The concept of imagery is a very simple one and although it is used a good deal in poetic writing it is of course found in other kinds of writing too. An **image** is language used in such a way as to help us to see, hear, taste, feel, think about or generally understand more clearly or vividly what is being said or the impression that the writer wishes to convey.

Images can work in several ways in the mind of the reader. On a simple level an image can be used literally to describe something. For example, in *Upon Westminster Bridge* (see page 12) the lines '...silent, bare/Ships, towers, domes, theatres, and temples lie/Open unto the fields, and to the sky;/All bright and glittering in the smokeless air' create a **literal image** in our minds of the scene that Wordsworth wishes to convey.

Often, though, images are **non-literal** or **figurative**: the thing being described is compared to something else with which it has something in common to make the description more vivid to the reader. You will, no doubt, already be familiar with images, such as similes and metaphors, which work in this way. However, just in case you need it, here is a reminder of the difference between the two, along with a definition of personification.

The simile

Similes are easy to spot because they make the comparison quite clear often by using the words 'as' or 'like'. For example, looking back at *Upon Westminster Bridge* once more the lines 'This City now doth, like a garment, wear/The beauty of the morning...' simply but effectively convey a sense of the beauty of the scene which 'clothes' the city but which also serves to conceal the less attractive aspects of the city which lie beneath the 'garment'.

The metaphor

In some ways a metaphor is like a simile in that it too creates a comparison. However, it is less direct than the simile in that it does not use 'as' or 'like' to create the comparison. Often the metaphor actually describes the subject as *being* the thing to which it is compared. For example, Wordsworth concludes *Upon Westminster Bridge* with the line, 'And all that mighty heart is lying still!'. Literally, of course, the city is not a heart, but metaphorically-speaking it can be seen as the 'heart' of the country, the capital city, and the centre of government.

Personification

Personification occurs when poets attribute an inanimate object or abstract idea with human qualities or actions. For example, in *Upon Westminster Bridge*, Wordsworth speaks of the river as if it were alive – 'The river glideth at his own sweet will'.

Aural imagery

Some kinds of images rely not upon the 'pictures' that they create in the mind of the reader but on the effect that they have on the ear, or a combination of both.

Alliteration involves the repetition of the same consonant sound, usually at the beginning of each word, over several words together. Larkin uses this technique in *Naturally the Foundation Will Pay Your Expenses* (see page 9), for example. It can be seen in phrases such as 'I pondered pages... Crowds, colourless and careworn... Still act their solemn-sinister...' and much of its impact lies in the effect that the repetition of the sounds creates on the reader's ear as well as the mind's eye.

Another kind of aural device is **assonance**. This involves the repetition of a vowel sound to achieve a particular kind of effect. The long, drawn out 'o' sounds created in the first line of *Frog Autumn* (see page 13), 'Summer grows old, cold-blooded mother' creates an impression of lethargy and lack of vitality as summer passes and winter approaches.

A third aural device is that of **onomatopoeia**. This refers to words that by their sound reflect their meaning. On a simple level words like 'bang' or 'thud' actually sound like the noises they describe.

It must be stressed, however, that the important thing is not so much to be able to spot the different kinds of images that might be present in a poem but to understand why the poet has used a particular image and be able to see how it works in the mind of the reader. Being able to say 'the poet uses alliteration in stanza three' is of no value in terms of the critical appreciation of a poem, but being able to show what the alliteration contributes to the overall effect of the poem is valuable.

For more on these individual forms of imagery see the Glossary, page 256.

Activity

1 Read the poem on page 16 and list five or six images that Hughes uses. Make brief notes on what these images mean to you, what they make you think about or anything that you find striking about them.
2 Join with two or three other students and compare your ideas. Decide together the meaning of the key images and their effects in the poem.
3 Write a short essay (about two pages in length) outlining your own thoughts and responses to the poet's use of imagery here.

Wind

[personification] This house has been far out at sea all night,
[onom] The woods crashing through darkness, the booming hills, *[sound]*
[power] Winds stampeding the fields under the window
[powerless] Floundering black astride and blinding wet

Till day rose; then under an orange sky
The hills had new places, and wind wielded
Blade-light, luminous black and emerald, *[colour]*
[crazy] Flexing like the lens of a mad eye.

[powerless] At noon I scaled along the house-side as far as
The coal-house door. Once I looked up –
Through the brunt wind that dented the balls of my eyes
[force] —The tent of the hills drummed and strained its guyrope,

The fields quivering, the skyline a grimace, *[weak]*
At any second to bang and vanish with a flap:
The wind flung a magpie away and a black-
Back gull bent like an iron bar slowly. The house

Rang like some fine green goblet in the note
That any second would shatter it. Now deep
In chairs, in front of the great fire, we grip
Our hearts and cannot entertain book, thought, *[fear]*

Or each other. We watch the fire blazing,
And feel the roots of the house move, but sit on,
Seeing the window tremble to come in, *[overpowering, frightening]*
Hearing the stones cry out under the horizons.

Ted Hughes

Rhyme

Rhyme can make an important contribution to the 'musical quality' of a poem and like rhythm it affects the sound and the overall impact of the piece. The system of rhyme within a poem, or **rhyme scheme**, can influence this effect in a variety of ways. It might act as a unifying influence and draw a poem together, or it could give a poem an incantatory quality or add emphasis to particular elements of the vocabulary (or diction). There are various kinds of rhymes and rhyme schemes and although most rhymes work on the basis of the rhyme occurring at the end of a line, some occur within the line. These are called **internal rhymes**.

In the same way that rhythm in a poem often follows a recognized pattern, so does rhyme. Working out the rhyme scheme is quite a straightforward business and is done by indicating lines that rhyme together through giving them the same letter of the alphabet. As an example, read the short poem that follows on page 17.

Eight O'Clock

He stood, and heard the steeple	a
Sprinkle the quarters on the morning town.	b
One, two, three, four, to market-place and people	a
It tossed them down.	b
Strapped, noosed, nighing his hour,	c
He stood and counted them and cursed his luck;	d
And then the clock collected in the tower	c
Its strength, and struck.	d

A. E. Housman

Housman uses an abab, cdcd rhyme scheme, i.e. alternate lines rhyme within stanzas. Let us now consider some examples of traditional forms and patterns. Pairs of lines that rhyme are called **couplets** or **rhyming couplets**. Two lines that rhyme together and that are written in iambic pentameter (see page 20) are known as **heroic couplets**. Sometimes a whole poem can consist entirely of rhyming couplets or the couplet can be used as part of a larger rhyme scheme. A Shakespearian sonnet uses the couplet to draw the poem to an end, as in Shakespeare's *Sonnet XVIII*, for example:

So long as man can breathe or eyes can see,
So long lives this, and this gives life to thee.

Rhyming couplets tend to create a bold, assertive effect and strongly convey a point or message. They can also be used for comic effect, to deflate an argument or character.

The **quatrain** is a set of four rhyming lines. Usual rhyme schemes are abab, abcb, aaaa, or abba. In *Jerusalem*, Blake uses the abcb scheme –

And did those feet in ancient time
Walk upon England's mountains green?
And was the holy Lamb of God
On England's pleasant pastures seen?

The quatrain is a flexible form that is used to create many effects but often, as here, it produces a sense of unity within compact and regular stanzas.

A **sestet** is a six-line stanza that can be arranged in a number of ways. The last six lines of an Italian sonnet (see page 25) are also called the sestet. In '*The lowest trees have tops, the ant her gall*', Dyer uses a regular ababcc rhyme scheme:

The lowest trees have tops, the ant her gall,
The fly her spleen, the little spark his heat;
The slender hairs cast shadows, though but small,
And bees have stings, although they be not great;
Seas have their source, and so have shallow springs:
And love is love, in beggars and in kings.

The **octave** is an eight-line stanza and can be constructed in a number of ways. It can be formed by linking two quatrains together or it can have a rhyme scheme that integrates all eight lines. It is also the name given to the first eight lines of an Italian sonnet.

As with all the elements of a poem though, the important thing is not to be able to spot the use of rhymes or even to work out the rhyme scheme but to ask yourself: 'Why has the poet used rhyme in this way and what does it contribute, together with all the other features, to the overall impact of the poem?'. The answer to this question is what really matters.

Summary

Here are some effects that rhyme might have on a poem.
- It can make a poem sound pleasing to the ear and perhaps add a musical quality. Conversely, it can create a jarring effect.
- It could serve to emphasize certain words – very often the words that rhyme are given a certain prominence.
- It can act as a kind of unifying influence on the poem, drawing lines and stanzas together through the pattern it imposes on them.
- It can give a poem an incantatory or 'ritualistic' feel.
- It can influence the rhythm of the verse.
- It can give a sense of finality – the rhyming couplet is often used to give a sense of 'ending'.
- It can exert a subconscious effect on the reader, drawing together certain words or images, affecting the sound, or adding emphasis in some way.

Activity

1 Read this poem carefully to yourself and write down your initial ideas on how the poet uses rhyme and with what effect.
2 In a small group, compare your ideas. Discuss how you think the use of rhyme affects the poem and what it contributes to its overall impact.

Ending

The love we thought would never stop
now cools like a congealing chop.
The kisses that were hot as curry
are bird-pecks taken in a hurry.
The hands that held electric charges
now lie inert as four moored barges.
The feet that ran to meet a date
are running slow and running late.
The eyes that shone and seldom shut
are victims of a power cut.
The parts that then transmitted joy
are now reserved and cold and coy.
Romance, expected once to stay,
has left a note saying GONE AWAY.

Gavin Ewart

Rhythm

When you were thinking about definitions of poetry at the beginning of this unit you might well have thought about rhythm as being one of the features that can set poetry apart from other kinds of writing. Although it is by no means true of all poems, one of the basic differences between a poem and a piece of prose is that a poem can contain some form of regular beat or rhythm.

Often this sense of rhythm can exert a profound influence on the overall effect of the poem giving it its feeling of 'movement' and life. The poet can use rhythm to create many different effects or to emphasize a certain aspect or idea in the poem. Very often it is also an important contributing factor to the mood or atmosphere and to what is sometimes referred to as the 'musical quality' of a poem. Music can be gentle and flowing, harsh or discordant, stilted and uneven in phrasing, or regular in tempo. It can have a rhythm that reflects a serious or solemn mood or a rhythm that suggests the comic or absurd. Just the same is true about the rhythms of poetry.

Here are some examples of the ways in which poets use language to create varying rhythms.

Syllable stress   Language possesses natural rhythms which are built into it and which we use automatically every time we pronounce words. For example, if we think of a word like 'delicately' it comes quite naturally to us to stress the first syllable and not the second. Not to do so would be to mispronounce the word. Poets often use these natural rhythms within words to help contribute to the overall rhythmic effect.

Emphatic stress   Poets sometimes choose to place emphasis on a particular word or phrase in order to achieve a particular result. The stress might be shifted to reinforce a particular tone or sometimes to affect the meaning. For example, think about Wordsworth's famous line 'I wandered lonely as a cloud' and how different emphases can change the overall effect:

'*I* wandered lonely as a cloud' ,   'I *wandered* lonely as a cloud',
'I wandered *lonely* as a cloud',   'I wandered lonely as a *cloud*'
and so on. The natural rhythm will often tell you what is right.

Phrasing and punctuation   The rhythm of a poem (or any other piece of writing) can be influenced by factors such as word order and length of phrases or sentences and these in turn can be influenced by the choice of punctuation marks, line and stanza breaks, and use of repetitions.

Metre   Technically speaking the whole notion of rhythm in poetry is closely tied up with the idea of metre. This concept originated from the principles of Classical Greek and Latin verse and was adopted by English poets from early times. Such principles stated that a line of verse should follow a precise and regular pattern in terms of the number of syllables it contained and the stress pattern that it used. This pattern was then repeated throughout the poem. Regular patterns of these stressed and unstressed syllables are called **metres** (see also syllable stress, above).

On a basic level the pattern created by a regular metre can be seen in nursery rhymes and limericks. For example, each stanza of *Mary Had a Little Lamb* follows this pattern:

Mary had a little lamb,
Its fleece was white as snow.
And everywhere that Mary went
The lamb was sure to go.

In identifying the metre of a poem the first thing to do is to establish how the rhythm pattern is made up. To help do this the syllables are divided up into groups of two or three (depending on the particular pattern) and each of these groups is called a **foot**. The number of **feet** in a line can vary. Here are the main patterns:

one foot — monometer   five feet — pentameter
two feet — dimeter   six feet — hexameter
three feet — trimeter   seven feet — heptameter
four feet — tetrameter   eight feet — octameter

The process of identifying the metre is called **scansion**. In scansion a $'$ or a — above a word indicates a stressed syllable while a $\smile$ is used to denote an unstressed syllable and feet are divided up using vertical lines $|$. (A double vertical line $\|$ indicates **caesura** which simply means a brief pause in the middle of a line of poetry.) For example, look at these lines by Keats:

When I | have fears | that I | may cease | to be
Before | my pen | hath gleaned | my teem | ing brain,

Each line consists of five metrical feet. Each foot consists of an unstressed and a stressed syllable. A foot that is made up in this way ($\smile'$) is called an **iambic foot (iamb)** and a line that is made up of five feet is called a **pentameter**. These lines, therefore are written using a metrical form called **iambic pentameter**.

If you were to look at the whole of this poem you would find that Keats also uses a rhyme scheme. Verse which is written in iambic pentameter and which does not use a rhyme scheme is called **blank verse**. This is one of the most frequently used forms in English poetry and it has been estimated that three-quarters of all English verse is written in blank verse. One of its attractions is that it is a metrical form that very closely follows the patterns of natural speech and for this reason was used as the staple form by dramatists such as Shakespeare as well as by poets such as Milton and Wordsworth. It also can capture a reflective, thoughtful mood. The following example (on page 21) shows Wordsworth's use of the form as he describes skating on the frozen lake as a boy.

The Prelude

Book 1 (1850)
And in the frosty season, when the sun
Was set, and visible for many a mile
The cottage windows blazed through twilight gloom,
I heeded not their summons: happy time
It was indeed for all of us – for me
It was a time of rapture! Clear and loud
The village clock tolled six, – I wheeled about,
Proud and exulting like an untired horse
That cares not for his home. All shod with steel,
We hissed along the polished ice in games
Confederate, imitative of the chase
And woodland pleasures, – the resounding horn,
The pack loud chiming, and the hunted hare.
So through the darkness and the cold we flew,
And not a voice was idle; with the din,
Smitten, the precipices rang aloud;
The leafless trees and every icy crag
Tinkled like iron; while far distant hills
Into the tumult sent an alien sound
Of melancholy not unnoticed, while the stars
Eastward were sparkling clear, and in the west
The orange sky of evening died away.

William Wordsworth

Although the iambic foot is the most common form there are other syllable patterns which poets use to create different effects. For example, the **trochaic foot (trochee)** consists of a stressed syllable followed by an unstressed one ($^{/\smile}$). A well-known poem which makes use of the trochaic foot (trochee) is Blake's *The Tyger*.

Tyger! | Tyger! | burning | bright
In the | forests | of the | night.

One of the effects of the trochaic metre is that the stressed first syllable adds emphasis and power to the words.

The **dactylic foot (dactyl)** consists of a stressed syllable followed by two unstressed ones ($^{/\smile\smile}$) as in Tennyson's *The Charge of the Light Brigade*.

Half a league, | half a league,
Half a league | onward

The dactylic metre reflects the rhythm of the horse at gallop giving a kind of 'drumming of hooves' feel to the poem. With its two unstressed syllables following the stressed one, this metre can also be used to create a sad, reflective, sometimes heavy mood.

The **anapaestic foot (anapaest)** consists of two unstressed syllables followed by a stressed one ($\breve{}\breve{}/$) while the **spondaic foot (spondee)** simply has two stressed syllables ($//$). Hardy uses both in his poem *A Wife Waits*.

$$\text{Will's} \mid \text{at the dance} \mid \text{in the Club} \mid \text{-room below,}$$
$$\text{Where} \mid \text{the tall liqu} \mid \text{or cups foam;}$$
$$\text{I} \mid \text{on the pave} \mid \text{ment up here} \mid \text{by the Bow,}$$
$$\text{Wait, wait,} \mid \text{to} \mid \text{steady} \mid \text{him home.}$$

The anapaests here create a sense of movement, and perhaps underlying tension, reflecting the wayward husband's revelry whereas the spondee, at the beginning of the final line, gives a sense of the wife's patience and resignation as she waits to help her drunken husband home. Note how the reversal of the rhythm pattern at the end reflects the husband's return.

Twentieth-century poets have tended to move away from strict metrical forms but metre can still be an important element in modern poetry. By its nature though, metre is a mechanical and repetitive device which often is at variance with the natural rhythms that a poem may contain. Few poets stick religiously to the metrical pattern that they adopt and poetry should always be read according to the natural rhythms of the language rather than its metrical plan.

Remember when you are writing about a poem that identifying its metrical pattern is of little value in itself. You will gain little reward in an exam for simply mentioning the metre of a poem. The key thing is that you are able to say what it contributes to the effect of the poem overall. Do not worry if you cannot remember the technical terms – the main thing is that you are able to describe what is happening. Technical terms are a kind of shorthand way of doing this but they are by no means essential. What matters is your understanding of how the poem works as a piece of writing.

Activity | Read through this poem by Hardy several times. Try to get a feel of the rhythm pattern. You could try tapping it out if it helps. Attempt to describe the kind of rhythm pattern that Hardy uses. What kind of 'feel' do you think it gives to the poem? Write a short description of the effect that both rhyme and rhythm create in *The Voice*.

The Voice

Woman much missed, how you call to me, call to me,
Saying that now you are not as you were
When you had changed from the one who was all to me,
But as at first, when our day was fair.

Can it be you that I hear? Let me view you, then,
Standing as when I drew near to the town
Where you would wait for me: yes, as I knew you then,
Even to the original air-blue gown!

Or is it only the breeze, in its listlessness
Travelling across the wet mead to me here,
You being ever dissolved to wan wistlessness,
Heard no more again far or near?

    Thus I; faltering forward,
    Leaves around me falling,
Wind oozing thin through the thorn from the norward
    And the woman calling.

Thomas Hardy

The Voice is one of a number of poems that Hardy wrote soon after the death of his wife, Emma. His feelings of loss were intensified by the fact that in the later years of their marriage they had grown apart. Here he remembers the love that they shared in their younger days. The poem begins with a regular rhythm created through a repetition of dactyls:

Woman much | missed, how you | call to me, | call to me,
Saying that | now you are | not as you | were
When you had | changed from the | one who was | all to me,

The dactyls help to create a mood of sad reflection and the repetition of:

call to me, | call to me

introduces a slightly haunting feel, suggestive of a calling voice being carried on the wind. The rhyming of 'call to me' with 'all to me' creates a link between the imagined caller and the poet and emphasizes how much he misses her now. Similarly, the rhyme of the second and fourth lines of the stanza emphasizes the contrast between the poet's present pain and the happiness the couple enjoyed in years past – 'you are not as you were/when our day was fair'.

The second stanza echoes the rhythm of the first in its repetition of dactyls:

Can it be | you that I | hear? ‖ Let me | view you, then,

and the sense of the poet's uncertainty is increased through his questioning and the caesura in the line. In stanza three again we have the repetition of the dactyls and the questioning continues as the poet wonders whether he really hears the voice of his loved one or if it is simply a trick of the wind:

Or is it | only the | breeze, in its | listlessness

Again we have the echoing rhyme, this time of 'listlessness'/'wistlessness'.

In the final stanza, however, the regular pattern the poet has established is broken. The caesura of 'Thus I; ‖ faltering forward' creates a halting, stumbling feel to the line reflecting the breakdown in the poet as his grief overwhelms him. The trochees of 'faltering forward' and 'falling' dominate the stanza and underline the sense of pain and despair that the poet feels – a pain that is made almost tangible through the image:

Wind oozing | thin through the | thorn from the | norward

There is a partial return of the dactyls here but, as the final dactyl trails away unfinished, they are dominated by the emphatic stress of the trochees in the last words of each line of this stanza. The final line itself echoes the opening line of the poem but now the dactyls have been replaced by the more emphatic trochees as the poet is left with the haunting voice in his mind:

And the | woman | calling.

We are left with the two words 'falling/calling' which create a striking effect through a combination of the rhyme and the trochaic metre and encapsulate the poet's experience here.

This poem clearly illustrates the contribution that rhythm can make to the overall effect of the poem but its importance, as here, cannot be appreciated in isolation. Its use is inextricably bound up with the language of the poem and the ideas that the poet wants to express.

Form

There are many different ways in which poems can be structured. One thing is certain though. A poet does not simply choose a certain form at random. It will have been carefully chosen and will have a direct bearing on what the poet hopes to achieve through the poem. In considering the form of a particular poem, therefore, we are back to that central question – why? In this case 'Why has the poet chosen to use this particular form?'

Form can refer to the way that the poem is actually written down on the page or to the way that the lines are organized, grouped, or structured. (This is sometimes called **poetic form**.) In terms of its structure, poetry can be divided into two categories. First, there is the kind of poetry where the lines follow on one from another continuously without breaks, such as in Wordsworth's *The Prelude*, Milton's *Paradise Lost* or Keats' *Endymion*. The technical term for this is **stichic poetry**, but do not worry too much about the technical terms; the important thing is to be able to recognize that poems differ in the way that they are put together.

Secondly, there is the kind of poetry where the lines are arranged in groups which are sometimes called verses but are more correctly referred to as **stanzas**. This is called **strophic poetry**. Keats uses this form in *The Eve of St. Agnes*, as does Blake in *The Tyger*, Heaney in *Mid-Term Break*, and Hughes in *Crow*, for example.

There are many different kinds of stanza, with variations depending on the number of lines they contain. (See section on Rhyme, page 16 and Glossary, page 256 for further descriptions.)

The Sonnet

The Sonnet is a very popular form in English poetry and it is one that you are likely come across in your studies. In basic terms a sonnet is a fourteen-line poem and the lines are usually arranged in one of two ways. First, there is the **Petrarchan** or **Italian Sonnet** (so called simply because it is named after the Medieval Italian writer, Petrarch). This kind of sonnet is arranged with a first part that consists of eight lines (the octave) and a second and concluding part of six lines (the sestet). There can be variations in the rhyme scheme but generally it follows the pattern *abbaabba cdecde*. If you look back at Wordsworth's *Upon Westminster Bridge* (see page 12) you will see that it follows this pattern.

The other form is the **Shakespearian** or **English Sonnet**. The rhyme scheme of this divides up into three quatrains and a concluding couplet. The rhyme scheme in this kind of sonnet usually follows the *abab cdcd efef gg* pattern.

Free Verse

Although forms which adhere to a strict pattern are still frequently used by poets in the Twentieth Century, there has been a trend towards poetry that does not have the constraints of metre or rhyme upon it and Free Verse has become predominant. This form of verse often does not have lines that are equal in length or that have a regular metre and often it does not rhyme. To a large extent this flexibility allows poets the freedom to create forms to suit their own purposes and create the effects that they want in their writing.

Certain forms of poetry have been used to express themes which can be broadly grouped together. (This is sometimes called **thematic form**.) For example, the Ode, the Ballad, the Elegy, the Aubade, the Pastoral, the Lyric, the Epic, and the Song all refer to particular kinds of poetry that have a broad thematic link in common. (See Glossary for more information on specific forms, page 256.)

Obviously the 'form' of a poem in terms of its physical structure is inseparably linked to the idea of its thematic 'form'. In turn, the whole concept of form is interlinked with other features such as rhyme, rhythm, and the poet's overall intention. What is important is that you are able to suggest reasons why a poet has chosen a particular form and comment on how it contributes, along with all these other features, in creating the poem's overall effect.

Handling 'difficult' poetry

It is, of course, far too simplistic to think in terms of 'easy' poetry and 'hard' poetry. Like some of the poems in this unit, poetry can often be 'easy to read' but, in fact, deal with complex themes and ideas that need careful thought. However, in the course of your A-level study, you might come across poetry that presents you with rather different problems.

These problems can arise for a number of reasons but here are some of the most common.

- You could encounter a problem of vocabulary – it may be that the poet uses difficult words that you do not understand or that the poem was written in a different age and so aspects of the language have changed.
- The poem could be concerned with concepts, ideas, or themes completely outside your sphere of experience.
- The poem might contain references that are difficult or obscure in some way, e.g. references based on classical mythology.
- It might use imagery that is difficult to decipher.
- The style in which the poem is written could be complex and you might need to do some detective work to unravel its meaning.

Some of these problems may be particularly apparent when studying poetry that was written in a different age to our own. Perhaps the most extreme example of this that you might encounter in A-level study would be in the study of the works of Chaucer who we will look at later in the Special Feature. However, the works of writers such as Shakespeare (see Special Feature in Unit 3, page 51) and Milton can also lead to feelings of apprehension.

So let us look at some examples of Milton's poetry and think about the kind of things you can do to help yourself when tackling such writers as this.

Milton lived and wrote in the Seventeenth Century, eventually siding with the Puritans during the English Civil War. He became their 'Secretary for the Foreign Tongues', translating political documents. He was also a leading author of the Puritan pamphlets which were issued to try to justify Cromwell's reign and the execution of Charles I.

Although he wrote poetry throughout his life, producing various works including *L'Allegro* (1632), *Il Penseroso* (1632), *Comus* (1634), and *Lycidas* (1637), it was in the latter part of his life that his great long, or 'epic', poems were written. These are the ones you are most likely to find set for study at A-level. *Paradise Lost* (1667) and *Samson Agonistes* (1671), in particular, frequently appear on A-level syllabuses.

Paradise Lost concerns itself with the Fall of Adam and Eve and was originally published in ten books although later it was issued in twelve books – the traditional number for an 'epic'. When set for A-level two books are usually specified for study. Here is an extract from *Book IX* where Satan, in the form of the serpent, seeks his prey, Eve, and finds her gardening. Read it through carefully.

Paradise Lost

Book IX
Nearer he drew, and many a walk traversed
Of stateliest covert, cedar, pine, or palm;
Then voluble and bold, now hid, now seen,
Among thick-woven arborets, and flowers

Imbordered on each bank, the hand of Eve:
Spot more delicious than those gardens feigned
Or of revived Adonis, or renowned
Alcinous, host of old Laertes' son,
Or that, not mystic, where the sapient king
Held dalliance with his fair Egyptian spouse.
Much he the place admired, the person more.
As one who, long in populous city pent,
Where houses thick and sewers annoy the air,
Forth issuing on a summer's morn to breathe
Among the pleasant villages and farms
Adjoined, from each thing met conceives delight –
The smell of grain, or tedded grass, or kine,
Or dairy, each rural sight, each rural sound;

Milton

Activity

> **1** Write a brief summary of what Milton is saying here. (Limit this to a maximum of 45 words.)
> **2** What immediate problems, if any, did you encounter in terms of understanding the detail of this passage?

Summary

You may find that the following cause you some problems.
- Some of Milton's vocabulary consists of words that are unfamiliar to you – words like 'arborets', 'sapient', 'dalliance' or 'tedded'.
- Milton mentions characters that you have not heard of before – 'Alcinous' or 'old Laertes', for example.
- The word order is sometimes different to that which you are used to.
- The passage consists mainly of description with very little action.

Obviously, one of the problems in reading and understanding poetry that was written possibly hundreds of years ago is that the language we use today is not quite the same as the language that was used then. Words may have changed in meaning, hold different connotations, or may simply have been outmoded.

The second problem here is that the references or allusions used would have been understood and have held some significance to a reader in the poet's own age but often mean little to us today. These are not difficulties confined to poetry written a long time ago (a reading of T. S. Eliot's *The Wasteland* will convince you of that) but the chances of encountering them are probably greater the older the poetry is. However, good editions usually contain notes and glossaries to help the reader understand these more obscure references and so appreciate the text more fully.

Milton uses many references and allusions to Classical literature and to the Bible in his work and a knowledge of Greek and Roman mythology helps a good deal in studying his poetry. His readers in the Eighteenth Century would have possessed this kind of background and would understand immediately the Biblical references and Classical allusions. For them they would serve, as they were intended to do, to illuminate and illustrate the work. Most of us, as twentieth-century readers, do not have this kind of background and so often such references can initially act as barriers to meaning rather than assisting our understanding.

The question is – what can you do to help yourself overcome these initial difficulties? Well, three things would help to begin with:

- Buy a good dictionary if you do not possess one already and use it. Make sure that you look up every word that you come across that you do not understand. It can be a good idea to make a list of these.
- Look up and make a note of references that you do not understand. You might need to consult Classical dictionaries or encyclopedias for some of these.
- Ask yourself questions. Never be satisfied with ignoring difficult words or references. Always ask yourself questions like 'Why is that reference used?', 'What does it mean?', 'What does it add to the sense or effect of the poem?'

Now, let's assume that you have had the chance to do a bit of research on the passage from *Paradise Lost* on page 26. How does it help you gain a deeper understanding of the extract?
Here are some definitions of 'difficult' words:
voluble – smoothly (flowing) or rolling
arborets – shrubberies
sapient – wise
dalliance – playing or exchanging caresses and embraces
tedded – new mown grass spread for drying

And here are some notes on the references Milton uses:
...gardens of Adonis – who was 'revived' by Prosperpina after being killed by a wild boar – to emphasize that Eden was even more 'delicious' than the garden in which Adonis was brought back to life.
...garden of Alcinous – he was the king of Phaecia who royally entertained Odysseus ('Old Laertes' son') – again comparing Eden with this garden.
...sapient king – King Solomon was the 'sapient king' and this is a reference to the garden in which he entertained his wife, the Pharaoh's daughter.

As you will see all three of these references are used to compare the beauty of the Garden of Eden with other splendid gardens from the Bible or mythology. You will have noticed that all these references form part of an elaborate simile which is used to create a vivid impression of the splendid nature of Eden, but this is not the only simile he uses in the extract.

Activity | Look back at the extract on page 26 again and with a partner or in a small group discuss Milton's use of imagery here.

The simile form is an important part of the imagery of *Paradise Lost*. Some of Milton's images are drawn on a grand scale and can be elaborate and quite complicated to unravel. The key thing is that very often poetry needs working at in order to arrive at some kind of understanding of it.

Summary

Here are some suggestions to help you with that process.
- Read the piece several times and adopt a systematic approach.
- Use the parts of the poetry that you understand as clues to help you understand more difficult sections.
- Highlight particularly difficult words, phrases, lines, images, etc.
- Look up words that you do not understand in a good dictionary.
- Refer to the notes or glossary that the text contains.
- Do some background reading about the writer and their period.

Putting it into practice

Now have a look at a quite different kind of poem and see how you handle an appreciation of it. The poem is by Samuel Taylor Coleridge, probably most famous for his narrative poem, *The Ancient Mariner*. He also wrote some poems that became known as *Conversation Poems* because of the way that they seem to address the reader in the style of an intimate and private talk. Read the poem through carefully.

Frost At Midnight

The Frost performs its secret ministry,
Unhelped by any wind. The owlet's cry
Came loud – and hark, again! loud as before.
The inmates of my cottage, all at rest,
Have left me to that solitude, which suits
Abstruser musings: save that at my side
My cradled infant slumbers peacefully.
'Tis calm indeed! so calm, that it disturbs
And vexes meditation with its strange
And extreme silentness. Sea, hill, and wood,
With all the numberless goings-on of life,
Inaudible as dreams! the thin blue flame
Lies on my low-burnt fire, and quivers not;
Only that film,[1] which fluttered on the grate,
Still flutters there, the sole unquiet thing.
Methinks, its motion in this hush of nature
Gives it dim sympathies with me who live,
Making it a companionable form,
Whose puny flaps and freaks the idling Spirit

By its own moods interprets, everywhere
Echo or mirror seeking of itself,
And makes a toy of Thought.

                           But O! how oft,
How oft, at school, with most believing mind,
Presageful, have I gazed upon the bars,
To watch that fluttering *stranger*! and as oft
With unclosed lids, already had I dreamt
Of my sweet birth-place, and the old church-tower,
Whose bells, the poor man's only music, rang
From morn to evening, all hot Fair-day,
So sweetly, that they stirred and haunted me
With a wild pleasure, falling on mine ear
Most like articulate sounds of things to come!
So gazed I, till the soothing things, I dreamt,
Lulled me to sleep, and sleep prolonged my dreams!
And so I brooded all the following morn,
Awed by the stern preceptor's face, mine eye
Fixed with mock study on my swimming book:
Save if the door half opened, and I snatched
A hasty glance, and still my heart leaped up,
For still I hoped to see the *stranger's* face,
Townsman, or aunt, or sister more beloved,
My play-mate when we both were clothed alike!

   Dear Babe, that sleepest cradled by my side,
Whose gentle breathings, heard in this deep calm,
Fill up the interspersed vacancies
And momentary pauses of the thought!
My babe so beautiful! it thrills my heart
With tender gladness, thus to look at thee,
And think that thou shalt learn far other lore,
And in far other scenes! For I was reared
In the great city, pent 'mid cloisters dim,
And saw nought lovely but the sky and stars.
But *thou*, my babe! shalt wander like a breeze
By lakes and sandy shores, beneath the crags
Of ancient mountain, and beneath the clouds
Which image in their bulk both lakes and shores
And mountain crags: so shalt thou see and hear
The lovely shapes and sounds intelligible
Of that eternal language, which thy God
Utters, who from eternity doth teach
Himself in all, and all things in himself.
Great universal Teacher! he shall mould
Thy spirit, and by giving make it ask.

Therefore all seasons shall be sweet to thee,
Whether the summer clothe the general earth
With greenness, or the redbreast sit and sing
Betwixt the tufts of snow on the bare branch
Of mossy apple-tree, while the nigh thatch
Smokes in the sun-thaw; whether the eave-drops fall
Heard only in the trances of the blast,
Or if the secret ministry of frost
Shall hang them up in silent icicles,
Quietly shining to the quiet Moon.

Samuel Taylor Coleridge
(Published 1798)

1 In all parts of the kingdom these films are called strangers and supposed to portend the arrival of some absent friend [Coleridge's note]

Activity

1 Discuss the poem with a partner or in a small group. Then, on your own, make a list of the key points arising from your discussion.
2 Now have a closer look at the poem. Consider the following questions about the early part of the poem. Discuss them with a partner making notes on the following as you go.
   • Why do you think Coleridge describes the Frost's ministry as secret?
   • What kind of atmosphere does he create in lines 1–7?
   • What kind of scene is set within the cottage?
   • How would you describe the poet's mood here?
   • Look at lines 15–23. What is the significance of '...that film, which fluttered on the grate'?
3 Now, on your own, look at the second section of the poem. Describe what is happening here. How has the mood changed?
4 The focus shifts again in the third section. How? Comment on Coleridge's use of imagery here.
5 How effective do you find the concluding section? Refer to the text to support your comments.
6 What use do you think Coleridge has made of rhythm here and what relationship does this have with the overall form of the poem.
   (A consideration of the *kind* of poem this is may help you here).
7 Now write your own critical appreciation of this poem covering all the aspects of it that you feel are of significance. (Your essay should be between 3 to 4 pages in length.)

Special Feature: Geoffrey Chaucer

Chaucer is generally considered to be the most important writer of the Middle Ages and his work certainly had a great influence on our literature and language, laying the foundations for many writers who were to come after him. It is no surprise, therefore, to find Chaucer featured on a variety of A-level English syllabuses. In fact, he is probably the most featured writer after Shakespeare.

This special feature will examine ways of approaching the reading of Middle English and the context within which *The Canterbury Tales* are set. The final section suggests various things that you can do in order to help develop your understanding of the particular Chaucer text that you are studying.

Reading Middle English

In the initial stages of your study of Chaucer you may encounter problems of understanding that are not present in other types of poetry. When you first open your copy of whichever Chaucer text you are studying, probably the first thing to strike you will be that it appears to be written in another language. Initially, this can be quite unsettling. Do not be put off, though, because once you have become used to the language things will seem much simpler. The language itself is nowhere near as daunting as it can look at first sight.

The first thing to bear in mind is that it is *not* written in another language – it is very definitely written in English. Admittedly, it is a rather different form of English to our present-day language because it is the English that was used in the Fourteenth Century. It is called Middle English and evolved as a mixture of different language elements. French was influential in its development. From the time of the Norman Conquest in 1066 until the mid-thirteenth century, French was the language of the Court and the upper middle-classes. Latin also made an important contribution to Middle English, being the language of legal and ecclesiastical documents and the preferred language of scholarly communication in the Middle Ages. These elements, combined with the predominant east Midland dialect (the dialect of Chaucer), gradually evolved into Middle English. This is the form of the language from which modern English developed and has both similarities and differences to it.

In studying Chaucer for the first time your first task is to become familiar with these similarities and differences. There are a number of things that you can do to help you to quickly become quite fluent in reading Chaucer in the original. So let us start by having a closer look at some of the features of Chaucer's language.

Reading Chaucer

Let us begin by looking at the opening lines of Chaucer's *General Prologue*:

Whan that Aprill with his shoures soote
The droghte of March hath perced to the roote,
And bathed every veyne in swich licour
Of which vertu engendred is the flour;
Whan Zephirus eek with his sweete breeth
Inspired hath in every holt and heeth
The tendre croppes,

(Lines 1–7)

Activity

> **1** Read these few lines aloud pronouncing each word just as it looks and write down a 'translation' of what you think it means. Make a note of any words that puzzle you or cause you a problem in the translation.
> **2** Now do exactly the same thing with these lines from the opening of *The Franklin's Tale.*

In Armorik, that called is Britayne,
Ther was a knyght that had loved and dide his payne
To serve a lady in his beste wise;
And many a labour, many a greet emprise
He for his lady wroghte, er she were wonne.

(Lines 1–5)

Let's see how you got on. Translated literally the lines from the *General Prologue* could read:

When that April with his showers sweet
The drought of March hath pierced to the root,
And bathed every vein in such liquor
Of which energy engendered is the flower.
When Zephirus also with his sweet breath
Breaths upon every wood and heath
Upon all the tender croppes;

Activity

> This still has some way to go before the meaning is clear in modern English.
> **1** Think carefully about the lines and then write your own version of what it means. You can write this in prose if you wish. Do not worry about an exact line-for-line translation.
> **2** First, compare your version with the one below and then compare both with your initial translation.

Here is one possible translation:

When the sweet showers of April have pierced the drought of March to its roots and bathed every vein in the powerful moisture that gives birth to the flowers. When Zephirus too, with his sweet breath, has breathed upon the delicate shoots in every wood and heath;

How did you get on? Your version will no doubt differ slightly. There are a number of ways that this could be written down and yet the sense would remain the same. One of the reasons for this is that sometimes the sense of a particular Middle English word can be expressed through a number of modern English alternatives. For example, 'vertu' can mean *virtue* in modern English, although here it conveys the sense of the rain having the power to give life to the plants. Similarly, 'engendred' can mean *engendering* or *procreation* although here we could translate it as *gives birth*, as we have done, or even *produces* would be in keeping with the sense of the line.

Here's a translation of the opening of *The Franklin's Tale*. Compare it with your version.

In Amorica, which is also known as Brittany, there lived a knight who loved and took trouble to serve his lady to the best of his ability. He undertook many labours and great enterprises for her before he won her.

Where did your problems with these lines occur? The place names of Armorik and Britaine perhaps caused you a little difficulty. 'Armorica' is simply another name, an ancient name for Brittany. 'Britaine' looks very similar to Britain so this might have misled you. Perhaps certain expressions, such as '...and dide his paine', also caused you some difficulty.

Activity | From your work on these two short extracts, make a list of the ways in which you have found Chaucer's English to differ from modern English.

Summary   You may have noticed some, or all, of the following points.
- Some words are identical to their modern English counterparts (e.g. 'bathed', 'every', 'called', 'loved').
- Some words look and sound very similar to their modern English counterparts (e.g. 'whan', 'greet', 'wonne').
- Some words look completely unfamiliar (e.g. 'soote', 'swich', 'eek').
- Some words might remind you of modern English words but actually mean something different (e.g. 'inspired', 'holt').
- Some of the words seem to be in rather a strange order.
- There are references to people, places, etc. that you might not have come across before (e.g. 'Zephirus').

The context of the tales

If you study Chaucer for A-level it is likely that you will read one of the stories which make up *The Canterbury Tales*. Whichever particular tale you are studying, though, it is important that you are able to set the tale into the wider context of *The Canterbury Tales* as a whole rather than just look at it in isolation. Each of the tales is set within the fictional framework established by Chaucer in the *General Prologue to the Canterbury Tales* which is a kind of introduction in which Chaucer sets the scene, introduces the pilgrims, describes them, and so forth.

The basic background to the tales is straightforward. A group of pilgrims are travelling from London to Canterbury to worship at the shrine of Thomas à Becket. They meet at the Tabard Inn at Southwark in London ready to begin their journey and the landlord, or Host, as he is known, suggests that they all take part in a story-telling competition to help to pass the time on their journey. The Host will judge the stories and the winner will receive a free meal at the inn on their return from Canterbury.

You will probably find in your edition of the particular tale that you are studying other material which is not actually part of the tale itself but which will help you to establish some background to the character telling the tale. This material usually includes at least two extracts taken from elsewhere in *The Canterbury Tales*:

- most editions contain the section taken from the *General Prologue* which describes the particular pilgrim who is telling the tale
- most editions also contain the relevant lines that link the tale in question to the one that immediately precedes it. This often involves an exchange between the pilgrims and the Host and which can help to throw light on characters and how they relate to one another

For example, here is what Chaucer has to say about The Miller in the *General Prologue*.

The Millere was a stout carl for the nones;
Ful byg he was of brawn, and eek of bones.
That proved wel, for over al ther he cam,
At wrastlynge he wolde have alwey the ram.
He was short-sholdred, brood, a thikke knarre;
Ther was no dore that he nolde heve of harre,
Or breke it at a renning with his heed.
His berd as any sowe or fox was reed,
And therto brood, as though it were a spade.
Upon the cop right of his nose he hade
A werte, and theron stood a toft of herys,
Reed as the brustles of a sowis erys;
His nosethirles blake were and wyde.
A swerd and bokeler bar he by his syde.

His mouth as greet was as a greet forneys.
He was a janglere and a goliardeys,
And that was moost of synne and harlotries.
Wel koude he stelen corn and tollen thries;
And yet he hadde a thombe of gold, pardee.
A whit cote and a blew hood wered he.
A baggepipe wel koude he blowe and sowne,
And therwithal he broghte us out of towne.

(Lines 545–566)

Activity	Read this description to get the general sense of it. What kind of picture does it give you of The Miller? How might this kind of information help you if you were studying *The Miller's Tale*?

The narrator's voice

The Canterbury Tales, then, is a story about a group of people telling stories. The characters are, of course, the invention of Chaucer but he also writes himself into the script by taking the role of one of the pilgrims. In fact, in his role as Sir Topas, he gives himself the worst tale of all to tell and is interrupted by the Host who can listen to no more and so he never actually finishes it.

Throughout the tales there is always the sense of the presence of two narrators; first of all the character telling the story but secondly, hidden somewhere behind the first narrator there is Chaucer himself, masterminding the whole scheme.

Activity	What do you think Chaucer gains by having his tales narrated by fictitious characters within a fictitious framework rather than simply telling the tales directly himself?

There are several factors that you might consider here.

- The idea of the group of pilgrims gives a sense of unity and structure to what might otherwise have been a loosely linked collection of stories.
- Links can be made between the character telling the tale and the actual tale itself and this can add another dimension to both tale and teller.
- The whole narrative scheme is given a depth and complexity in terms of its overall effect on the audience that would have been lacking in a simple single narration scheme.
- It allows him to get away with telling stories and making comments that may be ribald or contentious by distancing himself from them and attributing them to his characters. This can add to the ironic effect he often creates.

In most parts of most of the tales Chaucer keeps to the background but watch out for his voice coming through. Sometimes he will comment or make an aside or observation or sometimes even endow his character with a language or mode of expression which is very much Chaucer's own. In other words he has it both ways. Using *The Miller's Tale* as an example again, here Chaucer is able to convince his audience of the Miller as an independent character that he has no control over and urges them to choose another tale if they are likely to be offended by the Miller's bawdy offering.

The key thing throughout is to be aware of the subtlety with which Chaucer uses a variety of narrative voices to achieve just the effect that he wants. To summarize, following these steps should help you to tackle your Chaucer text confidently.

Summary

- Read the tale you are studying through fairly quickly to get a general sense of what it is about. Do not worry too much at this first stage if there are words, phrases, or sections of it that you do not understand.
- Avoid using your glossary too much during this 'first read' stage. This can interrupt your reading and make it more difficult to get the overall 'feel' of the story.
- Then look back over the tale and focus on the individual words, phrases, or sections that gave you problems and use the glossary to help form a picture of their meaning.
- Most editions of a particular tale will contain quite detailed line-referenced notes. Make full use of these – they will help you establish the meaning of more difficult sections and also fill in some useful background information that will add to your understanding of the tale.
- Try listening to a recording of the tale read by a professional. This will help you to gain an impression of the sound of the language and you will hear rhymes and rhythms that are invisible when looking at the printed page.
- Avoid using a modern English translation. If you go straight to a translation this will really inhibit you from coming to terms with the language for yourself. It is far better to be able to read the original for yourself than have to rely on a ready-made translation.

3 Drama

• •

Objectives

- To prepare yourself for writing about drama
- To consider some of the features to look for in evaluating drama texts
- To study dramatists who often feature on examination syllabuses
- To prepare for studying set drama texts
- To prepare for a context-based question on a drama text

What is drama?

A dictionary definition will state that:

❝ drama is something intended specifically for performance on stage in front of an audience. **❞**

This definition points to the fact that drama is written to be seen rather than read and its meaning can only be fully appreciated when actually seen in performance. This makes it a much more 'public' form than prose or poetry in that the experience of the play in performance is a shared experience. This essential aspect of drama is easy to lose sight of when sitting in a classroom, or on your own, grappling with the language of a drama text.

Visualizing the script

It is essential, then, that you are aware that in approaching a play you are dealing with a work that is very different from, say, a novel and that you will need to employ quite different strategies to handle it. You must be able to visualize the play in your head – be able to bring the play alive in your mind and see and hear the action as if you were at the theatre. Developing the ability to do this can be difficult simply by reading from the printed page. However, there are things you can do, from the outset, to help.

- Recognize that reading a play is essentially a group activity and so work with others as much as possible.
- Go and see plays performed as often as possible. (Do not restrict yourself to the ones you are studying, or just to professional productions.)
- Keep a notebook or log of plays that you see noting your responses – thoughts and feelings about performances and ideas on production.
- Take part in 'acting out' parts of a play – this will help you to appreciate the staging implications of a text in a way that straight reading never can.
- Listen to audio tapes or video recordings of plays. (These do not replace seeing the play 'live' but they are better than only reading the scripts.)

With this key point in mind, let us consider some aspects of plays that you will need to examine in the texts that you study.

Opening scenes

The way that a play opens is obviously crucial to engaging the audience's attention and writers can take many options here depending on the effects that they wish to achieve. In looking at an opening scene, whether of a text you are studying for the examination or a passage you are confronted with for the 'unseen', there are some key questions that are worth asking. The central questions are: 'What effect does the writer want this scene to have on the audience?' and 'What purpose does the scene serve to the play as a whole?'. Here are some possible answers to these questions.

- The scene provides an explanation of the plot so far, background information and details the audience need to understand what is going on. (This is sometimes called **exposition** [see page 48].)
- The scene creates a setting or background against which the play is set.
- The scene creates a mood or creates tension which captures the audience's attention immediately (the opening scene of *Hamlet* is a good example of this).
- The scene introduces characters, situations, and relationships.
- The scene provokes a sense of intrigue which captures the audience's attention and makes them want to know more.

Activity

1 Read carefully the opening to Brian Friel's *Making History* on page 40. Think about what Friel hopes to achieve here and what effect it would have on the audience.

> **2** Discuss this opening with a partner focusing on these aspects:
> - your impression of the two characters and their concerns
> - the information conveyed to the audience here and the techniques that Friel uses to put it across
> - the kind of atmosphere created and how Friel creates it

Making History

Act I Scene 1
(*A large living room in* **O'Neill's** *home in Dungannon, County Tyrone, Ireland. Late August in 1591. The room is spacious and scantily furnished: a large, refectory-type table; some chairs and stools; a sideboard. No attempt at decoration.*

O'Neill *moves around this comfortless room quickly and energetically, inexpertly cutting the stems off flowers, thrusting the flowers into various vases and then adding water. He is not listening to* **Harry Hoveden** *who consults and reads from various papers on the table.*

O'Neill *is forty-one. A private, sharp-minded man at this moment uncharacteristically outgoing and talkative. He always speaks in an upper-class English accent except on those occasions specifically scripted.* **Harry Hoveden**, *his personal secretary, is about the same age as* **O'Neill**. **O'Neill** *describes him as a man 'who has a comforting and a soothing effect'.*)

Harry:	That takes care of Friday. Saturday you're free all day – so far. Then on Sunday – that'll be the fourteenth –
	O'Hagan's place at Tullyogue. A big christening party. The invitation came the day you left. I've said you'll be there. All right?
	(*Pause*)
	It's young Brian's first child – you were at his wedding last year. It'll be a good day.
	(*Pause*)
	Hugh?
O'Neill:	Yes?
Harry:	O'Hagan's – where you were fostered.
O'Neill:	Tell me the name of these again.
Harry:	Broom.
O'Neill:	Broom. That's it.
Harry:	The Latin name is *genista*. Virgil mentions it somewhere.
O'Neill:	Does he really?
Harry:	Actually that *genista* comes from Spain.
	(**O'Neill** *looks at the flowers in amazement.*)
O'Neill:	Good Lord – does it? Spanish broom – magnificent name, isn't it?
Harry:	Give them plenty of water.
O'Neill:	Magnificent colour, isn't it?
Harry:	A letter from the Lord Deputy –
O'Neill:	They really transform the room. Splendid idea of yours, Harry. Thank you.
	(**O'Neill** *silently mouths the word* Genista *again and then continues distributing the flowers.*)

Harry: A letter from the Lord Deputy 'vigorously urging you to have your eldest son attend the newly established College of the Holy and Undivided Trinity in Dublin founded by the Most Serene Queen Elizabeth'. That 'vigorously urging' sounds ominous, doesn't it?

O'Neill: Sorry?

Harry: Sir William Fitzwilliam wants you to send young Hugh to the new Trinity College. I'm told he's trying to get all the big Gaelic families to send their children there. He would like an early response.

O'Neill: This jacket – what do you think, Harry? It's not a bit ...excessive, is it?

Harry: Excessive?

O'Neill: You know ... a little too – too strident?

Harry: Strident?

O'Neill: All right, damn it, too bloody young?

Harry: (*Looking at his papers*) It's very becoming, Hugh.

O'Neill: Do you think so? Maybe I should have got it in maroon.
(*He goes off to get more flowers.*)

Harry: A reminder that the Annual Festival of Harpers takes place next month in Roscommon. They've changed the venue to Roosky. You're Patron of the Festival and they would be very honoured if you would open the event with a short –
(*He now sees that he is alone. He looks through his papers.*
Pause. **O'Neill** *enters again with an armful of flowers.*)

Brian Friel

This opening scene starts the play off in quite a private and intimate setting. The stage directions at the beginning describe the setting and what is going on and this will help you to visualize the scene in your mind. Although the audience will not be so fully aware of what is happening here the activity taking place will capture their attention. The two characters, O'Neill and Harry, seem to have very different concerns at the opening of the play. O'Neill is immersed in the domestic – arranging the flowers in the room and seeking Harry's opinion about his attire. Harry, on the other hand, is concerned with imparting business and political news to O'Neill. Within this apparently low-key opening Friel makes it clear that O'Neill is a prominent public figure from the details that are mentioned – his presence being requested at important domestic and public occasions and the letter from the Lord Deputy trying to persuade him to send his son to Trinity College confirm this.

Notice how Friel's economical technique allows him to give the audience a good deal of information and establishes the central character of O'Neill right at the outset. If you were to study the whole of this play you would find that Friel also establishes one of the central themes of the play here – that of the conflict between O'Neill the private man and O'Neill the public figure. He is also able to give a clear indication of O'Neill's stature and importance both as a political figure and as a man with pastoral responsibilities towards his people.

Activity	1 Read the following extract which is the opening scene from Sheridan's comedy, *The Rivals*.
	2 Discuss the scene with a partner and consider these points:
	• the effect of the opening on the audience
	• the intention of the playwright
	• the techniques used
	• the purpose of any stage directions

The Rivals

Act I, Scene 1
(*Scene, a street in Bath.*
Coachman *crosses the stage. Enter* **Fag** *looking after him.*)

Fag: What! – Thomas! – Sure 'tis he? – What! – Thomas! – Thomas!

Coachman: Hey! – Odds life! – Mr Fag! – give us your hand, my old fellow-servant.

Fag: Excuse my glove, Thomas: I'm devilish glad to see you, my lad: why, my prince of charioteers, you look as hearty! – but who the deuce thought of seeing you in Bath!

Coachman: Sure, Master, Madam Julia, Harry, Mrs Kate, and the postillion be all come!

Fag: Indeed!

Coachman: Aye! Master thought another fit of the gout was coming to make him a visit: so he'd a mind to gi't the slip, and whip we were all off at an hour's warning.

Fag: Aye, aye! hasty in everything, or it would not be Sir Anthony Absolute

Coachman: But tell us, Mr Fag, how does young Master? Odd! Sir Anthony will stare to see the Captain here!

Fag: I do not serve Captain Absolute now–

Coachman: Why sure!

Fag: At present I am employed by Ensign Beverley.

Coachman: I doubt, Mr Fag, you ha'n't changed for the better.

Fag: I have not changed, Thomas.

Coachman: No! why didn't you say you had left young Master?

Fag: No – Well, honest Thomas, I must puzzle you no farther: briefly then – Captain Absolute and Ensign Beverley are one and the same person.

Coachman: The devil they are!

Fag: So it is indeed, Thomas; and the *Ensign* half of my master being on guard at present – the *Captain* has nothing to do with me.

Coachman: So, so! – what, this is some freak, I warrant! Do, tell us, Mr Fag, the meaning o't – you know I ha' trusted you.

Fag: You'll be secret, Thomas.

Coachman: As a coach-horse.

Fag: Why then the cause of all this is – L, O, V, E, – love, Thomas, who (as you may get read to you) has been a masquerader ever since the days of Jupiter.

Coachman: Aye, aye; I guessed there was a lady in the case: but pray, why does your master pass only for Ensign? – now if he had shammed General indeed –

Fag: Ah! Thomas, there lies the mystery o'the matter. Harkee, Thomas, my master is in love with a lady of a very singular taste: a lady who likes him better as a half-pay

	Ensign than if she knew he was son and heir to Sir Anthony Absolute, a baronet with three thousand a year.
Coachman:	That is an odd taste indeed! – but has she got the stuff, Mr Fag; is she rich, hey?
Fag:	Rich! – why, I believe she owns half the stocks! Zounds! Thomas, she could pay the national debt as easy as I could my washerwoman! She has a lap-dog that eats out of gold – she feeds her parrot with small pearls – and all her thread-papers are made of bank-notes!
Coachman:	Bravo! – faith! – odd! I warrant she has a set of thousands at least: but does she draw kindly with the Captain?
Fag:	As fond as pigeons.
Coachman:	May one hear her name?
Fag:	Miss Lydia Languish – but there is an old tough aunt in the way; though by the by – she has never seen my master – for he got acquainted with Miss while on a visit in Gloucestershire.
Coachman:	Well – I wish they were once harnessed together in matrimony. But pray, Mr Fag, what kind of a place is this Bath? I ha' heard a deal of it – here's a mort o' merry-making – hey?
Fag:	Pretty well, Thomas, pretty well – 'tis a good lounge. In the morning we go to the pump-room (though neither my master nor I drink the waters); after breakfast we saunter on the parades or play a game at billiards; at night we dance: but damn the place, I'm tired of it: their regular hours stupefy me – not a fiddle nor a card after eleven! – however Mr Faulkland's gentleman and I keep it up a little in private parties; I'll introduce you there, Thomas – you'll like him much.
Coachman:	Sure I know Mr Du-Peigne – you know his master is to marry Madam Julia.
Fag:	I had forgot. But Thomas you must polish a little – indeed you must: here now – this wig! – what the devil do you do with a wig, Thomas? None of the London whips of any degree of ton wear wigs now.
Coachman:	More's the pity! more's the pity, I say. Odds life! when I heard how the lawyers and doctors had took to their own hair, I thought how 'twould go next – odd rabbit it! when the fashion had got foot on the Bar, I guessed 'twould mount to the Box! – but 'tis all out of character, believe me, Mr Fag and lookee, I'll never gi' up mine – the lawyers and doctors may do as they will.
Fag:	Well, Thomas, we'll not quarrel about that.
Coachman:	Why, bless you, the gentlemen of they professions ben't all of a mind – for in our village now tho'ff Jack Gauge the exciseman has ta'en to his carrots, there's little Dick the farrier swears he'll never forsake his bob, though all the college should appear with their own heads!
Fag:	Indeed! well said Dick! but hold – mark! mark! Thomas.
Coachman:	Zooks! 'tis the Captain – is that the lady with him?
Fag:	No! no! that is Madam Lucy – my master's mistress's maid. They lodge at that house – but I must after him to tell him the news.
Coachman:	Odd! he's giving her money! – well, Mr Fag –
Fag:	Goodbye, Thomas – I have an appointment in Gyde's Porch this evening at eight; meet me there, and we'll make a little party.
	(*Exeunt severally*)

Sheridan

Presenting character

A key element in the impact of a dramatic production is the extent to which the playwright achieves a convincing sense of character. However, the nature of drama is such that the playwright employs very different methods of characterization to those employed by a novelist. Novelists can provide the reader with as much background information as they wish, they can enter the minds of the characters, let their readers know what characters think, feel, are planning to do. A playwright does not have all these options.

Activity

> Focusing on a play that you are studying, think carefully about the ways the characters are presented to the audience to give a full and rounded impression of them. Make a list of these methods and devices.

Perhaps the most straightforward way in which a playwright can define exactly how they intend a character to appear to the audience is through detailed and explicit stage directions. So it is important that when you begin to study a play you pay close attention to this information. When watching the play on the stage, of course, you will not be reading stage directions but you will actually be seeing them in performance.

Some playwrights give a great deal of information through their descriptions of how characters are meant to appear. Look carefully at this description from the opening of John Galsworthy's *Strife*, for example:

Strife

Act I

(It is noon. In the Underwoods' dining-room a bright fire is burning. On one side of the fireplace are double doors leading to the drawing-room, on the other side a door leading to the hall. In the centre of the room a long dining-table without cloth is set out as a board table. At the head of it in the Chairman's seat, sits **John Anthony***, an old man, big, clean shaven, and high-coloured, with thick white hair, and thick dark eyebrows. His movements are rather slow and feeble, but his eyes are very much alive. There is a glass of water by his side. On his right sits his son,* **Edgar***, an earnest-looking man of thirty, reading a newspaper. Next to him* **Wanklin***, a man with jutting eyebrows, and silver-streaked light hair, is bending over transfer papers.* **Tench***, the secretary, a short and rather humble, nervous man, with side whiskers, stands helping him. On* **Wanklin's** *right sits* **Underwood***, the Manager, a quiet man, with a long, stiff jaw, and steady eyes. Back to the fire is* **Scantlebury***, a very large, pale, sleepy man, with grey hair, rather bald. Between him and the Chairman are two empty chairs.)*

Wilder: *(Who is lean, cadaverous, and complaining, with drooping grey moustaches, stands before the fire)* I say, this fire's the devil! Can I have a screen, Tench?

John Galsworthy

Activity

> In a small group, read these stage directions carefully. Imagine you are a producer and a team of actors discussing preliminary views of these characters. Think about their appearances and personalities.

Galsworthy here presents anyone reading the text with a good deal of guidance on how to visualize the characters. Some playwrights provide little or no such direct guidance on how to interpret their characters but rely on other methods to convey a sense of character. These include:

- how characters speak (also embedded in stage directions)
- how characters are described by other characters
- what the characters say and do

Most playwrights (including Galsworthy) use a combination of all these methods in order to give a sense of fully-developed characters, although in some cases playwrights deliberately create stereotypical characters in order to achieve their particular effect. Some of the 'stock' characters to be found in Restoration Comedy, such as *The Rivals*, are examples of this.

Asides and soliloquies

To succeed in creating a convincing character, the dramatist needs to give the audience some sense of deeper, inner thoughts and feelings. Unlike the novelist, however, who can describe these as fully as desired to the reader, the dramatist has much more limited means at their disposal.

Two methods that are often used to provide some insight into characters' minds are the aside and the soliloquy. The **aside** is a kind of 'stage whisper', a behind-the-hand comment. Sometimes it is directed to another character but often it is aimed at the audience or the character 'speaks to themselves'. Asides tend to be short, often a single sentence, sometimes a single word. They are used by the playwright to convey small pieces of information concerning the plot or character to the audience. For example, in Congreve's *The Way of the World* one of the central characters, Mirabell, has insincerely courted Lady Wishfort as a cover for his real love of her niece, Millament. Lady Wishfort has discovered the truth and, although she gives nothing away in conversation, her aside shows that despite all she is till susceptible to his charms.

Lady Wishfort: (*Aside*) Oh, he has witchcraft in his eyes and tongue! When I did not see him, I could have bribed a villain to his assassination; but his appearance rakes the embers which have so long lain smothered in my breast.

Although asides are usually short comments sometimes they can be more extended. In *The Rivals* the characters almost give the audience a running commentary on what is going on and how they are feeling. In the following extract Absolute has angered his father by refusing to marry the girl his father has selected for him. He then has found out that she is actually the same girl as the one he loves and so he decides to appear penitent to his father (without letting him in on what is really happening!). It is worth noting that lines which can be taken as asides in performance are not always marked (*Aside*) in the script. One television adaptation of this play actually had the characters addressing the camera directly as though speaking confidentially and directly to the viewer, making them privy to the intrigue.

The Rivals

Act III, Scene 1
(*Scene, the North Parade.*
Enter **Absolute**.)

Absolute: 'Tis just as Fag told me, indeed. Whimsical enough, faith! My father wants to force me to marry the very girl I am plotting to run away with! He must not know of my connection with her yet awhile. – He has too summary a method of proceeding in these matters – and Lydia shall not yet lose her hopes of an elopement. – However, I'll read my recantation instantly. My conversion is something sudden, indeed, but I can assure him it is very *sincere*. – So, so – here he comes. He looks plaguy gruff.
(*Steps aside*)
(*Enter Sir Anthony.*)

Sir Anthony: No – I'll die sooner than forgive him. *Die*, did I say? I'll live these fifty years to plague him. – At our last meeting, his impudence had almost put me out of temper. An obstinate, passionate, self-willed boy! Who can he take after? This is my return for getting him before all his brothers and sisters! – for putting him, at twelve years old, into a marching regiment, and allowing him fifty pounds a year, besides his pay ever since! But I have done with him – he's anybody's son for me. – I never will see him more – never – never – never – never.

Absolute: Now for a penitential face.
(*Advances*)

Sheridan

The aside is an extremely useful device by which the playwright can give hints concerning plot or character to the audience. Through the soliloquy, the playwright has much more scope for developing a character's thoughts and feelings aloud, allowing the audience to see into the mind of the character. The **soliloquy** is an expanded and more fully developed speech and is usually delivered when the character is alone on the stage. Often soliloquies allow characters to reveal their true feelings, plans, or motives as they do not need to maintain any public image that they may project in front of the other characters. We will consider the role of the soliloquy in Shakespearian drama on page 56 but many playwrights in many different kinds of play make use of asides and soliloquies to create the effect they want.

Returning to *The Rivals*, the maid, Lucy, who pretends to be a 'simpleton', is, in fact, a cunning operator. When she is left alone at the end of a scene, this soliloquy reveals her true nature to the audience and so adds to their amusement as they see how she is playing all the characters off against one another.

The Rivals

Act I, Scene 2

Lucy: Ha! ha! ha! So, my dear simplicity, let me give you a little respite – (*Altering her manner*) let girls in my station be as fond as they please of appearing expert, and knowing in their trusts; commend me to a mask of silliness, and a pair of sharp eyes for my own interest under it! Let me see to what account I have turned my simplicity lately – (*Looks at a paper*) *For abetting Miss Lydia Languish in a design of running away with an ensign – in money – sundry times – twelve pound twelve – gowns, five – hats, ruffles, caps, etc., etc. – numberless! From the said Ensign, within this last month, six guineas and a half* – about a quarter's pay! Item, *from Mrs Malaprop, for betraying the young people to her –* when I found matters were likely to be discovered – *two guineas, and a black paduasoy.* Item, *from Mr Acres, for carrying divers letters* – which I never delivered – *two guineas, and a pair of buckles.* Item, *from Sir Lucius O'Trigger – three crowns – two gold pocket-pieces – and a silver snuff-box!* – Well done, *simplicity!* – yet I was forced to make my Hibernian believe, that he was corresponding, not with the aunt, but with the niece: for, though not over rich, I found he had too much pride and delicacy to sacrifice the feelings of a gentleman to the necessities of his fortune. (*Exit*)

Sheridan

Soliloquies are frequently used at some special moment in the play or when a character is undergoing some kind of emotionally or psychologically heightened experience. For example, when a character is distressed or suffering some kind of confusion of mind or alternatively when a character is feeling exultant or wants to work through their own thoughts and feelings.

Although technically speaking, we think of characters being alone on the stage, or at least out of earshot of other characters when they deliver their soliloquy, a soliloquy-like effect can be created in other ways. Sometimes a character may be in the presence of others but they are so wrapped up in their own world that it is as though they are talking to themselves. Although technically speaking not a soliloquy, this can serve much the same function.

It has often been noted that both the aside and the soliloquy are artificial devices and that in 'real life' people do not go around delivering speeches to themselves. In fact, they are just two of many conventions that we accept when watching a play which can be termed 'dramatic licence'. In the context of the theatre we forget their artificiality and accept them quite naturally.

Activity

1 Working in pairs, select a character from a play that you are studying. One assumes the role of that character, the other the mirror image. The 'character' asks questions of the image about their thoughts, feelings, motivations, etc. and the image answers. This role play should teach you as much about what your chosen character is *not* as what they *are*.

2 You can then select another character and swap roles.

Issues and themes

Complex though the formation and development of characters may be, they are themselves part of a more complex web that makes up the play as a whole. Within this web the playwright will have interwoven certain themes and issues. In studying a play, you will need to be able to identify these and to look at how the playwright explores them through the drama. Such ideas can be presented to the audience in two key ways. First, we can detect ideas, issues, thoughts, etc. expressed by the actual characters in a play. Secondly, we can detect themes, issues, or ideas that the playwright wants the play as a whole to project.

Sometimes a playwright will have major characters hold views or follow a philosophy that ultimately is shown to be counter to the message that the play as a whole conveys. This is often done to show the problems caused by or shortcomings of certain courses of action or philosophies. The issues that a play might raise can be many and varied but they are almost always presented via action centering on human relationships and conflicts.

Activity

> List the major characters in a play that you are studying. Draw up a chart which shows briefly the ideas, philosophies, values etc. held by each character, as shown through the action of the play. Then think about these ideas and against each jot down the dramatist's view.

Plot and structure

Obviously plot is central to most plays although there are certain kinds of play (some of Samuel Beckett's for example) where the very lack of a plot, or at least something that we would ordinarily recognize as a plot, is essential for the effect. At its simplest the **plot** is the story of the play – what actually happens. Having said that, there is much more to plot than simple 'story-line'. The whole notion of plot and its development is bound up with the way that the play is put together, with its structure. The creation of an order or pattern needs careful planning and the playwright needs to consider a number of factors. Generally speaking an effective plot should:

- maintain the interest of the audience from beginning to end
- move the action on from one episode to the next
- arouse interest of the audience in character and situation
- create high points or moments of crisis at intervals
- create expectation and surprise

Usually, the structure of a play follows a basic pattern which consists of a number of identifiable elements.

1 **Exposition:** this opens the play and often introduces the main characters and provides background information.

2 **Dramatic incitement:** the incident which provides the starting point for the main action of the play.

3 **Complication:** this usually forms the main action of the play in which the characters respond to the dramatic incitement and other developments that stem from it.

4 **Crisis:** the climax of the play.

5 **Resolution:** this is the final section of the play where things are worked out and some kind of conclusion is arrived at.

Let us look at this structure as applied to *The Rivals* to see how it works out. Sheridan's play, because of the complexities and confusions of the plot, may seem to have no structure at all on first reading (or viewing). However, a closer study of it reveals that it is very carefully structured indeed.

1 **Exposition:** the opening scene is a classic example of an exposition (see script on pages 42–43). Two servants, Fag and Thomas, through their conversation provide the audience with all the information that they need to follow the action. We are introduced to the stories of the two pairs of lovers (Jack and Lydia and Faulkland and Julia) whose fortunes run parallel to each other throughout the play and reach their resolution in the final scene.

2 **Dramatic incitement:** we are made aware of this through the exposition where we are told that Jack Absolute is wooing the beautiful Lydia Languish by pretending to be a character called Ensign Beverley.

3 **Complication:** there are many complications and twists to the plot – Jack's father, Sir Anthony arranges for his son to marry a young woman (who happens to be Lydia), Lydia's aunt forbids her to see Ensign Beverley (although she would be happy if she knew he was, in fact, Sir Anthony's son) and many more complications develop.

4 **Crisis:** the main crisis comes when Lydia finds out who her beloved Ensign Beverley really is, thus shattering her notions of a romantic elopement and she refuses to have any more to do with him.

5 **Resolution:** the final scene brings the reconciliation of Jack and Lydia and other strands of the plot which have created problems and complications for most of the other characters are also resolved.

In addition to the main plot involving Lydia and Jack, Sheridan makes use of various sub-plots (the most obvious being the action involving Julia and Faulkland). **Sub-plots** are secondary plots, sometimes separate from the main action but often linked to it in some way. Sub-plots tend to echo themes explored by the main plot or shed more light on them. They contribute to the interest of the play but do not detract from the main plot.

The pace of the action is also integral to the idea of plot and structure. Varying the pace at which the plot unfolds is another factor in maintaining the interest of the audience. Variations in the lengths of scenes and in mood, setting, and action can all influence a play's dramatic effectiveness.

Activity | Examine carefully the structure of a play that you are studying. Draw a diagram to represent the way that the play develops, making brief notes of key moments.

Approaching your script

There are a number of things you can do to deepen your understanding of your drama text for the examination. Here are some suggestions.

Summary

Plays in performance

- See a live performance of the play.
- Failing that see a video recording or a film of it.
- Make notes on performances in a play log book to help you to remember those important initial impressions.
- Read your drama text thoroughly prior to seeing it performed.
- Listen to the play on audio tape.
- See as many other plays as you can to broaden your experience of drama and the theatre.

Directing the text

- Work with others dramatizing for yourselves scenes from the text.
- Talk to others about staging implications.
- Imagine you are a director – plan carefully how you would stage a production of the play, the kind of actors you would cast, how you would bring your own interpretation out live on the stage, etc.
- Use diagrams, drawings and models to work out sets, stage layout, and props for selected scenes.

Studying the text

- Think about the characters – look at key speeches, look for shifts in focus, different ways of interpreting what they do and say.
- Look for various possible 'meanings' and 'patterns' in the play.
- Consider how/if the theatrical effects are signalled.
- Think about the pace and variety of the action.
- Think about the overall shape and structure of the play and the impact that this could have on an audience.
- Consider the particular characteristics and qualities of the play you are studying.
- Think about relationships between these various elements of the play and how together they present a whole.
- Apply the broader knowledge you have about the nature of plays and drama.

All these activities will help you to formulate and develop your own informed critical response to the play and therefore fulfil the objectives which lie at the heart of your study of drama.

Special Feature: William Shakespeare

● ●

Shakespeare has always held a dominant position as far as the drama element of English Literature syllabuses is concerned, and you will have encountered at least one of his plays before you start your A-level studies. Without a doubt, his works appear more frequently on A-level syllabuses than any other author and a detailed study of at least one of his plays is likely to be a major feature of your study of English Literature at A-level.

Exactly which play (or plays) you study will depend on which particular syllabus you are following, which text(s) your teacher or lecturer has selected, or which text(s) your learning modules cover. Having said that, some of Shakespeare's plays appear much more frequently than others on A-level syllabuses.

Shakespeare's plays

There are various ways in which the plays of Shakespeare can be categorized but a useful and simple method is to divide them into Histories, Tragedies, and Comedies. The main texts set for study at A-level are as follows:

Histories	Tragedies	Comedies
Richard II	*Hamlet*	*The Taming of the Shrew*
Henry IV (Part 1)	*Macbeth*	*Love's Labour's Lost*
Henry IV (Part 2)	*Othello*	*A Midsummer Night's Dream*
Henry V	*King Lear*	*Much Ado About Nothing*
Richard III	*Romeo and Juliet*	*The Merchant of Venice*
Antony and Cleopatra		*As You Like It*
Coriolanus		
Julius Caesar		

In addition, there are two further categories for a handful of plays that do not fit easily into the three broad areas.

The Problem Comedies	The Romances
Troilus and Cressida	*Cymbeline*
All's Well That Ends Well	*The Winter's Tale*
Measure for Measure	*The Tempest*

Let's have a closer look at some of the features of plays in each of these categories.

The Histories

The main history plays that you are likely to encounter in studying English at A-level are *Richard II*, *Henry IV Part 1*, *Henry IV Part 2*, *Henry V*, and *Richard III*, all of which focus on a specific period of English history. Added to these five, the Roman history plays, *Coriolanus*, *Julius Caesar*, and *Antony and Cleopatra*, are also favourites. It appears that Shakespeare was the first dramatist to write a real history play and to treat his material as a dramatist rather than a mere chronicler of events. His development of character and ideas and themes in these plays make them far more than simple chronicles as he adapts historical fact to suit his dramatic purpose.

Although every one of Shakespeare's Histories is very different in many respects, they do have certain features in common too. For example history plays usually:

- present famous historical figures and moments of crisis in their lives
- concern themselves with the order and stability of the state
- contain rebels who create problems
- contain heroes who are fallible
- concern the gap between an ideal notion of kingship and the less tidy reality
- accept the inevitability of disorder
- show that the failings and ambitions of individuals can disrupt the social order

Activity

> Take the history play that you are studying for your course, or one you have studied in the past, and decide how many of the above features you can identify in it. Make a note of how each feature can be seen in the particular play you have chosen.

The Tragedies

The idea of disorder also lies at the heart of the Tragedies. The Roman history plays are often included as tragedies. The four that are regarded as 'the great' Tragedies are *Hamlet*, *King Lear*, *Othello*, and *Macbeth*. These plays are very frequently set for study at A-level. At the heart of each of these plays is the central character – after whom the play is named – (the **eponymous hero** to give the technical term) and the action focuses very much on this central character. However, other characters are involved too and often several innocent victims are claimed before the play reaches its end.

Overall, Shakespeare's Tragedies have much in common with one another and with the concept of dramatic tragedy in general. Here are some key features.

- At the beginning of the play something occurs that disrupts the normal order of things.
- Chaos or disorder in society results.
- Extreme emotions are involved.

- Social restraint disintegrates.
- A climax is reached, usually with the death of the main character (and several others), before order is restored. This purging of emotions which affects the audience at the end of a tragedy is sometimes referred to as **catharsis**.

Activity

> If you are studying one of Shakespeare's Tragedies think about how the play fits this general pattern. Note down one thing that happens in the play which corresponds to each of the above features.

The Comedies

The term 'comedy' in modern usage tends to make us think of something fairly lightweight that makes us laugh. However, in its original sense, and certainly as applied to the plays of Shakespeare, the term simply means a play that has a happy ending; the action that leads to this ending may be funny and light in tone but equally it could deal with serious, even dangerous, life-threatening situations. In this sense a comedy can deal with issues that are just as serious as those raised by other kinds of plays.

Shakespearian comedy can vary considerably both in style and the mood the play creates. Early comedies, such as *The Comedy of Errors*, *The Taming of the Shrew*, *Love's Labour's Lost*, *A Midsummer Night's Dream*, and *Much Ado About Nothing*, or the later comedies, *As You Like It*, and *Twelfth Night*, might reasonably be called romantic comedies as love plays a central role in them. The general pattern for these comedies is as follows.

- Life is going on as normal.
- Characters fall in love.
- Various mishaps and misunderstandings threaten the happy outcome.
- The problems are resolved.
- The play ends happily with the various lovers united.

However, in some, notably *Much Ado About Nothing*, a good deal in the play verges on the tragic and in some ways is reminiscent of *Romeo and Juliet*. This serious edge is clearly there in *The Merchant of Venice* too, so much so that although the play ends happily for all (except for Shylock – almost a tragic figure at the end) that the term **tragicomedy** has been applied to it. The basic pattern, then, is very similar to that of the tragedies.

- An event occurs.
- This leads to disorder and disruption.
- Confusion results.
- The problems are resolved.

The difference comes in the way that the action is resolved and the focus that is maintained. In a comedy serious issues may be raised and addressed but the focus is very much on the foolishness of human behaviour. Within this structure, though, evil forces may be at work and the play deals with the powerful forces that motivate the characters to do what they do – sexual appetite, lust for power, greed, and envy. These forces are nowhere more evident than in what are referred to as the Problem Plays or Problem Comedies.

The Problem Comedies

Generally the Problem Comedies are taken to be *Measure for Measure*, *Troilus and Cressida*, and *All's Well That Ends Well*. In many ways these plays fall somewhere between tragedy and comedy but avoid becoming tragic because they end 'happily', at least in so far as no one dies at the end of the play. They are also known as the Problem Plays or Dark Comedies.

A dark tone and flawed characters typify these plays. They are more likely to disturb the audience rather than amuse them as they raise unsettling issues about the darker side of human nature. Like the other types of plays we have looked at, they centre on a disorder within society, but whereas the comedies operate very much in a world of fantasy and make-believe, these plays operate in a very much bleaker and coldly realistic environment.

It has been said that in writing these plays Shakespeare was experimenting with a dramatic form which brought together comedy and tragedy and this experimentation culminated in The Romance Plays.

The Romance Plays

Once again we see the idea of disorder presented through the Romances or Last Plays, *Pericles*, *Cymbeline*, *The Winter's Tale*, and *The Tempest*. Unlike the Problem Comedies, which have a coldly realistic setting, these plays make much more use of fantasy elements and magic to explore the central ideas. They operate in make-believe worlds and the plots often take improbable or incredible turns and twists. However, these features of the plays are essential to the effects that they create and the purpose they hope to achieve.

There are certain key ideas that can be seen emerging through all four plays which can help you to gain some idea of what they are about.

- The play centres on a noble family and a king.
- An evil or misguided deed is done.
- This causes great suffering to characters and years of separation.
- Through the suffering something new begins to emerge.
- In the end this new element transforms the old evil.
- An act of forgiveness resolves the problems and reconciliation takes place.

In simple terms the general pattern can be seen as:

PROSPERITY ⟶ DESTRUCTION ⟶ RECREATION

In many ways the unusual, and sometimes bizarre events that occur in the romances can present added difficulties, particularly when you are trying to establish the plot and character in your mind. However, like the other kinds of Shakespearian drama, these plays also fit into a broader pattern. At their heart are the same features that are present in the other kinds of plays we have discussed. There is order and disorder; love and harmony; conflict and discord; life falls short of the ideal world and human imperfection figures.

Activity

What type of Shakespeare play are you studying? Draw up a table of the key events and the plot structure thinking about the overall pattern that is created.

Character

An essential part of the study of your particular play will be to study the characters themselves and Shakepeare's methods of creating and presenting them.

Activity

Choose one of the central characters from the Shakespeare play that you are studying. Imagine that you are an actor who has been offered that part in a forthcoming production. Collect evidence from the play to support your view of the character and the way that you intend to play them on stage. Your evidence should consist of the following:
• what the character says about themselves
• what others say about the character
• what the character does when speaking
• what the character does when silent
• how the character's words match their actual deeds or their underlying motives
• how the character is viewed by those around them

This activity should help you form your own view of a character. Remember, though, there is often more than one way of looking at a character. Characters in plays, like people, are rarely seen in clear-cut, black-and-white terms. As part of your preparation for the examination, it would be useful for you to make notes on each of the characters in the play(s) you are studying making sure that you do the following.

Summary

• Consider all possible interpretations of the character.
• Assess the role or function that the character performs in the play.
• Examine in detail the key speeches the character makes and the scenes in which they appear.
• Gather a range of evidence from the play to support your view of the character.

Soliloquies and asides

In most of his plays Shakespeare makes full use of the dramatic devices of asides and soliloquies as a means of developing aspects of character.

In Shakespeare's *Othello* there is substantial use of both long and short asides. Often they reveal to the audience the wicked plan developing in Iago's mind and give a glimpse into his thoughts and the delight he takes in his evil. In this unusually long aside we are shown his thoughts taking shape as he watches Desdemona and Cassio.

Othello

Act II Scene 1

Iago: (*Aside*) He takes her by the palm. Ay, well said, whisper. With as little web as this will I ensnare as great a fly as Cassio. Ay, smile upon her, do. I will gyve thee in thine own courtship. You say true, 'tis so indeed. If such tricks as these strip you out of your lieutenantry, it had been better you had not kissed your three fingers so oft, which now again you are most apt to play the sir in. Very good: well kissed, an excellent courtesy! 'Tis so indeed. Yet again your fingers to your lips? Would they were clyster-pipes for your sake!

The repeated use of asides also give us an insight into Othello's growing torment. For example, in this extract Iago urges him to secretly observe his conversation with Cassio, to convince Othello (quite wrongly) that Cassio and Desdemona are having an affair. In fact, he and Cassio are talking about Bianca.

Act IV Scene 1

Othello: (*Aside*) Look, how he laughs already!
Iago: I never knew a woman love man so.
Cassio: Alas, poor rogue! I think i'faith she loves me.
Othello: (*Aside*) Now he denies it faintly, and laughs it out.
Iago: Do you hear, Cassio?
Othello: (*Aside*) Now he importunes him to tell it o'er.
        Go to, well said, well said!
Iago: She gives it out that you shall marry her.
        Do you intend it?
Cassio: Ha, ha, ha!
Othello: (*Aside*) Do you triumph, Roman? Do you triumph?
Cassio: I marry her! What! A customer! Prithee bear some charity
        to my wit: do not think it so unwholesome. Ha, ha, ha!
Othello: (*Aside*) So, so, so, so: they laugh that win.

And so Othello's jealousy builds and is communicated to the audience through the cumulative tension created by the asides.

Soliloquies, too, are used extensively to convey both information and inward emotion to the audience. In *Hamlet*, for example, it is possible to trace the development of Hamlet's shifting emotions during the course of the play through the sequence of soliloquies he delivers at various points in the action.

In *Henry IV, Part 1* the following soliloquy allows us, the audience, to see the true nature of Prince Hal early on in the play. We see him in a light that none of the other characters can. He has been a complete disappointment to his father, King Henry, and all the 'responsible' authority figures in the play because of the wild and dissolute life he has been leading in the company of the old reprobate, Falstaff, and his dubious tavern and whorehouse companions. However, at the end of Act I Scene 2, after bantering with these 'companions' in the tavern and becoming involved in the planning of a robbery, the Prince is left alone on the stage and delivers this soliloquy.

Henry IV, Part 1

Act I Scene 2

Prince:
I know you all, and will awhile uphold
The unyok'd humour of your idleness.
Yet herein will I imitate the sun,
Who doth permit the base contagious clouds
To smother up his beauty from the world,
That, when he please again to be himself,
Being wanted he may be more wonder'd at
By breaking through the foul and ugly mists
Of vapours that did seem to strangle him.
If all the year were playing holidays,
To sport would be as tedious as to work;
But when they seldom come, they wish'd-for come,
And nothing pleaseth but rare accidents:
So, when this loose behaviour I throw off,
And pay the debt I never promised,
By how much better than my word I am,
By so much shall I falsify men's hopes;
And, like bright metal on a sullen ground,
My reformation, glittering o'er my fault,
Shall show more goodly, and attract more eyes
Than that which hath no foil to set it off.
I'll so offend to make offence a skill,
Redeeming time when men think least I will.

Activity

> 1 Think about what Prince Hal is actually saying here. What does he reveal to the audience? Why do you think Shakespeare has placed this soliloquy at such an early point in the play?
> 2 Choose a soliloquy from the play you are studying and examine it carefully considering the following points:
> • what the audience learns from the soliloquy
> • why the playwright places the soliloquy at that particular point in the action of the play
> • what the dramatic effect of the soliloquy is in the context of the play as a whole

Verse and prose

It has often been said that Shakespeare's greatness is rooted in his ability to use language to suit all moods, occasions, and characters. Much of his work is written in blank verse (see Unit 2, page 20) – a flexible form which he adapts to suit many purposes, from moments of intense passion to bawdy bantering. However, we must not lose sight of the fact that Shakespeare makes substantial use of prose too which prompts the question 'Why does he switch between verse and prose in his plays?'.

A common answer to this question is that the 'high' characters use poetry, in keeping with their elevated natures and substance of their dialogue, while the 'low' or comic characters use the more plebian prose. An alternative answer is that Shakespeare uses prose for sub-plots or to indicate madness or a highly-wrought emotional state in a character. It is easy to find examples to support these ideas but it is also easy to find examples to disprove it too. The truth is that all these explanations are too general and simplistic to help us much and the real explanation is rather more complex.

For example, *Hamlet* begins with the guards, Francisco and Barnado, 'ordinary' and minor characters, speaking in verse. This helps to create a solemn and dignified tone with which to open the play in keeping with the serious events that are about to unfold with the appearance of the Ghost. When Ophelia becomes mad she speaks prose but she also speaks prose in the 'play-within-the-play' scene where she is perfectly sane. Hamlet himself speaks both prose and verse depending on the situation and who he is speaking to, the Players speak prose when they are not performing and verse when they are in role.

In looking at Shakespeare's use of verse and prose, therefore, you need to look at the context of the specific episode to really determine why Shakespeare has chosen to use language in the form he has. In every instance there will be a good dramatic reason on which his decision is based. It is worth remembering that Shakespeare's prose is not an unplanned, casual form. It is as much an art-form as his verse and is just as carefully structured and organized.

Activity

> Make a note of where switches between verse and prose occur in the text you are studying. Choose four of these points. Give reasons why you think the switch is made in each case.

Structure

The structure of each play is integral to the way in which Shakespeare shapes the central issues that are developed. The structure of his plays (or any play) can be viewed in two ways. What is sometimes called the **dynamic structure** of the play consists of the sequence of events which build up in a 'cause and effect' fashion to create the plot of the play and so drives the play forward.

Underlying this obvious structure, though, it is often possible to detect another that is less obvious but just as important. This second structure is reflected through various parallels and cross-references or repeated images, symbols, or language that create a kind of network of threads that run through the play. This kind of structure is sometimes called the **symmetric structure** and it can exert a powerful influence on the overall effect of a play.

In *Hamlet*, for example, the repeated parallels between Hamlet and Laertes as avenging sons or Hamlet's repeated consideration of death with its associated imagery are just two elements which help to form a whole web of patterning that is developed throughout the play. Similarly, in *King Lear*, the thread of 'blindness' to the truth as well as physical blindness presented through Gloucester and Lear create parallels which impose a kind of structure on the play.

Activity | Draw two diagrams – one to represent the dynamic structure of the Shakespeare play that you are studying; the other to represent the symmetric structure.

The context question

Many syllabuses feature what is known as a 'context' question on a Shakespeare text. This consists of an extract from a play that you have studied. Sometimes this will be a single speech; sometimes a dialogue between two or more characters.

Questions on the context passage come in two different forms:

- specific questions which focus entirely on the material in the passage
- questions based on the passage but which also want you to refer to other parts of the play

(It is quite possible to get both types of question within the same context.)

Always be clear in your own mind which kind of question you are answering and pay attention to what the question is asking you. If the question asks, 'From the passage, what do you learn about the speaker's character?' and you include information from elsewhere in the play you will be wasting precious time. Similarly, if you are asked to 'Comment on the importance of this scene to the overall effect of the play' and you only comment on the scene itself, you will be throwing potential marks away.

Approaching the context

There are several simple steps you can take to help you to handle the context question effectively:

1 Read the passage very carefully at least twice before attempting to answer any of the questions.

2 Read all the questions carefully before starting to write any answers. If you do not, you run the risk of including material in one answer which is required by another question.

3 Identify the key words and phrases in the question. This will help you to focus your mind on exactly what the question is asking you to do.

4 Roughly plan out (either in your head or on paper) what information you will include for each question.

Types of questions

The following are given as examples of question types but obviously wording and focus can vary.

1 'Comment on the effectiveness of this extract.'

Although superficially this may appear fairly open-ended it is really looking for some quite specific comments about any or all of the following features:

- language – the effectiveness of vocabulary, imagery, etc.
- action – the way the plot develops and links to other parts of the play
- character – significant or revealing points with regard to character
- themes – the relevance of the passage to the themes expressed through the play
- form – the way the passage is written, e.g. verse or prose, and the effect created by the particular form used

2 'What does the passage reveal about the speaker's character and state of mind at this point in the play?'

This kind of question suggests that there is something in the extract which is of particular significance in terms of character. Avoid just writing all you know about that character and focus on what specifically is shown through the passage.

3 'What is the dramatic significance of this passage?'

The idea of dramatic significance can be a little puzzling at first but actually it is quite straightforward. It really is a signal to let you know that you should comment on some or all of the following:

- how the content of the passage relates to and contributes to the whole plot
- what and how it contributes to your understanding of character(s)
- its relevance to the underlying themes of the play
- its contribution to the creation of atmosphere and mood
- its contribution to the overall impact on the audience both at this point in the play and to play as a whole

4 'Comment on the language used in the passage.'

This question is sometimes phrased as 'Comment on the way in which the passage is expressed' and is asking you to focus in detail on the language used in the passage in terms of the effect it creates. The key here is to avoid general comments and deal with specific words, phrases, and images, writing about the particular effects that they create. Here are some points to consider for this kind of question:

- the tone of the language
- the mood created
- the images used and their effect
- the way the language is structured and the impact this has
- the effect of the particular form chosen, e.g. blank verse, prose, etc.
- the rhythm created and its effect

Some Exam Boards have abandoned the approach to the context question which asks a number of separate questions in favour of a single question which then includes some suggested points for candidates to consider. For example, the AEB adopt this approach in the following 1996 exemplars. The passage, taken from *King Lear* (Act IV Scene 7) is followed by this question:

'Show how Shakespeare builds our sympathy for both Lear and Cordelia in this recognition scene.

You may wish to consider in your response:
the relationship of Lear and Cordelia
the language they use
the nature of the dramatic writing
the effect of this scene on your thoughts and feelings
the importance of this scene in the overall effect of the play'

Similarly, following an extract from Act I Scene 4 of *Much Ado About Nothing* the context question is this:

'How does Shakespeare present Claudio and Don Pedro to us at this moment in the play?
You may wish to consider in your response:
each man's attitude to love
the language
the dramatic effect on the audience'

Do not worry if you do not know these plays, the point is to get a feel for the kind of questions that are set. Try to obtain as many examples of recent past papers or exemplar material for the particular syllabus that you are studying and examine carefully the kind of questions that are asked.

Activity

1 Select an appropriate passage from the Shakespeare text that you are studying and construct a context question or series of questions of the type used on your particular syllabus. Also prepare specimen answers to your questions – a kind of 'mark scheme' if you like.
2 Exchange your 'context' passage and questions with a partner and have a go at answer their paper while they do yours. When you have finished read each other's responses and 'mark' the work.
3 Then meet as a group to discuss both the questions you devised and the various responses to them.

Critical notes and commentaries

There have probably been more critical works written on Shakespeare than any other writer. This can give the impression that in order to 'understand' his plays it is also necessary to be familiar with the massive body of scholarship that attaches itself to his works. This is not true.

When studying a Shakespeare play for A-level the first thing to do is to try to make sense of it in your own terms. Reading the writings of literary critics can help to show the range of views that it is possible to take on almost any aspect of a Shakespeare play, but you must not let these views substitute your own. Be aware that other views exist and often can be supported. Use them to help form your own ideas and sometimes to revise them but do not be overawed by them. Words in print are not automatically 'true'. If you put forward a view that you can support with direct reference to the text, then you have a valid view.

Many students seek the security of prepared commentaries, particularly in the early stages of their studies. There are various ones on the market but most of them have the same basic format of a scene-by-scene summary of the play and then sections on basic features of the play such as 'themes', 'character', and 'style'. Most include some kind of 'specimen questions'. This type of commentary is sometimes frowned upon by teachers but nevertheless many students do use them and providing you are aware of their limitations they can help you come to terms with a text early on in your studies. Be aware though that in order to be successful at A-level you need to go far beyond the level of discussion that they provide.

Which edition?

If you are working on A-level Literature in a class, the edition of the Shakespeare text may well be chosen for you by your teacher. If you are working in isolation or if you are providing your own text for your class then you might find yourself puzzling over which edition to choose. The 'Arden' edition is usually regarded as the most 'academic' and is packed with detailed notes covering a whole variety of things. Many of these notes can be useful but a great many of them are more relevant to undergraduate study and beyond.

There are then several editions (New Penguin, New Swan, Cambridge, Oxford, etc.) which contain some notes, usually at the back of the book, in a more accessible form. Some are specifically aimed at school or college students and contain notes, activities, suggested essay questions, etc. Finally, there are editions that simply contain the text alone. There are no notes or other 'trimmings' in these editions and they are very inexpensive.

The key thing to remember, though, is that although notes might help they are by no means essential. Indeed, sometimes they can even interfere with you coming to grips with the text itself. It would be easy to get the impression that Shakespeare study is so arcane that you can only understand it and engage in it if you have 'notes' to unlock the meaning for you. That would be a wrong impression. The two essential requirements are your mind and the text itself.

4 The Novel

● ●

Objectives	• To find ways of gaining an overview when studying a novel
	• To analyse more specific aspects of a novel, such as characterization and narrative viewpoint
	• To develop your own responses to novels
	• To prepare for studying a set text

What is a novel?

The word 'novel' usually means something new – a novelty. Some of the earliest novels, written in the Seventeenth and Eighteenth Centuries, would have been just that. One dictionary definition describes a novel as:

❝ a fictitious prose narrative or tale presenting a picture of real life, especially of the emotional crises in the life-history of the men and women portrayed. **❞**

Jane Austen's view was that a novel was:

❝ ...only some work in which the greatest powers of the mind are displayed, in which the most thorough knowledge of human nature, the happiest delineation of its varieties, the liveliest effusions of wit and humour, are conveyed to the world in the best chosen language. **❞**

A 'novelty' suggests something fairly lightweight, entertaining, and perhaps not of lasting significance. Early novels such as those of Samuel Richardson were sometimes serious and carried strong moral messages, but could often be rather sentimental. Nowadays we tend to make a distinction between 'literary' novels and popular fiction – but this dividing line can be blurred. As part of your A-level Literature course, you will be expected to study novels which are 'literary' and to develop the ability to recognize the differences. However, it can also be interesting to study popular, mass market novels and to consider how the conventions of writing fiction are applied in them.

Activity

> In a small group, imagine that one of you has never read or encountered a novel before. Other members of the group should try to explain what a novel is. Bear in mind the definitions given on page 63 but also use your own experience of reading novels. Feed back the most useful points in your explanation to the whole group.

Studying the novel

Every A-level Literature syllabus will require that you study at least one novel as a set text for examination. Usually this will be chosen for you from a short list issued by the Exam Board. If your syllabus has a coursework option or an additional set text examination paper where you are asked to study and compare two or more texts, you may also have the opportunity to study and write about novels you have chosen yourself.

At the outset, a set text novel can seem a daunting prospect. If yours happens to be Dickens' *Bleak House*, or Eliot's *Middlemarch*, it may well be the longest book you have ever read. If it is a twentieth-century novel which does not follow realistic conventions or a novel from an earlier period where the language is unfamiliar, you may feel that you will struggle to master it. Some novels are difficult, but usually they are rewarding and a 'good read' too, once you become engaged with the plot and characters and more familiar with the author's language and ideas. In this unit we will develop strategies for approaching them and identify the most important things to pay attention to.

One concept we need to keep in mind is that there are two main attitudes or positions we can take when we study a novel. The first attitude we can hold is that what is important is the content or the 'world' which the author has created. This is a world we can enter into, full of people, places, things, and events, to which we respond with liking or hatred, pity or criticism, as we do to the real world. Studying from this position, we will discuss the characters almost as if they were beings with the ability to choose their actions.

The second position we can take, is to see the novel as a 'text', as a created work of art, and to look at it in a much more detached and analytical way. Characters are devices which the author uses and manipulates to create a particular effect. Their only existence is in the precise words on the page.

Studying with this attitude, we will be more likely to consider what a character's role is in the construction of a plot, or the effect of using particular language to describe a place or person.

As you study a novel for A-level, you will most likely begin by responding from the first position, but you will also develop your understanding of the more analytical viewpoint. You will always need to know how the text is written as well as what it says.

When studying a set text novel, there are several aspects of the novel which you will need to know well. Most examination questions, though they may be worded in different ways, will focus on one of these.

- **An overview**   You need to have a clear understanding of the plot and central ideas, how events follow on and are related, and how the novel is structured. Questions might ask you to show how the novel's structure affects the reader's response, particularly if it is not a straightforward chronological narrative.
- **Narrative viewpoint**   Who tells the story? Why has the writer chosen this viewpoint? How does this affect the reader's response?
- **Characters**   Questions often focus on one or more characters, their development or their relationships.
- **The society, setting, or world in which the novel takes place**   Questions may centre on this, or may ask about the relationship between a character and the society in which he or she lives.
- **Language and style**   There may be distinctive qualities in the writer's choice of language, for example, in the use of imagery or comic exaggeration. Questions may ask you to consider why the writer has made these choices. What is their purpose and effect?

If you are studying novels for coursework, you may not need to explore all of these aspects in detail. You may decide to concentrate on one feature, particularly if you are going to compare two or more texts (see Unit 17).

Approaching the text

With a large text like a novel, we need to become familiar enough with it to 'find our way around' easily. We need to be able to locate incidents and important passages quickly. Here are some strategies that will help you to gain this familiarity.

- If you have time, read through the novel fairly quickly before you begin to study it. This gives you the opportunity to gain an overall impression of the novel and to read it, as it was intended, for entertainment. It will also help you to see how different aspects of the novel fit together when you begin to study it in depth. You will see how the plot is constructed and have an idea of what form of novel it is.
- Do some research. Find out what you can about the author and what was going on when the novel was written. Knowing something about the

historical and social background and about the conventions and beliefs of the time can help you to understand things which may otherwise seem strange or incomprehensible.

- Keep a separate notebook or 'log' for your work on each text. Try dividing a notebook into sections, one for each important aspect of the novel. You will need pages for each of the main characters, the setting, the narrator, themes and ideas, and language and style. As you work through the novel, jot down your observations about each aspect in the appropriate places. Include important quotations and page references. Then, when you need the information for a discussion or an essay on one of these topics, it will be easy to locate.
- Annotate the text carefully. Most literature examinations are 'open book' exams which means that you may take your own annotated copy of the text in with you. To gain most benefit from this, your annotations need to be clear, concise, and easy to recognize. You are not of course intended to write notes for entire essays into your texts. For advice on effective annotation and an example, see Unit 7, page 141 or Unit 14, page 217.

Let us turn now to explore some texts. As we examine different aspects of novels in this unit, we will look at examples from these three very different novels by writers often set at A-level.

- *Emma* by Jane Austen
- *Hard Times* by Charles Dickens
- *The Handmaid's Tale* by Margaret Atwood

Activity

> Use reference books and/or information provided in editions of these novels to find out what you can about each of these authors and their eras.

An overview

Novels come in many shapes and sizes, from short novellas (more like long short stories) with a few characters and fairly simple plots, to enormously large and complex works, with numerous characters, plots, and subplots and with many different strands which may or may not be interconnected.

There are also different genres or forms of novel. For example:

- **Fictional biography or autobiography** focus on the life and development of one character.
- **Picaresque novels** follow a central character on a journey through life in which they encounter a series of 'adventures' which form separate episodes.
- **Social or 'Protest' novels** use the characters and the world they inhabit as a way of criticizing or protesting about social or political issues.

Novelists sometimes choose to combine more than one of these types.

The plot, or storyline, of a novel can also be constructed in different ways. The simplest plots relate events in straightforward chronological order, from the point of view of a single narrator, but there have been many variations on this. For example:

- In *Hard Times*, Dickens moves from one group of people in Coketown to another. The connections between them all are not completely clear until the end, when we realize he has constructed a network of threads which link them.
- In *The Handmaid's Tale*, the narrative alternates between chapters which tell the story in the 'present' of the novel and others which are flashbacks. Entitled *Night* or *Nap*, these are times when the narrator has a chance to reminisce, dream or daydream about the past.
- Emily Brontë, in *Wuthering Heights* uses two narrators and departs from chronological order by plunging us into the middle of a mysterious situation and then going back in time to explain how it has come about. She then repeats this process to show how the situation is resolved.
- *Waterland* by Graham Swift, is built up like the reconstruction of a mosaic with each chapter contributing an event or some aspect of the historical background or the surroundings, until the last 'piece' falls into place. As a historian, he shows us that what happens to people is the result or culmination of many things which have occurred in the past, some significant, some apparently not.

Activity

> 1 Discuss the structure of your set text novel. Is it simply chronological or does it operate in some other way? What do you think is the effect of this structure?
> 2 Widen your discussion to cover any other novels you have read with interesting structures.

Opening pages

Usually, we can learn quite a lot about a novel by looking closely at the first few pages. The writer will be trying to engage our attention so that we want to read on. So it is quite likely that some of the important situations, characters, and themes will be presented right from the start.

Activity

> 1 Here are the opening pages of the three novels. Read them carefully.
> 2 Working with a partner, choose one of these and discuss it in detail, making notes on the following points.
> - Who is the narrator and what, if anything, can you find out about them? Is the narrative in the third person or the first person?
> - What characters (including the narrators) are introduced? What do you learn about them?

> - What situation is presented? Does the story begin in a particular place? If so, how is it described? What atmosphere is generated?
> - Does the writer begin by explaining clearly who is who and what is what? Or are you plunged into the middle of a situation and left to work out what is going on from hints the writer gives you?
> - Can you get a sense of the author's tone? Is the writing straight-forward? Might there be hidden messages or other levels of meaning?
> - What do you notice about the writer's style? What sort of imagery, vocabulary, and sentence structures are used?
> - What do you think this novel is going to be 'about'? Can you get a sense of any important ideas or themes that may be central to it?
> - In what ways does the writer arouse your curiosity? Do you want to read further? Why?
>
> **3** Present and compare your notes with the whole group. What similarities and differences are there between the three passages?
>
> **4** Try working on the opening pages of any other novel which you are studying in the same way.

Emma

Chapter 1

Emma Woodhouse, handsome, clever, and rich, with a comfortable home and happy disposition, seemed to unite some of the best blessings of existence; and had lived nearly twenty-one years in the world with very little to distress or vex her.

She was the youngest of the two daughters of a most affectionate, indulgent father and had, in consequence of her sister's marriage, been mistress of his house from a very early period. Her mother had died too long ago for her to have more than an indistinct remembrance of her caresses; and her place had been supplied by an excellent woman as governess, who had fallen little short of a mother in affection.

Sixteen years had Miss Taylor been in Mr Woodhouse's family, less as a governess than a friend, very fond of both daughters, but particularly of Emma. Between them it was more the intimacy of sisters. Even before Miss Taylor had ceased to hold the nominal office of governess, the mildness of her temper had hardly allowed her to impose any restraint; and the shadow of authority being now long passed away, they had been living together as friend and friend very mutually attached, and Emma doing just what she liked; highly esteeming Miss Taylor's judgement, but directed chiefly by her own.

The real evils, indeed, of Emma's situation were the power of having rather too much her own way, and a disposition to think a little too well of herself; these were the disadvantages which threatened to alloy to her many enjoyments. The danger, however, was at present so unperceived, that they did not by any means rank as misfortunes with her.

Sorrow came – a gentle sorrow – but not at all in the shape of any disagreeable consciousness. Miss Taylor married. It was Miss Taylor's loss which first brought grief. It was on the wedding-day of this beloved friend that Emma first sat in mournful thought of any continuance. The wedding over, and the bride-people gone, her father and herself were left to dine together, with no prospect of a third to cheer a long evening. Her father composed himself to sleep after dinner, as usual, and she had then only to sit and think of what she had lost.

Jane Austen

Hard Times

Chapter 1
The One Thing Needful
'Now, what I want is, Facts. Teach these boys and girls nothing but Facts. Facts alone are wanted in life. Plant nothing else, and root out everything else. You can only form the minds of reasoning animals upon Facts: nothing else will ever be of any service to them. This is the principle on which I bring up these children. Stick to Facts, sir!'
The scene was a plain, bare, monotonous vault of a schoolroom, and the speaker's square forefinger emphasized his observations by underscoring every sentence with a line on the schoolmaster's sleeve. The emphasis was helped by the speaker's square wall of a forehead, which had his eyebrows for its base, while his eyes found commodious cellarage in two dark caves, overshadowed by the wall. The emphasis was helped by the speaker's mouth, which was wide, thin, and hard set. The emphasis was helped by the speaker's voice, which was inflexible, dry, and dictatorial. The emphasis was helped by the speaker's hair, which bristled on the skirts of his bald head, a plantation of firs to keep the wind from its shining surface, all covered with knobs, like the crust of a plum pie, as if the head had scarcely warehouse-room for the hard facts stored inside. The speaker's obstinate carriage, square coat, square legs, square shoulders – nay, his very neckcloth, trained to take him by the throat with an unaccommodating grasp, like a stubborn fact, as it was – all helped the emphasis.
 'In this life, we want nothing but Facts, sir; nothing but Facts!'
The speaker, and the schoolmaster, and the third grown person present, all backed a little, and swept with their eyes the inclined plane of little vessels then and there arranged in order, ready to have imperial gallons of facts poured into them until they were full to the brim.

Charles Dickens

The Handmaid's Tale

Chapter 1
We slept in what had once been the gymnasium. The floor was of varnished wood, with stripes and circles painted on it, for the games that were formerly played there; the hoops for the basketball nets were still in place, though the nets were gone. A balcony ran around the room, for the spectators, and I thought I could smell, faintly like an after image, the pungent scent of sweat, shot through

with the sweet taste of chewing gum and perfume from the watching girls, felt-skirted as I knew from pictures, later in mini-skirts, then pants, then in one earring, spiky green-streaked hair. Dances would have been held there; the music lingered, a palimpsest of unheard sound, style upon style, an undercurrent of drums, a forlorn wail, garlands made of tissue-paper flowers, cardboard devils, a revolving ball of mirrors, powdering the dancers with a snow of light.

There was old sex in the room and loneliness, and expectation, of something without a shape or name. I remember that yearning, for something that was always about to happen and was never the same as the hands that were on us there and then, in the small of the back, or out back, in the parking lot, or in the television room with the sound turned down and only the pictures flickering over lifting flesh.

We yearned for the future. How did we learn it, that talent for insatiability? It was in the air; and it was still in the air, an afterthought, as we tried to sleep, in the army cots that been set up in rows, with spaces between so we could not talk. We had flannelette sheets, like children's, and army-issue blankets, old ones that still said U.S. We folded our clothes neatly and laid them on the stools at the ends of the beds. The lights were turned down but not out. Aunt Sara and Aunt Elizabeth patrolled; they had electric cattle prods slung on thongs from their leather belts.

Margaret Atwood

Narrative viewpoint

You will have noticed that in *Emma* and *Hard Times* the authors have chosen to use third-person narrative, while Margaret Atwood uses a first-person narrator for *The Handmaid's Tale*. There are advantages and disadvantages, and different possibilities in each.

Writing in the first person, the author takes on the role of a character (or characters) and tells the story 'from the inside'. This can strengthen the illusion that the novel is 'real', by making us, the readers, feel involved and able to empathize with the character. However, this usually also limits our perspective to this one character's perceptions: we only see other characters through their eyes. We cannot know of events the narrator does not witness unless they are reported by another character, for example in conversation.

As we have only this narrator's words to go on, we need to ask how far we can trust the narrator. He or she might be biased, deluded, blind to the true significance of events, or even deliberately deceiving the reader. Often, this very question adds interest to a first-person narrative.

The narrator in *The Handmaid's Tale* is Offred, a woman living in a future society in which people are restricted to very narrow, specific roles. Offred is a handmaid. Her job is to 'breed' to ensure the survival of her nation, while other women are responsible for domestic chores and some carry out the formal duties of a wife. Much of her narrative is in **stream of consciousness**, a form in which the writer aims to give a sense of how a character's mind works by tracking her thoughts as they flow from one topic to another. We have to piece together our impressions of Offred from what she reveals of her thoughts and feelings, her actions, and her attitudes to other characters.

Activity

> Here, early in the novel, Offred describes her living quarters and ponders her situation. Read the extract and make a note of everything that you learn about her as a person and as a storyteller. Consider also how far she engages your interest and sympathy.

The Handmaid's Tale

Chapter 2

A window, two white curtains. Under the window, a window seat with a little cushion. When the window is partly open – it only opens partly – the air can come in and make the curtains move. I can sit in the chair, or on the window seat, hands folded, and watch this. Sunlight comes in through the window too, and falls on the floor, which is made of wood, in narrow strips, highly polished. I can smell the polish. There's a rug on the floor, oval, of braided rags. This is the kind of touch they like: folk art, archaic, made by women, in their spare time, from things that have no further use. A return to traditional values. Waste not want not. I am not being wasted. Why do I want?

A bed. Single, mattress medium-hard, covered with a flocked white spread. Nothing takes place in the bed but sleep; or no sleep. I try not to think too much. Like other things now, thought must be rationed. There's a lot that doesn't bear thinking about. Thinking can hurt your chances, and I intend to last. I know why there is no glass, in front of the water-colour picture of blue irises, and why the window only opens partly and why the glass in it is shatterproof. It isn't running away they're afraid of. We wouldn't get far. It's those other escapes, the ones you can open in yourself, given a cutting edge.

So. Apart from these details, this could be a college guest room, for the less distinguished visitors; or a room in a rooming-house, of former times, for ladies in reduced circumstances. That is what we are now. The circumstances have been reduced; for those of us who still have circumstances.

But a chair, sunlight, flowers: these are not to be dismissed. I am alive, I live, I breathe, I put my hand out, unfolded, into the sunlight. Where I am is not a prison but a privilege, as Aunt Lydia said, who was in love with either/or.

Margaret Atwood

Summary

Probably you will have noted the following points.

- She notices and describes her surroundings in detail and specific details spark off trains of thought about her life in an interior monologue. She pays attention to these things because there is plenty of time to do so and nothing else to occupy her.
- She separates herself from the people in authority by referring rather anonymously to 'they' and 'them'.

- She feels limited by her life and is not satisfied living by the maxims she has been taught. She longs for something more –'Waste not want not. I am not being wasted. Why do I want?'.
- She is determined to survive, even if this means denying the truth sometimes – 'Thinking can hurt your chances, and I intend to last.'.
- She is optimistic enough to recognize what is good in her surroundings – 'But a chair, sunlight, flowers: these are not to be dismissed.'.
- Her language is usually simple and she does not use specific imagery. Many of her sentences are short or incomplete. Their confiding quality suggests we already know what she is talking about and who 'they' are, when in fact we know nothing about the regime in which she lives. She likes to play with words and double meanings in a wry, humorous way – 'The circumstances have been reduced; for those of us who still have circumstances.'.

••

Third-person narrative offers different possibilities. The author or narrator adopts a position which is 'godlike', or becomes a 'fly on the wall' reporting everything to us, the readers. This omniscient (all-knowing) narrator, from a vantage point outside the action, can relate events which may occur in different places, at different times, or even simultaneously. Often we are told how different characters feel so we see things from more than one perspective. Sometimes the author might tell the story dispassionately, without commenting or judging. Usually, however, authors make their presence felt. This might be through obvious authorial intrusion, where the writer butts into the narrative to express an opinion or comment on a situation, or it might be more subtle. For example, a character may be described in language we recognize as sarcastic, 'tongue-in-cheek', or ironic, making it clear that the author is critical or mocking; or positive or negative judgements may simply be revealed by the writer's choice of vocabulary. (See Unit 12, pages 196–203.)

We can easily detect Dickens' opinion of 'the speaker' in the opening page of *Hard Times*: describing his forehead as a 'square wall' and his voice as 'inflexible, dry, and dictatorial' is only the beginning of his portrait of the rigid Mr Gradgrind. A few pages later, he is concluding his description of Stone Lodge, Mr Gradgrind's 'matter of fact home' and his fact-ridden 'model' children. His bitter sarcasm is clear:

'...Iron clamps and girders... mechanical lifts... everything that heart could wish for.'

A moment later Dickens 'intrudes' in his own voice to express his doubts:

'Everything? Well I suppose so.'

Jane Austen does something similar, but rather more gently. Primarily, her opening paragraphs in *Emma* introduce her central character. Little in the way of judgement can be detected except where she informs us that:

'The real evils indeed of Emma's situation were the power of having rather too much her own way, and a disposition to think a little too well of herself.'

She does create characters who are 'types', such as Emma's father Mr Woodhouse, the anxious hypochondriac and Miss Bates, the non-stop talker. Their traits are exaggerated, but her mockery of them tends to be affectionate, without the ferocity of Dickens. Often, she comments ironically with the voice of 'society', when it is clear that her own intention is to question or poke fun at the conventional view as she does in the famous opening lines of *Pride and Prejudice*:

'It is a truth universally acknowledged, that a single man in possession of a good fortune must be in want of a wife.'

This question of the writer's stance towards characters or situations can be quite complex. Even in third-person narrative, things are often filtered through the perceptions of one particular character. We may need to consider carefully whether the author's views match those of this character or not. Alternatively, the author may choose to write with a 'voice' which is neither their own nor that of one of the characters in the novel.

Most of *Emma* is told from Emma's point of view, with her values and prejudices, but it is also possible to detect that Jane Austen shares some of her views and not others. Emma disapproves of two characters whose social status is inferior to her own. First, the self-satisfied Mrs Elton, who fails to recognize her position in Hartfield society and is much too familiar with Emma and her friends. She is:

'a vain woman, extremely well satisfied with herself, and thinking much of her own importance; that she meant to shine and be very superior, but with manners which had been formed in a bad school, pert and familiar; that all her notions were drawn from one set of people, and one style of living; that if not foolish she was ignorant, and that her society would certainly do Mr Elton no good...
...Happily it was now time to be gone. They were off; and Emma could breathe.'

On the other hand, she also disapproves of respectable young farmer Robert Martin, whom she considers a bad match for her young protégé, Harriet Smith:

'His appearance was very neat, and he looked like a sensible young man, but his person had no other advantage; and when he came to be contrasted with gentlemen, she thought he must lose all the ground he had gained in Harriet's inclination...
..."He is very plain, undoubtedly – remarkably plain: – but that is nothing, compared with his entire want of gentility. I had no right to expect much, and I did not expect much; but I had no idea that he could be so very clownish, so totally without air. I had imagined him, I confess, a degree or two nearer gentility."'

In the novel, it is clear that we are expected to agree with Emma about Mrs Elton. She is indeed an awful woman. However, where Robert Martin is concerned, we come to see that Emma is snobbish and misguided and that Jane Austen intends us to question her opinion.

Activity

> **1** Look once more at the openings of *Emma* and *The Handmaid's Tale*. Working with a partner, rewrite the first paragraph of *The Handmaid's Tale* in the third person and the first two paragraphs of *Emma* in the first person (with Emma as the narrator). Discuss the results. What is lost and what gained from changing the narrative viewpoint?
>
> **2** Think carefully about the narrative viewpoint in the novel you are studying. Who is the narrator? Can you trust their narrative? How aware are you of the author's presence? Look for examples of authorial intrusion.

Characters

Much of the interest in a novel lies in the characters whose world we enter and in whose lives we share. We usually respond to them first as people. We can analyse their personalities, trace how they are affected by events and empathize or disapprove of them. However, we do need to remember that they do not have lives outside the pages of the novel and so, it is rarely useful to speculate about their past or future experiences. More importantly, we need to pay attention to how they are presented.

It has already been suggested that it is useful to keep a 'log' to record key passages and quotations for each important character which can be built up as you work through the text.

Summary

Characters are revealed to us in various ways.
- **Description**   The author often provides an introductory 'pen-portrait' and then builds up our knowledge with details as the narrative proceeds. Key passages describe main characters or make us aware of how they change and develop.
- **Dialogue**   Other characters often give important clues when they discuss the character concerned. We may also find out a lot about someone from his or her own speech.
- **Thoughts and feelings**   The 'inner life' of a character can be revealed directly, particularly in a first-person narrative.
- **Actions and reactions**   How characters behave in various situations will inform our view of them.
- **Imagery and symbols**   Characters may be described using simile and metaphor, or may be associated symbolically with, for example, a colour or an element. In Emily Brontë's *Wuthering Heights*, Heathcliff is frequently linked with fire and with the colour black. Similarly, in Thomas Hardy's *Tess of the D'Urbervilles*, Tess is associated with the colour red which suggests danger or marks her out as a 'fallen woman' from the beginning. (See also the Special Feature on Forster, page 92.)

Activity

Here are some introductory character sketches from *Emma*, *Hard Times*, and *The Handmaid's Tale*. Working in a small group, make notes on these points.
- What kind of information does each author provide about the character in question?
- Do you learn anything of the character's inner life or just factual or superficial information?
- How does each writer use language in each case? Consider sentence structure, vocabulary, use of imagery, and other effects.
- What can you detect of the author's attitude to the character?

1

Mr John Knightley was a tall, gentleman-like, and very clever man; rising in his profession, domestic, and respectable in his private character; but with reserved manners which prevented his being generally pleasing; and capable of being sometimes out of humour. He was not an ill-tempered man, not so often unreasonably cross as to deserve such a reproach; but his temper was not his great perfection; and indeed, with such a worshipping wife, it was hardly possible that any natural defects in it would not be increased.

2

The Commander has on his black uniform, in which he looks like a museum guard. A semi-retired man, genial but wary, killing time. But only at first glance. After that he looks like a midwestern bank president, with his straight neatly brushed silver hair, his sober posture, shoulders a little stooped. And after that there is his moustache, silver also, and after that his chin, which really you can't miss. When you get down as far as the chin he looks like a vodka ad, in a glossy magazine, of times gone by.

His manner is mild, his hands large, with thick fingers and acquisitive thumbs, his blue eyes uncommunicative, falsely innocuous.

3

[Mr Bounderby] was a rich man: banker, merchant, manufacturer, and what not. A big, loud man, with a stare and a metallic laugh. A man made out of a coarse material, which seemed to have been stretched to make so much of him. A man with a great puffed head and forehead, swelled veins in his temples, and such a strained skin to his face that it seemed to hold his eyes open and lift his eyebrows up. A man with a pervading appearance on him of being inflated like a balloon, and ready to start. A man who could never sufficiently vaunt himself a self-made man. A man who was always proclaiming, through that brassy speaking-trumpet of a voice of his, his old ignorance and his old poverty. A man who was the Bully of humility.

4

Moira, sitting on the edge of my bed, legs crossed, ankle on knee, in her purple overalls, one dangly earring, the gold fingernail she wore to be eccentric, a cigarette between her stubby yellow-ended fingers. Let's go for a beer.

5

Harriet certainly was not clever, but she had a sweet, docile, grateful disposition; was totally free from conceit; and only desiring to be guided by any one she looked up to. Her early attachment to [Emma] herself was very amiable; and her inclination for good company, and power of appreciating what was elegant and clever shewed that there was no want of taste, though strength of understanding must not be expected.

Development of a character and a relationship

Now let us look at a character in more detail. If you are asked to explore the way a character is presented and how they change and develop in the course of a novel, it is a good idea to choose a few passages or episodes from different parts of the novel which feature the character to examine in detail. These may be descriptive passages, moments of dramatic action, episodes where the character contrasts or is in conflict with others, or where they face a decision.

Louisa Gradgrind

Dickens created the bleak world of Coketown, the setting of *Hard Times*, to expose and mock the philosophy of Utilitarianism. This set of beliefs saw people only in terms of their usefulness as workers or tools for industry and wealth-creation. No allowances were made for people having imaginations or emotional lives.

Many of Dickens' characters, such as Mr Bounderby, are caricatures whose traits are exaggerated in the extreme. The effect is comic, but they also allow Dickens to make serious points and express his anger. Sometimes, he is accused of creating only caricatures, unrealistic people without depth, but this is by no means always the case. In *Hard Times*, the caricatures are usually recognizable by their comical names, while the central characters who develop as 'real' people are allowed to have ordinary names. Louisa Gradgrind, a victim of her father's belief that facts are 'The one thing needful', is one of these. The account of how her life and development are distorted, and of how her father learns to regret his rigid methods, is moving.

Activity

> We first meet Louisa when her father is appalled to have discovered her with her brother Tom, spying on the local circus, a forbidden entertainment. Study the passage closely, and make notes on how Dickens presents her and her relationship with her father. Consider in particular:
> • the imagery used to describe Louisa's manner
> • what is revealed about each of them by the dialogue

Hard Times

Chapter 3
A Loophole

'In the name of wonder, idleness, and folly!' said Mr Gradgrind, leading each away by a hand; 'what do you do here?'

'Wanted to see what it was like,' returned Louisa shortly.

'What it was like?'

'Yes, father.'

There was an air of jaded sullenness in them both, and particularly in the girl: yet, struggling through the dissatisfaction of her face, there was a light with nothing to rest upon, a fire with nothing to burn, a starved imagination keeping life in itself somehow, which brightened its expression. Not with the brightness natural to cheerful youth, but with uncertain, eager, doubtful flashes, which had something painful in them, analogous to the changes on a blind face groping its way. She was a child now, of fifteen or sixteen; but at no distant day would seem to become a woman all at once. Her father thought so as he looked at her. She was pretty. Would have been self-willed (he thought in his eminently practical way), but for her bringing-up.

'Thomas, though I have the fact before me, I find it difficult to believe that you, with your education and resources, should have brought your sister to a scene like this.'

'I brought him, father,' said Louisa quickly. 'I asked him to come.'

'I am sorry to hear it. I am very sorry indeed to hear it. It makes Thomas no better, and it makes you worse, Louisa.'

She looked at her father again, but no tear fell down her cheek.

'You! Thomas and you, to whom the circle of the sciences is open; Thomas and you, who may be said to be replete with facts; Thomas and you, who have been trained to mathematical exactness; Thomas and you here!' cried Mr Gradgrind. 'In this degraded position! I am amazed.'

'I was tired. I have been tired a long time, ' said Louisa.

'Tired? Of what?' asked the astonished father.

'I don't know of what – of everything I think.'

'Say not another word, ' returned Mr Gradgrind. 'You are childish. I will hear no more.'

Charles Dickens

Louisa is presented in opposition to her father and his world of facts, but as yet the conflict is mostly within her, as her thwarted imagination fights for life. The images of light and an inward 'fire with nothing to burn' will recur frequently. She often gazes at the smoking chimneys of the Coketown factories which she knows must contain flames which have been suppressed, like her own imagination, and which burst out when darkness falls.

The dialogue reveals just how little capacity Gradgrind has for understanding his children. Notice the contrast between Louisa's short answers and her father's pompous, wordy style. She seems sullen, but also honest and very self-controlled. Her dry education has rendered her incapable of tears or emotional displays. His final accusation, that she is childish, is ironic. She has never been allowed to be a child. The passage does mark the first time Gradgrind is surprised by his children. Later it will be Louisa's tragedy which jolts him out of his complacency.

Now let us examine two further passages which reveal something of how their characters and their relationship alter.

Activity

> **1** Study the extracts carefully, together with the one on page 77. Discuss how the characters and their relationship are presented in each case.
> **2** Write a detailed comparison of the three passages. In what ways does Dickens convey the changes in Louisa's and Gradgrind's characters and in their relationship? Remember to consider:
> - the imagery used in the setting
> - characters dialogue, actions, and reactions

Hard Times

Chapter 15
Father and Daughter
[Mr Gradgrind has just proposed that in the name of reason, Louisa should undertake a loveless marriage to the appalling Mr Bounderby, a rich banker and merchant.]
'I now leave you to judge for yourself,' said Mr Gradgrind. 'I have stated the case, as such cases are usually stated among practical minds; I have stated it, as the case of your mother and myself was stated in its time. The rest, my dear Louisa, is for you to decide.'
From the beginning, she had sat looking at him fixedly. As he now leaned back in his chair, and bent his deep-set eyes upon her in his turn, perhaps he might have seen one wavering moment in her, when she was impelled to throw herself upon his breast, and give him the pent-up confidences of her heart. But, to see it, he must have overleaped at a bound the artificial barriers he had for many years been erecting, between himself and all those subtle essences of humanity which will elude the utmost cunning of algebra until the last trumpet ever to be sounded shall blow even algebra to wreck. The barriers were too many and too high for such a leap. With his unbending, utilitarian, matter of fact face, he hardened her again; and the moment shot away into the plumbless depths of the past, to mingle with all the lost opportunities that are drowned there.
Removing her eyes from him, she sat so long looking silently towards the town, that he said, at length: 'Are you consulting the chimneys of the Coketown works, Louisa?'
'There seems to be nothing there, but languid and monotonous smoke. Yet when the night comes, fire bursts out, Father!' she answered, turning quickly.
'Of course I know that, Louisa. I do not see the application of the remark.' To do him justice, he did not, at all.

Charles Dickens

Hard Times

Chapter 28
Down

[Long since married to Bounderby, Louisa has discovered and is tempted by the possibility of real love with another man. She returns to her father in great distress.]

When it thundered very loudly, [Mr Gradgrind] glanced towards Coketown, having it in his mind that some of the tall chimneys might be struck by lightning. The thunder was rolling into the distance, and the rain was pouring down like a deluge, when the door of his room opened. He looked round the lamp upon his table, and saw, with amazement, his eldest daughter.

'Louisa!'

'Father, I want to speak to you.'

'What is the matter? How strange you look! And good Heaven,' said Mr Gradgrind, wondering more and more, 'have you come here exposed to this storm?'

She put her hands to her dress, as if she hardly knew. 'Yes.' Then she uncovered her head, and letting her cloak and hood fall where they might, stood looking at him: so colourless, so dishevelled, so defiant and despairing, that he was afraid of her.

'What is it? I conjure you, Louisa, tell me what is the matter?'

She dropped into a chair before him, and put her cold hand on his arm.

'Father, you have trained me from my cradle.'

'Yes Louisa.'

'I curse the hour in which I was born to such a destiny.'

He looked at her in doubt and dread, vacantly repeating, 'Curse the hour? Curse the hour?'

'How could you give me life, and take from me all the inappreciable things that raise it from the state of conscious death? Where are the graces of my soul? Where are the sentiments of my heart? What have you done, O father, what have you done, with the garden that should have bloomed once, in this great wilderness here!'

She struck herself with both hands upon her bosom.

'If it had ever been here, its ashes alone would save me from the void in which my whole life sinks.'

Charles Dickens

Activity

1 Choose a character from a novel you are studying. Then select three or four passages from different parts of the novel which show 'key' moments for that character.

2 Analyse the passages carefully, paying close attention to how language and imagery are used to present the character at different times.

3 Using examples from these passages, write a short essay about the development of your chosen character.

4 Alternatively, choose an important relationship from a novel you are working on and follow steps 1 to 3.

The setting

The imaginary 'world' of a novel, into which the reader is invited, is often more than simply 'the place where the story happens'. The physical environment may be important in itself or as a backdrop to the action but it can also be used to reflect the characters and their experiences. It can also be symbolic of the ideas the writer wishes to convey. However, the 'world' of a novel will also portray a society with its own culture, politics, and values. Characters may exist comfortably in their worlds, but often, the whole thrust of a novel depends on the central character being a misfit, or being in conflict with some aspect of their 'society', whether this is their family, their social class, a religious group, or a state.

The world of a novel can be as small as a household or as large as a nation. Jane Austen set herself tight limits, saying that 'Three or four families in a country village is the very thing to work on.' *Emma* is set in Highbury, a 'large and populous village almost amounting to a town'. London is only sixteen miles distant, but far enough in those days to seem out of easy reach. The action concerns only a few of the 'best' families in the village – those with whom the Woodhouses, at the top of their social ladder, can associate, and one or two others of lower status who provide material for comedy.

Although Jane Austen is quick to make fun of hypocrisy and snobbery, she does not challenge the rigid class boundaries of Highbury; in fact in this novel she endorses them. Emma's attempts to disregard them are definitely seen as misguided. Her matchmaking with Mr Elton on behalf of her 'friend' Harriet Smith, pretty, but illegitimate and penniless, causes only pain and embarrassment.

Little space is given to describing places in *Emma*; it is the social world which is important. However, there are some occasions when the physical surroundings are given more prominence. Here, for example, are the grounds of Donwell Abbey, home of Mr Knightley.

Emma

Chapter 42
...it was in itself a charming walk and the view which closed it extremely pretty. – The considerable slope, at nearly the foot of which the Abbey stood, gradually acquired a steeper form beyond its grounds; and at half a mile distant was a bank of considerable abruptness and grandeur, well clothed with wood; – and at the bottom of this bank, favourably placed and sheltered, rose the Abbey-Mill Farm, with meadows in front, and the river making a close and handsome curve around it.

Jane Austen

Activity

> Discuss the following points.
> - If this property reflects its owner, what sort of a man would you expect him to be?
> - Compare the situation of the Abbey with that of Abbey-Mill Farm.

Jane Austen almost never uses imagery, in the poetic sense. However, here her description provides an image of the people associated with the places. Mr Knightley is the one real gentleman who is right for Emma. He is firm and honest, sees the truth and speaks it, but is not talkative. The grounds of his home are solid and impressive, slightly rugged and placed at a height; the bank is 'well clothed with wood', mirroring his reticence. Meanwhile, in its proper position, at the foot of the hill, but protected by it, lies the farm where eventually Harriet will take her place with Robert Martin.

In *Hard Times*, the world Dickens creates is that of a northern English industrial town, a larger world than Jane Austen's Highbury. Like some of his characters, the setting is a caricature. It is based on a real town, but has exaggerated features. His intention of protesting against the deadening effects of Utilitarianism is never clearer than when he introduces us to Coketown. He presents us with an environment where the physical surroundings reflect the social conditions. Read his description and then consider it through the activity which follows.

Hard Times

Chapter 5
The Key-note
Coketown, to which Messrs Bounderby and Gradgrind now walked, was a triumph of fact; it had no greater taint of fancy in it than Mrs Gradgrind herself. Let us strike the key-note, Coketown, before pursuing our tune.
It was a town of red brick, or of brick that would have been red if the smoke and ashes had allowed it; but, as matters stood it was a town of unnatural red and black like the painted face of a savage. It was a town of machinery and tall chimneys, out of which interminable serpents of smoke trailed themselves for ever and ever, and never got uncoiled. It had a black canal in it, and a river that ran purple with ill-smelling dye, and vast piles of building full of windows where there was a rattling and a trembling all day long, and where the piston of the steam-engine worked monotonously up and down, like the head of an elephant in a state of melancholy madness. It contained several large streets all very like one another, and many small streets still more like one another, inhabited by people equally like one another, who all went in and out at the same hours, with the same sound upon the same pavements, to do the same work, and to whom every day was the same as yesterday and tomorrow, and every year the counterpart of the last and the next.

Charles Dickens

Activity	How does Dickens present Coketown? Make notes on his use of: • simile and metaphor • colour and the senses • the rhythm of the passage • sentence construction

The world of *The Handmaid's Tale* is wider again. It is set in the future, in an imaginary state in America, The Republic of Gilead. Fearful about declining population, due to man-made environmental disaster, a dictatorship has assigned roles to all people, but particularly to women. Wives are idealized, non-sexual beings. They wear virginal blue, while those women capable of the all-important child-bearing are assigned to them as handmaids or breeders, dressed in red. This symbolizes blood, sex, and childbirth. It marks them out as 'fallen women'. Gilead is a state ruled by terror, in which it is highly dangerous to ask questions or to assert one's individuality in any way. We do not even discover the narrator's real name: she is merely the handmaid 'Of-Fred'.

None of this is made clear to us at the start of the novel. Only gradually as we read Offred's stream of consciousness narrative do we piece together enough information to understand what is going on. It is quite a way into the text before we are provided with some 'historical background'. Here, Offred, waiting to assist at a birth, remembers some of the teaching she received at the Red Centre, where the handmaids are trained.

The Handmaid's Tale

Chapter 19

The siren goes on and on. That used to be the sound of death, for ambulances or fires. Possibly it will be the sound of death today also. We will soon know. What will Ofwarren give birth to? A baby, as we all hope? Or something else, an Unbaby, with a pinhead or a snout like a dog's, or two bodies, or a hole in its heart or no arms, or webbed hands and feet? There's no telling. They could tell once, with machines, but that is now outlawed. What would be the point of knowing, anyway? You can't have them taken out; whatever it is must be carried to term.

The chances are one in four, we learned that at the Centre. The air got too full, once, of chemicals, rays, radiation, the water swarmed with toxic molecules, all of that takes years to clean up, and meanwhile they creep into your body, camp out in your fatty cells. Who knows, your very flesh may be polluted, dirty as an oily beach, sure death to shore birds and unborn babies. Maybe a vulture would die of eating you. Maybe you light up in the dark, like an old-fashioned watch. Death-watch. That's a kind of beetle, it buries carrion.

I can't think of myself, my body, sometimes, without seeing the skeleton: how I must appear to an electron. A cradle of life, made of bones; and within, hazards, warped proteins, bad crystals, jagged as glass. Women took medicines, pills, men sprayed trees, cows ate grass, all that souped-up piss flowed into the rivers. Not to mention the exploding atomic power plants, along the San Andreas fault, nobody's fault, during the earthquakes, and the mutant strain of syphilis no mould could touch. Some did it themselves, had themselves tied shut with catgut or scarred with chemicals. How could they, said Aunt Lydia, O how could they have done such a thing? Jezebels! Scorning God's gifts! Wringing her hands. It's a risk you're taking, said Aunt Lydia, but you are the shock troops, you will march out in advance, into dangerous territory. The greater the risk, the greater the glory. She clasped her hands, radiant with our phony courage. We looked down at the tops of our desks. To go through all that and give birth to a shredder: it wasn't a fine thought. We didn't know exactly what would happen to the babies that didn't get passed, that were declared Unbabies. But we knew they were put somewhere, quickly, away.

Margaret Atwood

Activity | Read the passage carefully and discuss in a small group what you learn about the following points.
- What has happened in Gilead in the past.
- What conditions are like in Gilead now.
- The laws and customs of Gilead in respect of pregnancy and childbirth.
- How propaganda and religion are used to ensure the women fit in with the needs of the regime.

In *Hard Times* and *The Handmaid's Tale*, the settings are very important. In both cases the writers have presented aspects they dislike about their own societies in an exaggerated form. This enables them to draw attention to these and to protest in an indirect way whilst being thought-provoking and entertaining. While Dickens demonstrates in Coketown the terrible results of extreme Utilitarianism, Margaret Atwood writes as a feminist, concerned about the environment and about women being defined and limited by their traditional roles. Both writers create worlds where people are reduced to particular functions. However, both have a hopeful note in that the 'human spirit' is not entirely crushed despite such repressive regimes. 'Fancy' and imagination may be buried and distorted in *Hard Times*, but they do not die completely. Similarly, through the very telling of her story we know that Offred is far more than just her 'viable ovaries'.

Activity | Study and make notes on the setting of the novel you are studying.
- What sort of 'world' is it? How large or small, open or restrictive? What are its rules, values, beliefs, and customs?
- Locate passages where the author describes the physical surroundings, comments on the social order, or where characters act or speak in a way which represents their society.
- Do the characters fit comfortably in their world or are they in opposition to it? Is this shown to be a good or bad thing?

Language and style

Unless we are studying linguistics, we do not usually discuss a writer's use of language in isolation from its content. What we are concerned with is how effectively language is used to create worlds or present characters, situations, and ideas. So you probably will have noticed that as we have looked at each of these aspects of the novel, we have always examined the writer's language and style at the same time.

Summary

Here are some of the features of language we have considered.
- **Narrative voice:** the choice of first-person or third-person narrative.
- **Imagery:** the use of simile and metaphor. Look particularly for recurring images or patterns of imagery.
- **Sentence/paragraph structure:** the use of sentences which are long or short, complete or incomplete, complex or simple.
- **Vocabulary:** the selection of one word or group of words rather than another.

For some examples, look again at the extracts from *Hard Times* which present Louisa Gradgrind and Coketown. Style is also discussed in Unit 12, pages 194–203.

Set text examination questions

Novels are long and complex, and you will have devoted a substantial amount of time on your course to studying your text. As with any other set text, the time you are given to write about your set text novel in A-level Literature examinations is very short – perhaps as little as 45 minutes. This means you will only be able use a very small part of your knowledge about the text. In your answer, you must be relevant and selective.

Examination questions will focus your attention on one aspect of the text, such as a character. You need to keep this idea in your mind throughout and make sure every point you make is relevant to the question.

It is vital in questions on the novel that you are selective, i.e that you have the ability to home in quickly on episodes in the text which are most useful in answering the question and choose quotations which best illustrate your ideas. Examiners frequently complain that students are not sufficiently selective about what they include.

However little time you have, it is a good idea to give a small part of that to planning your answer. Even two or three minutes can be enough to help you work out what it is essential to mention and to find a sense of direction in your writing.

For detailed guidance on all aspects of revising set texts and developing exam-writing skills see Unit 16, pages 233–240.

Coursework with novels

In coursework, you can explore a topic in more detail and in a more leisurely way than you can under the pressure of examination time limits. If you are concentrating on one novel text for coursework, any of the aspects covered in this unit will provide the basis for a coursework essay question.

Many students also choose to study novels for the comparative element of the course. Reading two or more novels which have something in common, and working out the connections and contrasts between them, can be very satisfying. You could also write comparatively about the novels featured in this unit; despite the fact that they are widely different, there are some interesting ways they can be linked. For example:

- *Hard Times* and *The Handmaid's Tale* are both novels which present repressive societies which limit the potential of the individuals in them. In each case, a central character is damaged and restricted by the regime in which she lives, but struggles to cope and retain some sense of self.

- In *Emma* and *Hard Times* the authors use humour, through characters who are exaggerated or caricatures, to make serious moral points.

- *Emma* and *The Handmaid's Tale* both have something to tell us about the roles of men and women in different societies.

For more on writing coursework essays and framing suitable questions see Unit 17, pages 241–245.

Special Feature: E. M. Forster

Edward Morgan Forster was born in 1879 and was educated at Tunbridge School and King's College, Cambridge. Whilst at King's he became a member of an exclusive intellectual society which included the economist, John Maynard Keynes and the biographer and essayist, Lytton Strachey. After leaving Cambridge, Forster travelled in Italy and Greece and the first of his 'Italian' novels, *Where Angels Fear to Tread*, was published in 1905 followed by *The Longest Journey*, set entirely in England, in 1907. His second 'Italian' novel, *A Room With a View*, was published in 1908 and his second 'English' novel, *Howards End*, in 1910. Later Forster travelled extensively in India, particularly between 1912–13 and 1921–23, publishing his last novel, *A Passage to India*, in 1924. Although his novel *Maurice* was also completed during this period (1913), it was only circulated privately and was not published until after his death in 1970. This was because of society's then repressive attitude towards homosexuality, which is one of the themes of the novel. We must remember that Forster was writing only 30 years after Oscar Wilde had been imprisoned for what were termed 'homosexual offences'.

After 1924 Forster turned away from fiction and devoted his energies to a wide range of literary activities including biography, essays, and collaborating in the writing of the libretto for Britten's opera *Billy Budd*. As the first president of the National Council for Civil Liberties, Forster did much work in the defence of civil liberties. He also stood out against censorship, appearing as a witness for the defence in the trial of the publishers of D. H. Lawrence's controversial novel *Lady Chatterley's Lover* in 1960.

Returning to the focus of this special feature, the four novels that most frequently appear on A-level syllabuses are *Howards End*, *A Room With a View*, *Where Angels Fear to Tread*, and *A Passage to India*. This special feature will examine Forster's work focusing in particular on *A Room With a View* to illustrate some of the ideas and aspects explored.

Forster in context

In order to understand the kind of writer that Forster is and the central areas of interest of his work it can be very useful to know something about his background and the social and political contexts within which he wrote. Here are some key points that will help you to see his work in context.

- In essence, Forster was an Edwardian novelist – most of his novels being written before the First World War. This was a period when the British Empire was at its height and British influence and power was worldwide.

- It was also a time when there were great extremes of wealth and poverty; class divisions were very marked.
- Forster came from a middle-class background and enjoyed the comfort and privilege that this afforded.
- He was also an intellectual with a liberal view. He was very sensitive to the social inequalities and injustices that he saw around him. This made him aware of the contradictions of his own position. He enjoyed the benefits afforded by his class but at the same time wanted that class system reformed to create greater equality between people. In this sense he stood outside his class, viewing it in a detached, often critical way.
- It has been suggested that Forster's homosexuality meant that he felt inwardly alienated from his society and so this too allowed him to view it in a dispassionate way.
- He was associated with the Bloomsbury Group, a group of intellectuals who challenged the social, artistic, and sexual restrictions of Victorian society.
- Forster's travels gave him a first-hand view of the British abroad and the various attitudes they exhibited to different cultures, races, and classes.

Themes and ideas

Forster's background was embedded in the culture and values of the Middle Class but he was well aware of its weaknesses as well as its strengths:

'They gained wealth by the Industrial Revolution, political power by the Reform Bill of 1832; they are connected with the rise and organization of the British Empire; they are responsible for the literature of the Nineteenth Century.'

'Notes on the English Character' from *Arbinger Harvest*

Its hallmarks are 'Solidity, caution, integrity, efficiency. Lack of imagination, hypocrisy.' It is these last two characteristics that Forster is particularly interested in exploring and satirizing in his novels.

In *A Room With a View* he focuses on a number of ideas relating to the Middle Class, exposing their shortcomings and weaknesses through gentle comedy. The novel opens in Florence where Lucy Honeychurch is on holiday with her older cousin and chaperone, Miss Bartlett. In the following extract, Lucy and her cousin have just arrived at the Pension Bertolini to find that the rooms they have been given do not have a view. Mr Emerson, a fellow traveller, offers them his own and his son's rooms which do have views. Even at this early stage, Forster introduces some of the key themes of the novel.

Activity

1 Read the extract on page 88 carefully making a note of moments that you think are significant or which catch your attention. Choose brief quotations from the text to support your points.
2 When you have done that, compare your notes with a partner's.

A Room With a View

Chapter 1

'I wanted to see the Arno. The rooms the Signora promised us in her letter would have looked over the Arno. The Signora had no business to do it at all. Oh, it is a shame!'

'Any nook does for me,' Miss Bartlett continued; 'but it does seem hard that you shouldn't have a view.'

Lucy felt that she had been selfish. 'Charlotte, you mustn't spoil me: of course you must look over the Arno, too. I meant that. The first vacant room in the front –'

'You must have it,' said Miss Bartlett, part of whose travelling expenses were paid by Lucy's mother – a piece of generosity to which she made many a tactful allusion.

'No, no. You must have it.'

'I insist on it. Your mother would never forgive me, Lucy.'

'She would never forgive me.'

The ladies' voices grew animated, and – if the sad truth be owned – a little peevish. They were tired, and under the guise of unselfishness they wrangled. Some of their neighbours interchanged glances, and one of them – one of the ill-bred people whom one does meet abroad – leant forward over the table and actually intruded into their argument.

He said:

'I have a view, I have a view.'

Miss Bartlett was startled. Generally at a pension people looked them over for a day or two before speaking, and often did not find out that they would 'do' till they had gone. She knew that the intruder was ill-bred, even before she glanced at him. He was an old man, of heavy build, with a fair, shaven face and large eyes. There was something childish in those eyes, though it was not the childishness of senility. What exactly it was Miss Bartlett did not stop to consider, for her glance passed on to his clothes. These did not attract her. He was probably trying to become acquainted with them before they got into the swim. So she assumed a dazed expression when he spoke to her, and then said: 'A view? Oh, a view! How delightful a view is!'

'This is my son,' said the old man; 'his name's George. He has a view, too.'

'Ah,' said Miss Bartlett, repressing Lucy who was about to speak.

'What I mean,' he continued, 'is that you can have our rooms and we'll have yours. We'll change.'

The better class of tourist was shocked at this, and sympathized with the newcomers. Miss Bartlett, in reply, opened her mouth as little as possible, and said:

'Thank you very much indeed; that is out of the question.'

'Why?' said the old man, with both fists on the table.

'Because it is quite out of the question, thank you.'

'You see, we don't like to take –' began Lucy.

Her cousin again repressed her.

'But why?' he persisted. 'Women like looking at a view; men don't.' And he thumped with his fists like a naughty child, and turned to his son, saying, 'George, persuade them!'

'It's so obvious they should have the rooms,' said the son. 'There's nothing else to say.'

He did not look at the ladies as he spoke, but his voice was perplexed and sorrowful. Lucy, too, was perplexed; but she saw that they were in for what is known as 'quite a scene', and she had an odd feeling that whenever these ill-bred tourists spoke the contest widened and deepened till it dealt, not with rooms and views but with – well, with something quite different, whose existence she had not realized before. Now, the old man attacked Miss Bartlett almost violently: Why should she not change? What possible objection had she? They would clear out in half an hour.

Summary

There are a number of points that you might have focused on. Here are a selection.

- The dispute between Lucy and Charlotte as to who should have the room seems strained. Miss Bartlett seems to be adhering strongly to the 'etiquette' of the situation: '"You must have it," said Miss Bartlett, part of whose expenses were paid by Lucy's mother'. Lucy is equally aware of the stance that she should assume under the laws of politeness – 'She would never forgive me'. Her feeling is that Miss Bartlett is her 'elder' but not her 'better'.
- The unconventional nature of Mr Emerson's offer is stressed through the reactions of the others: 'The better class of tourist was shocked at this' – clearly this is not the 'done thing' to do and points to Mr Emerson's lack of gentlemanly manners and breeding. This is further emphasized by the fact Miss Bartlett replies opening 'her mouth as little as possible'.
- At first the difference between the characters here seems to be a simple one of class, but it is worth looking carefully at Lucy's reaction to the situation and thinking about the description of Mr Emerson who seems to act with a kind of childish innocence here.
- The conflict caused here over 'a room with a view' might itself signal (bearing in mind the novel's title) that this is significant beyond its surface meaning. Lucy's 'realization' also hints at this. The surface 'argument' highlights differences in conventions between social classes but the underlying conflict shows a contrast between sticking to a narrow-minded convention and possessing a generosity of spirit as seen in Mr Emerson.

Of course, it is impossible, from such a short extract to see the full range of the ideas that Forster explores in the novel. Social convention is just one of its themes and the novel ranges much wider on religion, attitudes to art and the nature of love. In the end the whole text reflects on the way in which people treat each other and themselves.

Presentation of character

As with other novelists featured in Unit 4, at the centre of Forster's novels is a fascination for characters and the way that they interact within the constraints placed upon them by their society. One of his main interests is to show the importance of finding fulfilment through relationships and the forces that combine together to prevent this happening. He represents life as a search for values, a kind of journey to find spiritual fulfilment and to reconcile discordant elements of human experience. The epigraph of *Howards End*, 'Only Connect', encapsulates this idea. As is said of Margaret's philosophy in that novel:

'Only connect! That was the whole of her sermon. Only connect the prose and the passion, and both will be exalted, and human love will be seen at its height. Live in fragments no longer. Only connect, and the beast and the monk, robbed of isolation that is life to either, will die.'

In the following extract from *A Room With a View*, Lucy has gone into Santa Croce in the company of Miss Lavish, an eccentric novelist who is also staying at the pension. However, she is abandoned by Miss Lavish who, to make matters worse, goes off with Lucy's guide book.

Activity

> **1** The novel is written in the third person but do you detect any differences in tone of voice in this extract? Make a note of any points in the text where you think you can hear Lucy's 'inner voice' as opposed to the voice of the author.
>
> **2** Discuss with a partner the effects that are achieved through these differences of narrative voice and how the character is presented.

A Room With a View

Chapter 2

Lucy waited for nearly ten minutes. Then she began to get tired. The beggars worried her, the dust blew in her eyes, and she remembered that a young girl ought not to loiter in public places. She descended slowly into the Piazza with the intention of rejoining Miss Lavish, who was really almost too original. But at that moment Miss Lavish and her local-colour box moved also, and disappeared down a side-street, both gesticulating largely.

Tears of indignation came to Lucy's eyes – partly because Miss Lavish had jilted her, partly because she had taken her Baedeker. How could she find her way home? How could she find her way about in Santa Croce? Her first morning was ruined, and she might never be in Florence again. A few minutes ago she had been all high spirits, talking as a woman of culture, and half-persuading herself that she was full of originality. Now she entered the church depressed and humiliated, not even able to remember whether it was built by the Franciscans or the Dominicans.

Of course, it must be a wonderful building. But how like a barn! And how very cold! Of course, it contained frescoes by Giotto, in the presence of whose tactile values she was capable of feeling what was proper. But who was to tell her which they were? She walked about disdainfully, unwilling to be enthusiastic over monuments of uncertain authorship or date. There was no one even to tell her which, of all the sepulchral slabs that paved the nave and transepts, was the one that was really beautiful, the one that had been most praised by Mr Ruskin.

The passage starts off in straightforward third-person narrative but very subtly Forster intersperses the narration with comments that appear to be Lucy's own thoughts and feelings. For example, '...she remembered that a young girl ought not to loiter in public places' and 'How could she find her way home?'. This style of narrative deepens our knowledge of individual characters. In this case:

- it creates a sympathetic link between character and reader without obvious signals from the writer
- it brings a sense of immediacy – emphasizing Lucy's insecurity here
- it adds to the humour by allowing us to see the naïvety of Lucy's thoughts

Activity

> Now read this next extract, thinking about the way that the characters are presented. Lucy is again unchaperoned as she walks alone into the Piazza Signoria at dusk. She is bored with the protection that she is constantly given by her cousin and is looking for some excitement. Discuss the passage with a partner and note down your ideas on the way that Forster presents this incident and the character of Lucy. Refer back to the bullet points above to help your discussion here.

A Room With a View

Chapter 4

But though she spent nearly seven lire the gates of liberty seemed still unopened. She was conscious of her discontent; it was new to her to be conscious of it. 'The world,' she thought, 'is certainly full of beautiful things, if only I could come across them.' It was not surprising that Mrs Honeychurch disapproved of music, declaring that it always left her daughter peevish, unpractical, and touchy. 'Nothing ever happens to me,' she reflected, as she entered the Piazza Signoria and looked nonchalantly at its marvels, now fairly familiar to her. The great square was in shadow; the sunshine had come too late to strike it. Neptune was already unsubstantial in the twilight, half god, half ghost, and his fountain plashed dreamily to the men and satyrs who idled together on its marge. The Loggia showed as the triple entrance of a cave, wherein dwelt many a deity, shadowy but immortal, looking forth upon the arrivals and departures of mankind. It was the hour of unreality – the hour, that is, when unfamiliar things are real. An older person at such an hour and in such a place might think that sufficient was happening to him, and rest content. Lucy desired more.

She fixed her eyes wistfully on the tower of the palace, which rose out of the lower darkness like a pillar of roughened gold. It seemed no longer a tower, no longer supported by earth, but some unattainable treasure throbbing in the tranquil sky. Its brightness mesmerized her, still dancing before her eyes when she bent them to the ground and started towards home.

Then something did happen.

Two Italians by the Loggia had been bickering about a debt. 'Cinque lire,' they had cried, 'cinque lire!' They sparred at each other, and one of them was hit lightly upon the chest. He frowned; he bent towards Lucy with a look of interest, as if he had an important message for her. He opened his lips to deliver it, and a stream of red came out between them and trickled down his unshaven chin.

Aspects of Forster's style

Forster novels display a number of distinctive elements of style. Here are some aspects of style to be attuned to when reading his novels.

- The plots of his novels are very carefully crafted with several interlocking strands carefully worked out and seldom leaving any loose ends. Within his plots Forster often makes use of climaxes (large and small) such as that presented in the last extract, or the visit to the Marabar Caves in *A Passage to India*, or Evie's wedding in *Howards End*.
- Imagery plays an important part and this is used in several ways. In reading the novels you will become aware of certain images which recur throughout the book. For example, in *A Room With a View*, we have already noted the significance of the title of the novel and therefore the potential importance of 'rooms with views' and 'rooms with no views'. However, there are other images of symbolic importance too, such as the idea of 'darkness' and 'light'.
- Forster's technique also makes use of contrasting imagery to develop aspects of his themes. As he presents the contrast between the imperfect world in which we exist and the perfect, transcendent world towards which his characters strive, he often uses the world of art to show the differing visions of life that his characters hold. In *A Room With a View*, for example, Cecil values the restrained qualities of Leonardo's work whereas Lucy herself embodies the more energetic qualities of Michelangelo's art. For Forster this symbolically represents the contrast between restraint and passion or disillusionment and fulfilment.
- Music plays a part large part in all five novels and Forster sees it as having the power to transcend the 'ordinary' elements of everyday life and lift the spirit on to a higher plane of awareness.
- Often closely associated with the musical imagery is an element of mysticism. This provides another way of escape from the metaphorical 'cages' Forster's characters create through failure to understand their self-deceptions and to 'connect' with one another.
- There is a strong sense of place and time in each of the novels. For example, the seasons play a prominent part in each of the novels. In *A Room With a View*, Lucy is kissed by George among the spring violets but when she next meets him it is autumn and the following spring we hear of their marriage and intention to return to Florence.
- All of Forster's novels reveal his talent for carefully observed dialogue. This is particularly evident in some of the conversations in the Italian novels and through the speech patterns of the Anglo-Indians in *A Passage to India*, where his dialogue reflects a conversation in English which conveys the intonations of the foreign speaker.

Activity

> 1 Read the extracts on pages 93–94, making a note of any stylistic features that strike you. Pick out any words, phrases, or ideas that you think might have a symbolic significance and explain what this might be.
> 2 Discuss your choices with a partner.

This first extract comes as Lucy goes out alone and witnesses a murder in the Piazza Signoria. Mr Beebe, a clergyman also staying at the pension, has tried to discourage her from going out alone but has failed.

A Room With a View

Chapter 3

'She oughtn't really to go at all,' said Mr Beebe, as they watched her from the window, 'and she knows it. I put it down to too much Beethoven.'
It is interesting to note that a little earlier Mr Beebe also made the comment:
'If Miss Honeychurch ever takes to live as she plays, it will be very exciting – both for us and for her.'

Chapter 4

Mr Beebe was right. Lucy never knew her desires so clearly as after music. She had not really appreciated the clergyman's wit, nor the suggestive twitterings of Miss Alan. Conversation was tedious; she wanted something big, and she believed that it would have come to her on the wind-swept platform of an electric tram.
This she might not attempt. It was unladylike. Why? Why were most big things unladylike? Charlotte had once explained to her why. It was not that ladies were inferior to men; it was that they were different. Their mission was to inspire others to achievement rather than to achieve themselves. Indirectly, by means of tact and a spotless name, a lady could accomplish much. But if she rushed into the fray herself she would be first censured, then despised, and finally ignored. Poems had been written to illustrate this point.
There is much that is immortal in this medieval lady. The dragons have gone, and so have the knights, but still she lingers in our midst. She reigned in many an early Victorian castle, and was queen of much early Victorian song. It is sweet to protect her in the intervals of business, sweet to pay her honour when she has cooked our dinner well. But alas! the creature grows degenerate. In her heart also there are springing up strange desires. She too is enamoured of heavy winds, and vast panoramas, and green expanses of the sea. She has marked the kingdom of this world, how full it is of wealth, and beauty, and war – a radiant crust, built around the central fires, spinning towards the receding heavens. Men, declaring that she inspires them to it, move joyfully over the surface, having the most delightful meetings with other men, happy, not because they are masculine, but because they are alive. Before the show breaks up she would like to drop the august title of the Eternal Woman, and go there as her transitory self.
Lucy does not stand for the medieval lady, who was rather an ideal to which she was bidden to lift her eyes when feeling serious. Nor has she any system of revolt. Here and there a restriction annoyed her particularly, and she would transgress it, and perhaps be sorry that she had done so. This afternoon she was peculiarly restive. She would really like to do something of which her well-wishers disapproved. As she might not go on the electric tram, she went to Alinari's shop.

This second extract comes from a part a little earlier in the book when Lucy is abandoned by Miss Lavish and meets the Emersons by chance in the church of Santa Croce. They overhear Mr Eager's talk about the Giotto frescoes and his remarks are in complete contrast to those of Mr Emerson.

A Room With a View

Chapter 2

The chapel was already filled with an earnest congregation, and out of them rose the voice of a lecturer, directing them how to worship Giotto, not by tactile valuations, but by the standards of the spirit.

'Remember,' he was saying, 'the facts about this church of Santa Croce; how it was built by faith in the full fervour of medievalism, before any taint of the Renaissance had appeared. Observe how Giotto in these frescoes – now, unhappily, ruined by restoration – is untroubled by the snares of anatomy and perspective. Could anything be more majestic, more pathetic, beautiful, true? How little, we feel, avails knowledge and technical cleverness against a man who truly feels!'

'No!' exclaimed Mr Emerson, in much too loud a voice for church. 'Remember nothing of the sort! Built by faith indeed! That simply means the workmen weren't paid properly. And as for the frescoes, I see no truth in them. Look at that fat man in blue! He must weigh as much as I do, and he is shooting into the sky like an air-balloon.'

He was referring to the fresco of the Ascension of St John. Inside, the lecturer's voice faltered, as well it might. The audience shifted uneasily, and so did Lucy. She was sure that she ought not to be with these men; but they had cast a spell over her. They were so serious and so strange that she could not remember how to behave.

'Now, did this happen, or didn't it? Yes or no?'

George replied:

'It happened like this, if it happened at all. I would rather go up to heaven by myself than be pushed by cherubs; and if I got there I should like my friends to lean out of it, just as they do here.'

'You will never go up,' said his father. 'You and I, dear boy, will lie at peace in the earth that bore us, and our names will disappear as surely as our work survives.'

The climax

At the end of *A Room With a View* it is clear to the reader that Lucy is in love with George but she represses her feelings and intends to go abroad. However, purely by chance she meets Mr Emerson who knows the truth. In this extract, which is in effect the climax of the action, Lucy turns to him for help.

A Room With a View

Chapter 19

'Lucy!' the voices called.

She turned to Mr Emerson in despair. But his face revived her. It was the face of a saint who understood.

'Now it is all dark. Now Beauty and Passion seem never to have existed. I know. But remember the mountains over Florence and the view. Ah, dear, if I were George, and gave you one kiss, it would make you brave. You have to go cold into a battle that needs warmth, out into the muddle that you have made yourself; and your mother and all your friends will despise you, oh my darling, and rightly, if it is ever right to despise. George still dark, all the tussle and the misery without a word from him. Am I justified?' Into his own eyes tears came. 'Yes, for we fight for more than Love or Pleasure: there is Truth. Truth counts, Truth does count.'
'You kiss me,' said the girl. 'You kiss me. I will try.'
He gave her a sense of the deities reconciled, a feeling that, in gaining the man she loved, she would gain something for the whole world. Throughout the squalor of her homeward drive – she spoke at once – his salutation remained. He had robbed the body of its taint, the taunts of their sting; he had shown her the holiness of direct desire. She 'never exactly understood,' she would say in after years, 'how he managed to strengthen her. It was as if he had made her see the whole of everything at once.'

Activity

> Bearing in mind what you have learned about the way in which Forster writes, prepare a short response to this extract commenting on the following elements of style:
> • imagery
> • description
> • presentation of character

Writing on Forster

Preparing yourself for exam questions on Forster clearly has much in common with your preparation for the other texts you are studying. Of course you will need to know the plot of the novel you are studying thoroughly and have at your fingertips detailed knowledge of events and character.

However, it will also be useful to recognize the topics on which questions often arise. Here are some of them:

- Character: both in terms of particular characters' importance to the novel and the ways in which Forster presents characters.
- Forster as a social satirist and humorist
- Forster as 'philosopher' commenting on fundamental elements to do with the 'human spirit' and 'inner being'.
- His use of language, imagery, symbolism, and other methods by which he suggests meaning to the reader.
- The different levels at which his novels operate. For example, they can be read as straightforward stories but they also operate on a symbolic level, present social comment or philosophical ideas, and draw attention to central elements of human nature, etc.

A consideration of all these elements will of course underpin your approach to the study of whichever Forster novel you are studying.

5 The Short Story

Objectives

- To prepare yourself for writing about short stories
- To consider some of the particular features of short stories
- To examine examples of the work of short story writers who often feature on examination syllabuses
- To prepare for studying set short story texts

What is a short story?

In one sense the answer to this question is so obvious it hardly seems worth a thought. A 'short story' is clearly a story that is short! Perhaps we need to rephrase the question and pose the question that the critic, Norman Friedman, once asked – 'What makes a short story?'

Activity

Think carefully about the short stories that you have read. Make a list of the differences between these stories and novels that you have studied (apart from the obvious point to do with length!).

Friedman answers this question by identifying two key features.
- A short story may be short because the material itself is narrow in its range or area of interest.

- A short story may be short because although the material has a potentially broad range the writer cuts it down to focus on one aspect and maximize the story's impact or artistic effect.

Many short stories do focus on a single incident, moment in time, or experience, but that is not always the case. Not all short stories are deliberately crafted by the writer as a vehicle for a single effect. In fact some stories gain their impact because they do not operate on a 'single effect' structure. Indeed, in some instances the 'single effect' type of story can appear contrived.

For many years the short story has suffered a good deal of critical neglect and has been regarded as an academically lightweight genre when measured against the much 'weightier' and prestigious novel form. However, recently there has been a recognition that the short story is something more than the novel's poor relation and it is not now uncommon to find a range of short stories on A-level syllabuses. If you are studying a short story text there are a number of areas that you will need to have some ideas about. Examination questions can be phrased in different ways but it is likely that they will focus on one or more of the following.

- **Plot and structure**   You will need a clear understanding of what happens in the story, the basic ideas that it deals with, how it is structured, and how the various elements of it relate to one another. How the story is structured can be of particular interest to the examiner if it varies from a straightforward chronological pattern.

- **Narrative viewpoint**   The question of who is telling the story is a very important one and raises questions about why the writer has chosen to present the story from this particular viewpoint and what effect this has on the reader's response.

- **Characters**   This is a favourite area for A-level questions. They often focus on one or more of the characters in the story or stories and may ask you to examine how the writer presents or develops the characters or to explore how they relate to each other.

- **Language and style**   You will also need a clear idea about the distinctive qualities of the writer's style. This will involve focusing closely on the specific detail and the writer's choice of language (the way this is used, and the effects that it creates).

Plot and structure

Activity

Think carefully about a short story that you have read and make a list of the features that you think are important in terms of making this story 'work'.

One thing you may have noted about short stories is that very often the story focuses on a single character in a single situation rather than tracing a range of characters through a variety of situations and phases of development as novels often do. However, often the focus for the story is a moment at which the central character(s) undergoes some important experience which presents a significant moment in their personal development. It can be seen as a 'moment of truth' in which something or some perception, large or small, changes within the character. In some stories, though, this 'moment of truth' is evident only to the reader and not the character(s).

Not all stories reach a climax, though. Some stories may offer a kind of 'snap-shot' of a period of time or an experience – a 'day in the life of...' kind of story might be like this. Other stories end inconclusively leaving the reader with feelings of uncertainty, while other kinds of story do not seem to have a discernible plot at all. This may lead the reader to feel completely baffled by what they have read and subsequently to tentatively explore a range of possible interpretations in his or her head. This might, of course, have been exactly the response that the writer intended.

This diagram presents one way of thinking about how alternative plots and structures of short stories work:

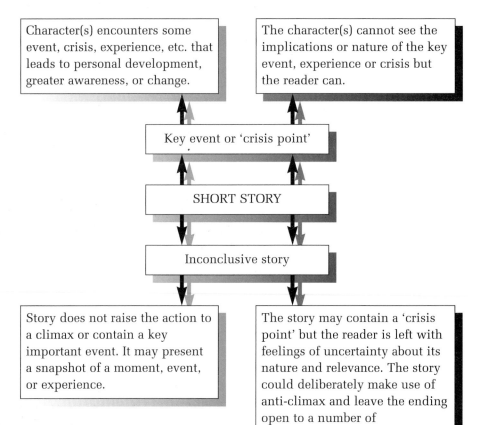

Character(s) encounters some event, crisis, experience, etc. that leads to personal development, greater awareness, or change.

The character(s) cannot see the implications or nature of the key event, experience or crisis but the reader can.

Key event or 'crisis point'

SHORT STORY

Inconclusive story

Story does not raise the action to a climax or contain a key important event. It may present a snapshot of a moment, event, or experience.

The story may contain a 'crisis point' but the reader is left with feelings of uncertainty about its nature and relevance. The story could deliberately make use of anti-climax and leave the ending open to a number of interpretations or questions.

Beginnings

Our very earliest experiences of stories (the fairy tales we listen to, and then the vast range of stories that we hear, read, and see presented in film and television as adults) teach us one thing – stories have a 'beginning', a 'middle', and an 'end'. Strictly speaking, though, it is not entirely true. There are stories that do not seem to have a beginning or an ending in the conventional sense. We will look at stories like these which seem to be 'all middle', so to speak, a little later. The vast majority of stories, however, do have some kind of beginning or opening section; a middle, where the characters, situation, and ideas are developed; and an ending that draws the story to a conclusion.

Here are some possible ways in which stories can open:
- the writer launches straight into the narrative
- the writer sets the scene by giving explicit background information
- the writer informs the reader using suggestion or implication rather than direct description
- the opening is direct and holds the reader's attention, perhaps capturing attention with a word or short phrase

Activity

> Read the following openings to four short stories. Then, in a small group, discuss your responses to them. Think carefully about how each writer approaches the opening to their story and try to identify the techniques that they use.

1 The Boarding House

Mrs Mooney was a butcher's daughter. She was a woman who was quite able to keep things to herself: a determined woman. She had married her father's foreman and opened a butcher's shop near Spring Gardens. But as soon as his father-in-law was dead Mr Mooney began to go to the devil. He drank, plundered the till, ran headlong into debt. It was no use making him take the pledge: he was sure to break out again a few days after. By fighting his wife in the presence of customers and by buying bad meat he ruined his business. One night he went for his wife with the cleaver and she had to sleep in a neighbour's house.

James Joyce

2 In Memoriam Brian Rosenfeld

'1939. It wasn't just the outbreak of war to us, but the fact that my mother decided to leave my father that week. Just like that. A personal holocaust. Fear was in the air, muted excitement; the measured tones of Neville Chamberlain oozed out of the dark brown canvas-webbed wireless set, gently, softly. He was an appeaser, like my ma, but he'd lost patience, as she had. The future would be different now.'

Elizabeth Troop

3 The Snow Pavilion

The motor stalled in the middle of a snowy landscape, lodged in a rut, wouldn't budge an inch. How I swore! I'd planned to be snug in front of a roaring fire by now, a single malt on the mahogany wine-table (a connoisseur's piece) beside me, the five courses of Melissa's dinner savourously aromatizing the kitchen; to complete the décor, a labrador retriever's head laid on my knee as trustingly as if I were indeed a country gentleman and lolled by rights among the chintz. After dinner, before I read our customary pre-coital poetry aloud to her, my elegant and accomplished mistress, also a connoisseur's piece, might play the piano for her part-time pasha while I sipped black, acrid coffee from her precious little cups.

Angela Carter

4 Dual Control

'You ought to have stopped.'
'For God's sake, shut up, Freda.'
'Well, you should have. You ought to have made sure she was alright.'
'Of course she's alright.'
'How do you know? You didn't stop to find out, did you?'
'Do you want me to go back? We're late enough as it is, thanks to your fooling about getting ready, but I don't suppose the Bradys'll notice if we're late. I don't suppose they'll notice if we never turn up, though after the way you angled for the invitation...'
'That's right, blame it all on me. We could have left half an hour ago if you hadn't been late home from the office.'
'How often do I have to tell you that business isn't a matter of nine to five?'
'No it's a matter of the Bradys, isn't it? You were keen enough we should get asked. Where were you anyway? Drinking with the boys? Or smooching with some floozie?'

Elizabeth Walter

Obviously the opening of a story is vital. If the reader's attention is not captured immediately the story contains no initial impact to encourage them to continue, to draw them into the story. However, bearing in mind the constraints of length under which the short story operates, it is also important that the opening compresses information that might have taken some time to explain so that the reader quickly and effectively gains a picture of what is going on. Short story writers are often faced with this question of how much they can omit while at the same time creating the impression of completeness and continuity in their stories.

Going back to the extracts that you have just discussed, you may have noticed that Extract 3 launches straight into the narrative. The car getting stuck in the snow captures the reader's attention straight away. This opening paragraph goes on to give quite a bit of information to set the scene very economically as the narrator reflects on the plans he had made for his evening.

In Extract 1, Joyce begins by setting the scene and providing the reader with some background information necessary to understand the context of the story. This opening paragraph concentrates on providing the reader with details of Mrs Mooney's background and her situation through succinct and straightforward description.

In Extract 4, on the other hand, we are told very little directly and we have to work out for ourselves what is happening or what has happened using clues suggested through the narrative. This approach can provide us with just as much information as straightforward description. In this instance we learn about the characters – what they are doing and what has happened – through the dialogue but it leaves a good deal to the reader's imagination too. (In fact, this story is told entirely through dialogue with no direct description.)

In contrast, Extract 2 begins with the arresting '1939' which immediately captures our attention. The short and direct paragraph clearly sets the context for the story and indicates to us the personal and domestic scene reflected against the magnitude of world events.

Narrative line

Short stories, like other fictional works, order the events that they describe in a particular way. Through the story-line the writer can create a wide range of effects, such as creating suspense, raising the action to a climax point, resolving problems, leading (or misleading) the reader in particular ways, and leaving endings open to a variety of interpretations.

Very often the narrative structure is a straightforward progression with one event following another and moving towards a conclusion where all is resolved. However, sometimes a writer might play around with this structure to create particular effects. Here are some points to consider when you focus on the narrative structure of a story.

- Make a list of the key events in the story.
- Look at the order in which these events are related by the writer.
- Look at the time structure of the story – is it told in simple chronological order or is there use of flashbacks or cutting back and forth?
- Are there any details or pieces of information that the writer omits or particular points that are emphasized?

Short stories often have a moment in the plot upon which the whole structure of the story turns and which affects the outcome of the tale. Sometimes this trigger can be a quite trivial incident or experience but it signifies a moment of revelation to the central character. *Hassan's Tower* by Margaret Drabble contains just such a moment for newly-married Kenneth on honeymoon with his wife, Chloë, in Morocco. They are a wealthy couple who appear to have everything that they could want in life but Kenneth is disappointed in his new wife and disillusioned with life in general. He is ill-at-ease in Morocco and goes about in constant fear of being robbed. Against his will his wife takes him to Hassan's Tower and wants to climb to the top to see the view. Reluctantly, he accompanies her and during the course of this seemingly unremarkable excursion he experiences a revelation that changes his whole outlook on his wife, his life, and those around him.

Hassan's Tower

The more he looked, the more he realized that the people on top of the tower were in their own way as astonishing a view as the more evidently panoramic vistas. The whole of the top of the tower was thick and covered with people: small children were crawling about, mothers were feeding their babies, young men were holding the hands of girls and indeed the hands of other young men, boys were sitting on the very edge and dangling their feet into space, and old women who would need a day to recover from the climb were lying back in the sun, for all the world as though they were grandmothers on a beach in England ...and as he gazed he felt growing within him a sense of extraordinary familiarity that was in its own way a kind of illumination ...He saw these people, quite suddenly, for what they were, for people, for nothing other than people; their clothes filled out with bodies, their faces took on expression, their relations became dazzlingly clear, as though the details of their strangeness had dropped away, as though the terms of common humanity (always before credited in principle, but never before perceived) had become facts before his eyes.

Margaret Drabble

Endings

There are as many ways of ending a story as there are of beginning it and the ending is clearly a very important element in the overall structure of a piece. In a short story it is often the ending which reveals meaning, points up a significant theme, or provides a resolution. This kind of ending should leave the reader contented and satisfied with a sense of a tale completed.

Equally though, a writer might create an 'open' ending, one that does not provide answers, an ending that might leave the reader pondering on what it all means or unsettle them. This could be, of course, just the kind of response that the writer is aiming for.

The ending with 'a sting in the tail' has become very popular in recent years, being popularized through the short stories of Roald Dahl. It is worth noting, though, that with this kind of ending we need to distinguish between a device which is merely used as a kind of 'trick' and a twist at the end which causes us to see something fundamental in the story as a whole.

Activity

> Choose three short stories that you know and reread them. Discuss the ending of each with a partner, thinking about the following questions.
> - Does the story have what you would recognize as a definite ending?
> - How does the ending relate to the rest of the story?
> - Does the writer draw attention to any specific points in the ending?
> - How would you have ended the story?

Narrative viewpoint

You will already be familiar with the term viewpoint in the sense of 'from whose point of view we see the events of the story'. However, it is perhaps worth bearing in mind that this term can encompass two related but distinct ideas. In addressing viewpoint we need to consider the question of who is actually seeing the events described and who is narrating them. They may be one and the same or quite separate and that the question is rather more complex than it might first appear.

It may be possible to approach the question of viewpoint by distinguishing between narrators who seem to address the reader directly from within the story (**internal narrators**) or those who have a more 'external' narrative viewpoint. As readers you need to be aware of how writers use viewpoint within their stories, be sensitive to subtle shifts and aware of the effects this can have on the narrative and your perception of it.

For more discussion of narrative viewpoint see Unit 4, pages 70–74.

Activity

> Look at these two extracts and think about the narrative viewpoints used in each.

1 Missy

'There you are, Mrs Ebbs, hold the cup steady. Can you manage, dear? Whoops! That's it. Now sit up properly, you'll slip down in the bed again, sit up against your pillows. That's it. Don't nod off again, will you? Now careful, Mrs Ebbs, I haven't got all day, dear. That's it, good girl.'
The voice came roaring towards her. The face was bland as suet. The face was a cow's face. An ox.
'Ox-face,' she said, but she had not said it.
She tipped the spoon and sucked in her soup, little bits of carrot and soft lentil sieving through the spaces between her teeth.
'All right now, Mrs Ebbs?'
Ox-face.
'I'm not deaf.'
Was she?

Susan Hill

2 A Tradition of Eighteen Hundred and Four, Christmas 1882

The widely discussed possibility of an invasion of England through a Channel Tunnel has more than once recalled old Solomon Selby's story to my mind. The occasion on which I numbered myself among his audience was one evening when he was sitting in the yawning chimney-corner of the inn-kitchen, with some others who had gathered there, and I entered for shelter from the rain. Withdrawing the stem of his pipe from the dental notch in which it habitually rested, he leaned back in the recess behind him and smiled into the fire. The smile was neither mirthful nor sad, not precisely humorous nor altogether thoughtful. We who knew him recognized it in a moment: it was his narrative smile. Breaking off our few desultory remarks we drew up closer, and he thus began...

Thomas Hardy

In Extract 2 you will notice immediately that Hardy is writing in the first person here. He is recounting a particular evening when he heard a story told by Solomon Selby. You obviously cannot tell from this brief opening but the bulk of the story is told as if by Solomon Selby as reported by Hardy. Think about what effect this has on the narrative. Notice too how Hardy economically sets the context of the story through implication – the title providing the date, 1804, coupled with the idea of an invasion through a 'Channel Tunnel' clearly sets the story against the background of the Napoleonic Wars. Hardy also economically sets the story in its more immediate context – the cosy inn of 1882, sheltering from the rain with others gathered round the fire, and the anticipation of a good story well told – all these details help to set the mood and draw the reader into the narrative.

Compare this with the approach adopted by Hill in Extract 1. She chooses a quite different way of telling her story. It is written in the third person and we are launched, without any preamble, into a 'situation'. It is not immediately clear what that situation is but it seems that someone, perhaps a nurse, is feeding soup to Mrs Ebbs. Although Hill partially adopts the stance of external narrator, some of the narrative views the scene through the eyes of Mrs Ebbs as she sees the face of the nurse peering towards her.

Activity

> Look at three or four short stories that you have studied. With a partner, discuss the narrative viewpoint that the writer adopts in each. Now write a short essay, illustrated by examples, on the way in which narrative viewpoint contributes to the overall effect of these stories.

Character

Although some critics argue that it is absurd to consider fictitious characters as if they were 'real' people, on the other hand, when we read stories we do create our own mental image of them based on our experiences of real life.

However, we must not lose sight of the fact that they are creations of the writer and do not have an existence outside the text. In many cases writers create their characters to serve particular functions within the narrative and present them in ways that give particular impressions. Therefore, we should look carefully at the kinds of characters the writer portrays, how they are presented, which of their features are stressed, and what role they perform. We must also think about how the characters interlock with all the other elements of the story to create a unified whole and how we respond to them as readers.

In Unit 4 you considered ways in which characters can be revealed to us in novels and these points also apply to the short story. It would be useful to look back at these points to refresh your memory (see page 74). Read the following extract and think about how the two characters are presented.

Halloran's Child

He was eating the rabbit he had shot himself on the previous day, separating the small bones carefully from the flesh before soaking lumps of bread in the dark salt gravy. When they were boys, he and his brother, Nelson Twomey, used to trap rabbits and other animals too, weasels and stoats – it was sport, they thought nothing of it, it was only what Farley the gamekeeper did.
Then, Nate had gone by himself into the wood and found a young fallow deer caught by the leg, and when he had eventually got it free the animal had stumbled away, its foot mangled and dropping a trail of fresh blood through the undergrowth. Nate had gone for his brother, brought him back and shown him.
'Well, it'll die, that's what,' Nelson had said, and shrugged his thin shoulders. It was the first glimpse Nate had of his brother's true nature, his meanness.
'Die of gangrene. That's poison.'
He had wept that night, one of the few occasions in his life, and he got up at dawn and gone out to search for the wounded animal, remembering the trembling hind quarters and the sweat which had matted its pale coat, the eyes, where the sticky rheum had begun to gather in the corners. He found only the blood, dried dark on the bracken. It led him towards where the bank of the stream fell away at his feet, and he could not follow further.

Susan Hill

| **Activity** | What impressions do you get of Nelson and Nate Twomey in this extract? Use specific references from the passage to support your ideas. |

One of the first striking things about this passage is the way that Hill emphasizes Nate's sensitivity and concern for the suffering of an innocent and helpless creature. He does, however, continue to shoot and eat rabbits and to kill chickens for food but these things are all part of the natural order of things and do not involve unnecessary or drawn-out suffering. What seems significant here is that it is not the killing but the pointless suffering of the innocent animal in the trap that appals him. In this respect he is quite different to his older brother, Nelson, who not only appears indifferent to the suffering of the animals but actually relishes the cruelty inherent in his work as a rat-catcher. There is a violence within Nelson that seems to simmer below the surface and that makes Nate in some way afraid of him. One of the effects of the description of the two brothers in this passage is to focus attention more closely on the characteristics of Nate. If you were to read the rest of the story you would find that Nate is the central character.

Activity

> 1 Now look back at the two extracts on pages 103–104 that you considered in terms of narrative viewpoint. Read them again but this time focus on any clues or hints that they might give concerning the characters. Discuss your ideas with a partner and jot down the main points of your discussion.
> 2 Choose two stories that you have read and studied and write brief notes on how the writer(s) reveal and present the central character(s).

Language and imagery

The style in which a story is written – the choices that writers make in the language they use and the ways in which they use it – is a key element in the overall effect that is created by a story in the mind of the reader. It might be written quite plainly using little figurative language or the writer might use imagery to help create the desired effect.

In *Halloran's Child*, Hill very often uses groups of images to build up a particular effect. Look at this passage, for example, which describes the Hallorans' daughter, Jenny.

Halloran's Child

They had only one child, the daughter, Jenny. She had never been truly well since the day she was born, and when she was a year old and began to walk her limbs seemed incapable of holding her up, she was unsteady and sickly. At the age of four she had rheumatic fever and almost died, and Halloran had said in public hearing that he wished for it, wished to have it over with, for who wanted an invalid for a child and how could he bear the anxiety? She had been forbidden to run or even walk far, though she went to school when she was five and there was treated like a fragile doll by the others, who had been put in awe of her. She played with no one, though sometimes, as she sat in a corner of the playground, one of them would take pity on her and bring pick-sticks or a jigsaw and do it with her for a little while. But she seemed to be separated from them, almost to be less than human, because of the transparency of her skin and her thin, delicate bones, because of the fine blueness tinging her lips and the flesh below her nervous eyes.

Susan Hill

Activity Read this extract carefully and pick out any images that are particularly effective. Describe what impressions are created by each of these and then compare your ideas with a partner.

Notice how Hill emphasizes the frailty of Jenny through a variety of images that build up to create a vivid impression of the sick child. She tells us that Jenny '...was treated like a fragile doll' that she seemed '...almost to be less than human, because of the transparency of her skin and her thin, delicate bones, because of the fine blueness tinging her lips and the flesh below her nervous eyes'. This creates an image of a fragile, young, featherless baby bird and gives an impression of vulnerability, of someone with a tenuous grip on life.

Later on in the story Jenny goes into hospital and when she comes out the fragility of her body is re-emphasized by Hill who describes her '...small legs poking out like sticks', her '...neck bent like a stalk', and introduces the idea that she is dying as Nate sees '...the deadness within the child's eyes'.

Nate goes to visit Jenny, and again Hill uses description relating to skin and eyes and bones to show the child's deteriorating condition:

'...she seemed to have shrunk, her flesh was thinner, scarcely covering her bones, and the skin was tight and shiny. Her eyes were very bright and yet dead, too.'

Again Hill uses imagery suggestive of a helpless creature:

'He looked down at her hand, resting on the sheet. It was like a small claw.'

and again images that hint of death:

'Her lips moved and there was no blood in them, they were thin and dry and oddly transparent, like the skin of a chrysalis.

This technique of using recurring images to build up a picture or atmosphere is a feature typical of Hill's style.

Activity Choose two or three stories that you have studied and think carefully about how they are written. Note down what seem to you to be particular features of the style of each. Include examples to illustrate your points.

The whole story

Annotation can be a very useful aid to exploring a text. It allows you to record those tentative first responses or ideas that are suggested to you as you read a text. Indeed, the process of noting points on the text itself can help you to focus on the meaning and implications of individual words and phrases.

Often these 'first impressions' tend to be lost or forgotten later but they do play a very important part in the development of your ideas about a particular text. Here is an example of a second year student's notes around the short story *I Spy* by Graham Greene. In this instance the student read the story and then began annotating it prior to a small group discussion in which students compared their ideas. Read *I Spy* for yourself and think about the annotations made around the text.

I Spy

Sense of secrecy

Sense of mystery, menace, potential danger, etc

Charlie Stowe waited until he heard his mother snore before he got out of bed. Even then he moved with caution and tiptoed to the window. The front of the house was irregular, so that it was possible to see a light burning in his mother's room. But now all the windows were dark. A searchlight passed across the sky, lighting the banks of cloud and probing the dark deep spaces between, seeking enemy airships. The wind blew from the sea, and Charlie Stowe could hear behind his mother's snores the beating of the waves. A draught through the cracks in the window-frame stirred his nightshirt. Charlie Stowe was frightened.

Searchlight – airships – wartime

1st World War

Sleeping mother – repetition of snore

Cold – out of bed! – darkness emphasized

Not modern

What is Charlie up to?

But the thought of the tobacconist's shop which his father kept down a dozen wooden stairs drew him on. He was twelve years old, and already boys at the County School mocked him because he had never smoked a cigarette. The packets were piled twelve deep below, Gold Flake and Players, De Reszke, Abdulla, Woodbines, and the little shop lay under a thin haze of stale smoke which would completely disguise his crime. That it was a crime to steal some of his father's stock Charlie Stowe had no doubt, but he did not love his father; his father was unreal to him, a wraith, pale, thin, indefinite, who noticed him only spasmodically and left even punishment to his mother. For his mother he felt a passionate demonstrative love; her large boisterous presence and her noisy charity filled the world for him; from her speech he judged her the friend of everyone, from the rector's wife to the 'dear Queen', except the 'Huns', the monsters who lurked in Zeppelins in the clouds. But his father's affection and dislike were as indefinite as his movements. Tonight he had said he would be in Norwich, and yet you never knew. Charlie Stowe had no sense of safety as he crept down the wooden stairs. When they creaked he clenched his fingers on the collar of his nightshirt.

Mention of father

'Manly' to smoke – grown up

More info about Charlie

Pressure from peers

Brands of cigarettes

A 'crime' stealing, guilty conscience

Why?

What does all this mean?

Father does not seem to bother with him – different to mum

Contrast with father

Zeppelins – bombing raids

Something mysterious about father

A sign of fear!

At the bottom of the stairs he came out quite suddenly into the little shop. It was too dark to see his way, and he did not dare touch the switch. For half a minute he sat in despair on the bottom step with

A sense almost of surprise

What to do next!

his chin cupped in his hands. Then the regular movement of the searchlight was reflected through an upper window and the boy had time to fix in memory the pile of cigarettes, the counter, and the small hole under it. The footsteps of a policeman on the pavement made him grab the first packet to his hand and dive for the hole. A light shone along the floor and a hand tried the door, then the footsteps passed on, and Charlie cowered in the darkness. At last he got his courage back by telling himself in his curiously adult way that if he were caught now there was nothing to be done about it, and he might as well have his smoke. He put a cigarette in his mouth and then remembered that he had no matches. For a while he dared not move. Three times the searchlight lit the shop, while he muttered taunts and encouragements. May as well be hung for a sheep, Cowardy, cowardy custard, grown-up and childish exhortations oddly mixed.

But as he moved he heard footfalls in the street, the sound of several men walking rapidly. Charlie Stowe was old enough to feel surprise that anybody was about. The footsteps came nearer, stopped; a key was turned in the shop door, a voice said: 'Let him in,' and then he heard his father, 'If you wouldn't mind being quiet, gentlemen, I don't want to wake up the family.' There was a note unfamiliar to Charlie in the undecided voice. A torch flashed and the electric globe burst into blue light. The boy held his breath; he wondered whether his father would hear his heart beating, and he clutched his nightshirt tightly and prayed, 'O God, don't let me be caught.' Through a crack in the counter he could see his father where he stood, one hand held to his high stiff collar, between two men in bowler hats and belted mackintoshes. They were strangers. 'Have a cigarette,' his father said in a voice dry as a biscuit. One of the men shook his head. 'It wouldn't do, not when we are on duty. Thank you all the same.' He spoke gently but without kindness; Charlie Stowe thought his father must be ill. 'Mind if I put a few in my pocket?' Mr Stowe asked, and when the man nodded he lifted a pile of Gold Flake and Players from a shelf and caressed the packets with the tips of his fingers. 'Well,' he said, 'there's nothing to be done about it, and I may as well have my smokes.' For a moment Charlie Stowe feared discovery, his father stared round the shop so thoroughly; he might have been seeing it for the first time. 'It's a good little business,' he said, 'for those that like it. The wife will sell out, I suppose. Else the neighbours'll be wrecking it. Well, you want to be off. A stitch in time. I'll get my coat.'

Marginal annotations (left):

- Fear of discovery builds up atmosphere of tension
- Panic
- Relief
- Recovers
- Gone so far, might as well go through with it
- Still afraid
- Why this word?
- Tension again
- 'Gentlemen' – very polite and formal
- Something out of the ordinary happening
- Police?
- Police again!
- Stocking up – may not be back for some time
- Why 'caressed'?
- A bit like Charlie, 'if he were caught now there would be nothing to be done about it'

Marginal annotations (right):

- Fear of his 'crime' being found out
- Tension
- Why 'curiously' adult? – he is realistic about what is happening
- Mixture of adult and child
- Supposed to be in Norwich
- Why not?
- Fear of being caught
- Like Charlie clenching his nightshirt
- Is he under arrest?
- Fear, uncertainty
- Why 'gently'/without kindness'? – an unusual combination
- Why ill
- Has to ask permission – under arrest?
- Or the last!
- The end of his family life
- Why would the neighbours do that?

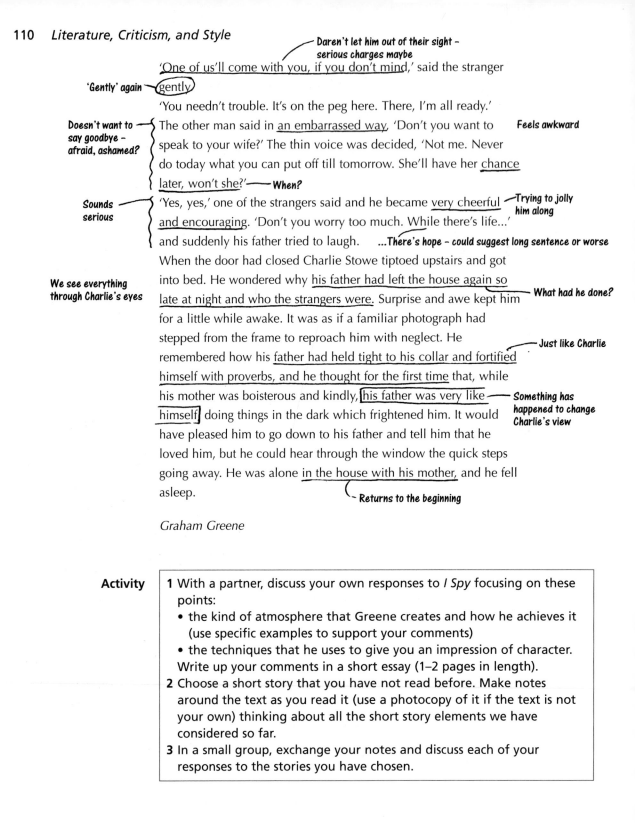

Daren't let him out of their sight –
serious charges maybe

'One of us'll come with you, if you don't mind,' said the stranger

'Gently' again ⟶ gently.

'You needn't trouble. It's on the peg here. There, I'm all ready.'

Doesn't want to say goodbye – afraid, ashamed?

The other man said in an embarrassed way, 'Don't you want to   Feels awkward
speak to your wife?' The thin voice was decided, 'Not me. Never
do today what you can put off till tomorrow. She'll have her chance
later, won't she?'——When?

Sounds serious

'Yes, yes,' one of the strangers said and he became very cheerful ⟶ Trying to jolly him along
and encouraging. 'Don't you worry too much. While there's life...'
and suddenly his father tried to laugh.   ...There's hope – could suggest long sentence or worse

When the door had closed Charlie Stowe tiptoed upstairs and got

We see everything through Charlie's eyes

into bed. He wondered why his father had left the house again so
late at night and who the strangers were. Surprise and awe kept him   — What had he done?
for a little while awake. It was as if a familiar photograph had
stepped from the frame to reproach him with neglect. He
remembered how his father had held tight to his collar and fortified   — Just like Charlie
himself with proverbs, and he thought for the first time that, while
his mother was boisterous and kindly, his father was very like —— Something has happened to change Charlie's view
himself doing things in the dark which frightened him. It would
have pleased him to go down to his father and tell him that he
loved him, but he could hear through the window the quick steps
going away. He was alone in the house with his mother, and he fell
asleep.

— Returns to the beginning

Graham Greene

Activity

1 With a partner, discuss your own responses to *I Spy* focusing on these points:
   • the kind of atmosphere that Greene creates and how he achieves it (use specific examples to support your comments)
   • the techniques that he uses to give you an impression of character. Write up your comments in a short essay (1–2 pages in length).
2 Choose a short story that you have not read before. Make notes around the text as you read it (use a photocopy of it if the text is not your own) thinking about all the short story elements we have considered so far.
3 In a small group, exchange your notes and discuss each of your responses to the stories you have chosen.

Special Feature: Jane Gardam

• •

Jane Gardam was born in Yorkshire in 1928 and after studying literature at London University she became a journalist and writer. She is well known for her novels for children and adults as well as for short stories in which she experiments with different forms and ideas. She won the Winifred Holtby Memorial Prize in 1976, was runner-up for the Booker Prize in 1978, won the Whitbread Literary Award in 1981 and her collection of short stories, *Pangs of Love and Other Stories*, from which *Stone Trees* is taken, received the Katherine Mansfield Award in 1984.

Stone Trees reflects both her urge to experiment with the short story form and her exploration of the inner emotions of her central character. Read the story through carefully.

Stone Trees

So now that he is dead so now that he is dead I am to spend the day with them.
The Robertsons.
On the Isle of Wight. Train journey train journey from London. There and back in a day.
So now that he is dead –
They were at the funeral. Not their children. Too little. So good so good they were to me. She – Anna – she cried a lot. Tom held my arm tight. Strong. I liked it. In the place even the place where your coffin was, I liked it, his strong arm. Never having liked Tom that much, I liked his strong arm.
And they stayed over. Slept at the house a night or two. Did the telephone. Some gran or someone was with their children. Thank God we had no children. Think of Tom/Anna dying and those two children left –
So now that you are dead –
It's nice of them isn't it now that you are dead? Well, you'd have expected it. You aren't surprised by it. I'm not surprised by it. After all there has to be somewhere to go. All clean all clean at home. Back work soon someday. Very soon now for it's a week. They broke their two week holiday for the funeral. Holiday Isle of Wight where you/I went once. There was a dip, a big-dipper dip, a wavy line of cliffs along the shore, and in this dip of the cliffs a hotel – a long beach and the waves moving in shallow.
Over stone trees.
But it was long ago and what can stone trees have been? Fantasy.
So now that you are dead so now –

Sweetie love so now that you are dead I am to spend the day with the Robertsons alone and we shall talk you/I later. So now –

The boat crosses. Has crossed. Already. Criss-cross deck. Criss-cross water. Splashy sea and look – ! Lovely clouds flying (now that you are dead) and here's the pier. A long, long pier into the sea and gulls shouting and children yelling here and there and here's my ticket and there they stand. All in a row – Tom, Anna, the two children solemn. And smiles now – Tom and Anna. Tom and Anna look too large to be quite true. Too good. Anna who never did anything wrong. Arms stretch too far forward for a simple day.

They stretch because they want. They would not stretch to me if you were obvious and not just dead. Then it would have been, hullo, easy crossing? Good. Wonderful day. Let's get back and down on the beach. Great to see you both. So now that you are dead –

We paced last week. Three

Tom. Anna. I.

And other black figures wood-faced outside the crematorium in blazing sun, examining shiny black-edged tickets on blazing bouquets. 'How good of Marjorie – fancy old Marjorie. I didn't even know she –' There was that woman who ran out of the so-called service with handkerchief at her eyes. But who was there except you my darling and I and the Robertsons and the shiny cards and did they do it then? Were they doing it then as we read the flowers? Do they do it at once or stack it up with other coffins and was it still inside waiting as I paced with portly Tom? Christian Tom – Tom we laughed at so often and oh my darling now that you are dead –

Cambridge. You can't say that Tom has precisely changed since Cambridge. Thickened. More solid. Unshaken still, quite unshaken and – well, wonderful of course. Anna hasn't changed. Small, specs, curly hair, straight-laced. Dear Anna how we sat and worked out all. Analysed. Girton. We talked about how many men it was decent to do it with without being wild and when you should decide to start and Anna said none and never. Not before marriage you said. Anna always in that church where Tom preached and Tom never looking Anna's way, and how she ached. So now that –

Sweet I miss you so. Now that you are –. My darling oh my God!

In the train two young women. (Yes thanks Anna, I'm fine. Nice journey. First time out. It's doing me good. Isn't it a lovely day?) There were these two women talking about their rights. They were reading about all that was due to them. In a magazine.

'Well, it's only right isn't it?'

'What?'

'Having your own life. Doing your thing.'

'Well–'

'Not – you know. Men and that. Not letting them have all the freedom and that. You have to stand up for yourself and get free of men.'

We come to the hotel and of course it is the one. The one in the dip of the cliffs almost on the beach, and how were they to know? It's typical though, somehow. We didn't like them my darling did we, after Cambridge very much? We didn't see them – dropped them in some way. We didn't see them for nearly two years. And we wondered, sometimes, whatever it was we had thought we had had in common – do-good, earnest Tom, healthy face and shorts, striding out over mountains singing snatches of Berlioz and stopping now and then to pray. And you were you and always unexpected – alert, alive, mocking, and forever young and now that you are –

But they were there again. In California. You at the university and I at the university, teaching a term; and there – behold the Robertsons, holding out their arms to save America. Little house full of the shiny-faced, the chinless – marriage counsellors, marriage-enrichment classes oh my God! And one child in Anna and one just learning to walk. We were taken to them by somebody just for a lark not knowing who they'd turn out to be and we said – 'Hey! Tom and Anna.'

And in Sacramento in a house with lacy balconies and little red Italian brick walls and all their old Cambridge books about and photographs we half-remembered, we opened wine and were very happy; and over the old white-washed fireplace there was Tom's old crucifix and his Cambridge oar. And I sat in the rocking chair she'd had at Girton and it felt familiar and we loved the Robertsons that day in sweaty, wheezing Sacramento because they were there again. This is no reason. But it is true.

We talked about how we'd all met each other first. Terrible party. Jesus College. Anna met Tom and I met you my darling and it was something or other – Feminism, Neo-Platonism, Third World – and there you were with bright, ridiculous, marvellous, mocking eyes and long hard hands and I loved you as everyone else clearly loved you. And the Robertsons talked sagely to one another. They were not the Robertsons then but Tom and Anna. We never became the anythings, thank God. There was no need because we were whatever the appearance might be one person and had no need of a plural term and now that –

Sweetie, do you remember the *smell* of that house? In Cambridge? And again in Sacramento? She liked it you know. She left dishes for a week and food bits and old knickers and tights in rolls on the mantelpiece and said, 'There are things more important.' Under the burning ethic there was you know something very desperate about Anna. Tom didn't notice her. Day after day and I'd guess night after night.' He sat in the rocking chair and glared at God. And meeting them again just the same, in Sacramento, you looked at the crucifix and the oar and at me, your eyes like the first time we met because there we both remembered the first time, long ago. Remembering that was a short return to each other because by then, by America, I knew that you were one I'd never have to myself because wherever you were or went folk turned and smiled at you and loved you. Well, I'd known always. I didn't face it at first, that one woman would never be enough for you and that if I moved in with you you would soon move on.

Everyone wanted you. When we got married there was a general sense of comedy and the sense of my extraordinary and very temporary luck.

It is not right or dignified to love so much. To let a man rule so much. It is obsession and not love, a mental illness not a life. And of course, with marriage came the quarrelling and pain because I knew there were so many others, and you not coming home, and teasing when you did and saying that there was only me but of course I knew it was not so because of – cheap and trite things like – the smell of scent. It was worst just before the Robertsons went away.

But then – after California – we came here to this beach once and it was September like now, and a still, gold peace. And the hotel in the dip, and the sand white and wide and rock pools. And only I with you. You were quieter. You brought no work. You lay on the beach with a novel flapping pages and the sand gathering in them. We held hands and it was not as so often. It was not as when I looked at you and saw your eyes looking at someone else invisible. God, love – the killing sickness. Maybe never let it start – just mock and talk of Rights. Don't let it near. Sex without sentiment. Manage one's life with dignity. But now that you are dead –

And one day on that year's peaceful holiday we walked out to the stone trees which now I remember. They told us, at the hotel, that in the sea, lying on their stone sides, on their stone bark and broken stone branches, were great prehistoric trees, petrified and huge and broken into sections by the millennia and chopped here and there as by an infernal knife, like rhubarb chunks or blocks of Edinburgh candy, sand coloured, ancient among the young stones.

Trees so old that no one ever saw them living. Trees become stone. I said, 'I love stone' and you said, 'I love trees,' and kicked them. You said, 'Who wants stone trees?' And we walked about on them, a stone stick forest, quite out to sea, and sat and put our feet in pools where green grasses swayed and starfish shone. And you said – despising the stone trees – there is only ever you – you know – and I knew that the last one was gone and the pain of her and you and I were one again. It was quite right that you loved so much being so much loved and I am glad, for now that you are dead –

I shall never see you any more.

I shall never feel your hand over my hand.

I shall never lean my head against you any more.

I shall never see your eyes which now that you are –

'The sandwiches are egg, love, and cheese, and there's chocolate. We didn't bring a feast. It's too hot.'

'It's lovely.'

'Drink?'

'I don't like Ribena, thanks.'

'It's not. It's wine. In tumblers. Today we're having a lot of wine in very big tumblers.'

(Anna Robertson of evangelical persuasion, who never acts extremely, is offering me wine in tumblers. Now that you are dead.)

'It's nice wine. I'll be drunk.'

The children say, 'You can have some of our cake. D'you want a biscuit?' They've been told to be nice. The little girl pats sand, absorbed, solemn, straight-haired, grave like Tom. The older one, the boy, eats cake and lies on his stomach aware of me and that my husband has died and gone to God.

And you have gone to God?

You were with God and you were my god and now that you –

The boy has long legs. Seven-year-old long legs. The boy is a little like you and not at all like Tom. He rolls over and gives me a biscuit. I'm so glad we had no children. I could not have shared you with children. We needed nobody else except you needed other girls to love a bit and leave – nothing important. You moved on and never mind. I didn't. I did not mind. The pain passed and I don't mind and I shall not mind now that you are dead.

The boy is really – or am I going mad altogether – very like you.

The boy is Peter.

Says, 'Are you coming out on the rocks?'

'I'm fine thanks, Peter. I'm drinking my wine.'

'Drink it later and come out on the rocks. Come on over the rocks.'

See Anna, Tom, proud of Peter being kind to me and only seven. They pretend not to see, fiddling with coffee flask, suntan oil. 'Wonderful summer,' says Anna. 'Wonderful.'

'Come on the rocks.'

'Peter – don't boss,' says Anna.

'Leave your wine and come,' says Peter, 'I'll show you the rocks.'

Do I go with this boy over the rocks my darling now that you are dead and I have no child and I will never see you any more.

Not any more.

Ever again.

Now that you are –

It is ridiculous how this boy walks.

How Anna wept.

'Look, hold my hand,' says Peter, 'and take care. We're on old trees. What d'you think of that? They were so old they turned to stone. It's something in the atmosphere. They're awful, aren't they? I like trees all leafy and sparkly.'

'Sparkly trees?'

'Well, there'd be no pollution. No people. Now just rotten stone.'

'I like stone.'

He kicks them, 'I like trees.'

And I sit down my love because I will not see you any more or hold your hand or put my face on yours and this will pass of course. They've told me that this sort of grief will pass.

But I don't want the grief to change. I want not to forget the feel and look of you and the look of your live eyes and the physical life of you and I do not want to cease to grieve.

'Look, hey, look,' says Peter and stops balancing. 'The tide is coming in.' The water slaps. The dead stone which was once covered with breathing holes for life takes life again, and where it looked like burned out ashy stone there are colours, and little movements, and frondy things responding to water, which laps and laps.

'Look,' says Peter, 'there's a starfish. Pink as pink. Hey – take my hand. Mind out. You mustn't slip.' (This boy has long hard hands.) 'The tide is coming in.'

How Anna cried.

The tide is coming in and it will cover the stone trees and then it will ebb back again and the stone trees will remain, and already the water is showing more growing things that are there all the time, though only now and then seen.
And Peter takes my hand in yours and I will never see you any more – How Anna cried. And things are growing in the cracks in the stones. The boy laughs and looks at me with your known eyes. Now that you are.

Jane Gardam

Activity

1 Discuss the plot of *Stone Trees*, making a note of the key points and any features that particularly strike you. Consider the story's structure. How do flashbacks and time shifts contribute to this? Draw a chart or a diagram to illustrate the structure of the story.

2 Now focus on the characters in the story and the ways in which Gardam creates and presents them. Using specific references from the text, show how she portrays them.

3 What ideas does Gardam explore through the story? Do you think she has a message for the reader? If so, what do you think it is?

4 Now write an essay discussing your interpretation of and responses to this short story. Use your ideas from questions 1–3 and ensure that you comment on the effect of the following:
  • characterization
  • plot and structure
  • use of language
  • theme

6 Non-fiction Prose

Objectives	• To explore different types of non-fiction prose texts
	• To consider the variety of aims and purposes of prose writers
	• To write about prose texts for coursework
	• To prepare for unseen practical criticism of prose texts

What is prose?

The simplest answer to this question is that any form of writing which is not poetry is prose, including, of course, novels and short stories. In this unit, we will consider prose writings other than fiction, but it does not follow that prose texts are unimaginative or contain only dry facts, as you will see in particular from the Special Feature on Swift on pages 127–138.

Prose writers can have many different purposes. These can include:

- describing or reporting events
- propounding new ideas or points of view
- teaching or explaining
- reflecting on or expressing opinions about people, events, or situations
- raising awareness of social issues or injustices
- persuading or influencing readers on political issues; for example, by presenting arguments from a particular point of view.
- entertaining or amusing by presenting topics in original or clever ways

Non-fiction prose texts appear rarely as set texts in A-level English syllabuses, but extracts are quite commonly set as unseens and they are often very rewarding to study for coursework. (A useful 'spin-off' from the study of prose texts is that they can help us to build up our understanding of the historical background against which all forms of literature are produced.)

Prose texts that you study for A-level Literature are likely to combine factual content, descriptive content, or the writer's opinions, with features which make them interesting enough to be read for recreation as well as information. When studying prose texts, our approach is not necessarily any different from when we study novels or even poetry. We still need to ask the key questions: What is the text about? How has the author chosen to write about it? Why is the author writing it? In more specific terms, we need to examine:

- the surface and deeper meanings presented
- the author's viewpoint. Is the text written in the first person or the third person? The effects of this choice in fiction texts are explored in Unit 4 (see pages 70–74), but in non-fiction prose, they can be even more important. Writing in the third person suggests a more objective view-point while writing in the first person tends to give a more opinionated or subjective view. Some texts will need careful thought to determine where the author stands in relation to their material and to the reader
- the structure of the text. In argumentative writing, for example, both sides of the issue may be presented in a measured way before making a judgement or the author may be concerned only with building up the evidence one-sidedly. In contrast, personal, reflective writing may be loose, informal, or even quite unconventional in the way it is structured
- the tone of the writing and the emotions behind the words
- use of imagery and vocabulary
- other stylistic features, such as length and construction of sentences

These aspects all need to be borne in mind as we go on to consider the main types of prose texts that you may encounter at A-level: essays, autobiography and diaries, documentary writing, and journalism. However, you may find that it is sometimes difficult to put texts into categories in this way: essays can be journalistic and a diary can 'document' events.

The essay

In its pure form, the published essay is relatively rare nowadays. However, it used to be a popular way for an author to explore a topic of interest or to convey opinions about current affairs. From the Seventeenth Century, essays were circulated in pamphlets or published in magazines. These remained very popular forms of mass communication until radio and television took over as more powerful vehicles for the expression of personal or political views.

Essays are written in many styles: they can be witty, angry, and satirical or gentle and thoughtful, but they usually present a personal or subjective view of a topic, and do not pretend to be objective.

Francis Bacon, a seventeenth-century politician and writer whose classical education pervades his work, wrote fifty-eight essays on topics such as Death, Travel, and Anger. *Of Studies*, the essay below, contains his advice on the subject of reading. Although these are expressions of his personal opinions, they are very formal, showing just how carefully prose can be constructed.

Because of its date and Bacon's frequent use of Classical allusions, at a first reading, this may seem quite a challenging text. The advice given in Unit 2 on studying difficult poetry (see page 25) is equally relevant when encountering more difficult prose texts. A good dictionary is always useful, but also be aware of the fact that some words have changed their meanings over the centuries. Some help is provided here by the footnotes.

Of Studies

Studies serve for delight, for ornament, and for ability.[1] Their chief use for delight, is in privateness and retiring;[2] for ornament, is in discourse; and for ability, is in the judgement and disposition of business. For expert men[3] can execute, and perhaps judge of particulars, one by one; but the general counsels,[4] and the plots and marshalling of affairs come best from those that are learned. To spend too much time in studies is sloth; to use them too much for ornament is affectation; to make judgement wholly by their rules is the humour of a scholar.
They perfect nature, and are perfected by experience, for natural abilities are like natural plants that need proyning[5] by study; and studies themselves do give forth directions too much at large, except they be bounded in by experience.
Crafty men contemn studies[6], simple men admire them, and wise men use them; for they teach not their own use; but that is a wisdom without them and above them, won by observation.
Read not to contradict and confute; nor to believe and take for granted; nor to find talk and discourse; but to weigh and consider. Some books are to be tasted, others to be swallowed, and some few to be chewed and digested: that is, some books are to be read only in parts; others to be read, but not curiously;[7] and some few to be read wholly and with diligence and attention. Some books also may be read by deputy, and extracts made of them by others, but that would be only in the less important arguments, and the meaner sort of books; else distilled books are like common distilled waters, flashy[8] things.
Reading maketh a full man; conference a ready man; and writing an exact man. And therefore, if a man write little, he had need have a great memory; if he confer little, he had need have a present wit;[9] and if he read little, he had need have much cunning, to seem to know that he doth not.

Francis Bacon

1 *for ability*: to make men able.
2 *retiring*: peace and solitude
3 *expert men*: men who have learned from practical experience and not through study.
4 *counsels*: ideas; advice
5 *proyning*: cultivating; pruning
6 *Crafty men contemn studies*: practical men avoid studies
7 *curiously*: with great care
8 *flashy*: insipid; weak
9 *present wit*: quick mind

Activity

Read the extract again carefully. Some explanations are offered, but make a note of any other unfamiliar words and look them up.

1 The first aim is to fully understand Bacon's meaning. Working alone or with a partner, write a summary, in simple modern English, which conveys the meaning of each section. (The original was not set out in paragraphs, but has been divided into manageable sections here.)

2 What do you think Bacon's aim is in this essay?

3 Now look closely at how Bacon constructs his sentences. For example, what do you notice about the first two sentences and the last two sentences here? What other patterns can you find?

4 What do you think is the effect on the reader of this style of writing?

This is stylized, formal writing. Perhaps the writer gives as much attention to weighing his words and impressively balancing his sentences, as to the content of his essay. Bacon is very sure of himself. His ideas, opinions, and judgements are presented as if they are statements of fact.

Autobiography and diaries

These forms of writing provide fascinating insights into the lives of people, past and present. Biographies document or celebrate the lives of famous – or infamous – people. They may be the product of the author's friendship with his subject or the result of extensive research. For example, two biographies of Charlotte Brontë, one by her contemporary and friend, Mrs Gaskell which is personal and anecdotatal, the other by the twentieth-century scholar, Winifred Gerin which is scholarly and objective, present very different insights into this Victorian writer.

Autobiographical writing might be a review of a whole lifetime or it may focus on particular events or a significant period in the author's life as Brian Keenan does in his autobiography *An Evil Cradling*. This is his account of the years he spent as a hostage in Beirut.

Activity

1 Read the following extract in which Keenan invites us to share his experience of confinement and isolation, something which most of us would fear.

2 Discuss the text with a partner and make notes on how Keenan uses language:
  • to involve the reader in his experiences
  • to convey the monotony of life in the cell
  • to describe how he is affected by captivity and how he copes with the situation
  In particular, consider:
  • the sentence patterns Keenan uses
  • the effect of his strong use of the first person

An Evil Cradling

Come now into the cell with me and stay here and feel if you can and if you will that time, whatever time it was, for however long, for time means nothing in this cell. Come, come in.

I am back from my daily ablutions. I hear the padlock slam behind me and I lift the towel which has draped my head from my face. I look at the food on the floor. The round of Arab bread, a boiled egg, the jam I will not eat, the slice or two of processed cheese and perhaps some houmus. Every day I look to see if it will change, if there will be some new morsel of food that will make this day different from all the other days, but there is no change. This day is the same as all the days in the past and as all the days to come. It will always be the same food sitting on the floor in the same place.

I set down my plastic bottle of drinking water and the other empty bottle. From bottle to bottle, through me, this fluid will daily run. I set the urine bottle at the far corner away from the food. This I put in a plastic bag to keep it fresh. In this heat the bread rapidly turns stale and hard. It is like eating cardboard. I pace my four paces backwards and forwards, slowly feeling my mind empty, wondering where it will go today. Will I go with it or will I try to hold it back, like a father and an unruly child? There is a greasy patch on the wall where I lay my head. Like a dog I sniff it.

I begin as I have always begun these days to think of something, anything upon which I can concentrate. Something I can think about and so try to push away the crushing emptiness of this tiny, tiny cell and the day's long silence. I try with desperation to recall the dream of the night before or perhaps to push away the horror of it. The nights are filled with dreaming. The cinema of the mind, the reels flashing and flashing by and suddenly stopping at some point when with strange contortions it throws up some absurd drama that I cannot understand. I try to block it out. Strange how in the daytime the dreams that we do not wish to remember come flickering back into the conscious mind. Those dreams that we desperately want to have with us in the daylight will not come to us but have gone and cannot be enticed back. It is as if we are running down a long empty tunnel looking for something that we left behind but cannot see in the blackness. The guards are gone. I have not heard a noise for several hours now. It must be time to eat. I tear off a quarter of the unleavened bread and begin to peel the shell from the egg. The word 'albumen' intrigues me for a while and I wonder where the name came from. How someone decided once to call that part of the egg 'albumen'. The shape of an egg has lost its fascination for me. I have exhausted thinking about the form of an egg. A boiled egg with dry bread is doubly taste-less. I make this meaningless remark to myself every day and don't know why.

Brian Keenan

Documentary writing

Sometimes authors use recorded facts and the words of writers, experts, or witnesses (i.e. 'documentation') to produce their own interpretation of events. The maker of a television documentary works in a similar way.

In *A Journal of the Plague Year*, Daniel Defoe writes in the role of a contemporary observer of the plague which swept the city in 1665 – 'a Citizen who continued all the while in London'. Anthony Burgess, in his introduction to the Penguin edition, points out that:

'...it reads like a rapid, colloquial, sometimes clumsy setting down of reminiscences of a great historical event that was lived through by a plain London merchant with a passion for facts, a certain journalistic talent, but... no literary pretensions whatever. In reality it is a rather cunning work of art, a confidence trick of the imagination... He wanted to write a popular novel but insisted on doing his homework first.'

Accordingly, the 'journal' presents documentary evidence, such as statistics relating to deaths from the plague, advertisements, and legal papers. In his role of observer, Defoe explains the significance of these, then goes on to make them relevant and personal by adding anecdotes about events he has 'witnessed'. So he both imparts a lot of information and engages his readers through the 'human interest' of his stories. In this extract, after setting out the legal orders which enforced the shutting up of the houses of people infected by the plague, he discusses the pros and cons of this practice before telling some stories to illustrate its results.

A Journal of the Plague Year

It is true that the locking up the doors of people's houses and setting a watchman there night and day to prevent their stirring out or any coming to them, when perhaps the sound people in the family might have escaped if they had been removed from the sick, looked very hard and cruel; and many people perished in these miserable confinements which, 'tis reasonable to believe, would not have been distempered if they had had liberty, though the plague was in the house; at which the people were very clamorous and uneasy at first, and several violences were committed and injuries offered to the men who were set to watch the houses so shut up; also several people broke out by force in many places, as I shall observe by-and-by. But it was a public good that justified the private mischief, and there was no obtaining the least mitigation by any application to magistrates or government at that time, at least not that I heard of. This put the people upon all manner of stratagem in order, if possible, to get out; and it would fill a little volume to set down the arts used by the people of such houses to shut the eyes of the watchmen who were employed, to deceive them, and to escape or break out from them, in which frequent scuffles and some mischief happened...

Nor, indeed, could less be expected, for here were so many prisons in the town as there were houses shut up; and as the people shut up or imprisoned so were guilty of no crime, only shut up because miserable, it was really the more intolerable to them.

It had also this difference, that every prison, as we may call it, had but one jailer, and as he had the whole house to guard, and that many houses were so situated as that they had several ways out, some more, some less, and some into several streets, it was impossible for one man so to guard all the passages as to prevent the escape of people made desperate by the fright of their circumstances, by the resentment of their usage, or by the raging of the distemper itself; so that they would talk to the watchman on one side of the house, while the family made their escape at another.

For example, in Coleman Street there are abundance of alleys, as appears still. A house was shut up in that they call White's Alley; and this house had a back-window, not a door, into a court which had a passage into Bell Alley. A watchman was set by the constable at the door of this house, and there he stood, or his comrade, night and day, while the family went all away in the evening out at that window into the court, and left the poor fellows warding and watching for near a fortnight.

Not far from the same place they blew up a watchman with gunpowder, and burned the poor fellow dreadfully; and while he made hideous cries, and nobody would venture to come near to help him, the whole family that were able to stir got out at the windows one storey high, two that were left sick calling out for help. Care was taken to give them nurses to look after them, but the persons fled were never found, till after the plague was abated they returned; but as nothing could be proved, so nothing could be done to them.

Daniel Defoe

A different technique is used by John Hersey in *Hiroshima*, which traces the experiences of six survivors of the first atomic bomb. He introduces each person individually, describing everyday details of their lives so that we can picture them in the moments before the bomb fell, before tracking each of them through the year which follows. This extract begins the tale of Toshiko Sasaki.

Hiroshima

Miss Toshiko Sasaki, the East Asia Tin Works clerk... got up at three o'clock in the morning on the day the bomb fell. There was extra housework to do. Her eleven-month-old brother, Akio, had come down the day before with a serious stomach upset; her mother had taken him to the Tamura Paediatric Hospital and was staying there with him. Miss Sasaki, who was about twenty, had to cook breakfast for her father, a brother, a sister, and herself, and – since the hospital, because of the war, was unable to provide food – to prepare a whole day's meals for her mother and the baby, in time for her father, who worked in a factory making rubber earplugs for artillery crews, to take the food by on his way to the plant. When she had finished and had cleaned and put away the cooking things, it was nearly seven. The family lived in Koi, and she had a forty-five minute trip to the tin works, in the section of town called Kannonmachi. She was in charge of the personnel records in the factory...

Miss Sasaki... sat down at her desk. She was quite far from the windows, which were off to her left, and behind her were a couple of tall bookcases containing all the books of the factory library, which the personnel department had organized. She settled herself at her desk, put some things in a drawer, and shifted papers. She thought that before she began to make entries in her lists of new employees, discharges, and departures for the Army, she would chat for a moment with the girl at her right. Just as she turned her head away from the windows, the room was filled with a blinding light. She was paralyzed by fear, fixed still in her chair for a long moment (the plant was 1,600 yards from the centre [of the explosion]). Everything fell, and Miss Sasaki lost consciousness. The ceiling dropped suddenly and the wooden floor above collapsed in splinters and the people up there came down and the roof above them gave way; but principally and first of all, the bookcases right behind her swooped forward and the contents threw her down, with her left leg horribly twisted and breaking underneath her. There, in the tin factory, in the first moment of the atomic age, a human being was crushed by books.

John Hersey

Activity

> **1** Read the extracts from *A Journal of the Plague Year* and *Hiroshima* again. Discuss the following points with a partner and make notes.
> - What sorts of factual information and detail does each writer provide?
> - How does each writer make his account personal and specific to the people described?
> - Which writer expresses more emotion?
> - Which writer draws the stronger emotional response from you as a reader? How and why?
>
> **2** Write a detailed comparison of these two extracts showing how each writer engages us in the experience of disaster. Use your notes as a starting point for your comparison.

Journalism

You may have noticed that many of the prose texts in this unit deal with disturbing or disastrous events. This seems particularly true when we look at journalistic writing, because typically it focuses on 'bad news'. Indeed, the exposure of injustice or suffering seems to inspire journalists to produce their most powerful work. Journalism can, of course, be very humorous, satirical, or entertaining but it is often intended to alert us to some form of wrongdoing.

John Pilger, an Australian journalist, has written bitingly about injustices all over the world. He has a particular concern to expose the ways in which the media and propaganda are used to distort people's perception of events. In the extract on page 125, he shows how the language used by those responsible for bombing campaigns in Vietnam and in the Gulf War blunted people's awareness of the human suffering involved.

Video Nasties

In 1972, I watched American B52s bombing southern Vietnam, near the ashes of a town called An Loc. From a distance of two miles, I could see three ladders of bombs curved in the sky; and, as each rung reached the ground, there was a plume of fire and a sound that welled and rippled, then quaked the ground beneath me.

This was Operation Arc Light, described by the Pentagon as 'high performance denial interdiction, with minimized collateral damage': jargon that echoes today. The B52s were unseen above the clouds; between them they dropped seventy tons of explosives in a 'long-box' pattern that extended several miles. Almost everything that moved inside the box was deemed 'redundant'.

On inspection, a road that connected two villages had been replaced by craters, one of them almost a quarter of a mile wide. Houses had vanished. There was no life; cooking pots lay strewn in a ditch, no doubt dropped in haste. People a hundred yards from the point of contact had not left even their scorched shadows, which the dead had left at Hiroshima. Visitors to Indo-China today are shocked by the moonscape of craters in Vietnam, Laos and Cambodia, where people lived.

The B52s now operating over Iraq are the same type of thirty-year-old aircraft. We are told they are bombing Saddam Hussein's Republican Guard, and the 'outskirts' of Baghdad. Before the introduction in Vietnam of military euphemisms designed to make palatable to Congress new hi-tech 'anti-people' weapons, the term used was carpet-bombing. This was vivid and accurate, for these aircraft lay carpets of death, killing and destroying comprehensively and indiscriminately. This is what they were built to do; and that is what they are no doubt doing in a country where most people neither have shelters nor are 'dug in'.

The other night, on television, a senior ex-RAF officer included the current B52 raids in his description of 'pinpoint strikes... part of the extraordinary precision work of the Allies'. John Major and Tom King constantly refer to this 'remarkable precision' and, by clear implication, the equally remarkable humanitarian benefits this brings to the innocent people of Iraq, although further information about these benefits is curiously unforthcoming.

...The principal weapons used against Iraq, such as the Tomahawk cruise missile, have a 'circular error probability'. This means they are targeted to fall within a circle, like a dart landing anywhere on a dart board. They do not have to hit, or even damage, the bull's-eye to be considered 'effective' or 'successful'. Some have hit the bull's-eye – the Tomahawk that demolished the Ministry of Defence building in Baghdad is the most famous – but many, if not most, clearly have not. What else have they hit? What else is within the circle? People, maybe? The numerous autocues say nothing.

General Powell has also referred to 'minimized collateral damage'. Like 'circular error probability' this term was invented in Vietnam. It means dead civilians: men, women, and children. Their number is 'minimized', of course...

John Pilger

Activity

> 1 Look at paragraphs 1 to 3. In what ways do Pilger's language, style, and attitude in the second paragraph differ from those of the first and third? What is his aim here? Find other examples of this in the text.
> 2 Pilger talks about 'military euphemisms'. A euphemism is a word or phrase which we use when stating the truth baldly would be too painful or embarrassing. Examine the words and phrases in quotation marks – the official jargon. What is their purpose and effect? Devise substitute phrases which would express the truth more graphically. Create some euphemisms of your own for the effects of warfare.
> 3 'The... remarkable humanitarian benefits this brings to the innocent people of Iraq, although further information about these benefits is curiously unforthcoming.' How would you describe Pilger's tone in this extract? Find other examples in the text to support your views.

Comparing prose texts

If your syllabus includes coursework, it will probably require that one element of this should be a comparative study of at least two complete texts. This element of your course may be taught in class or you may be given the opportunity to work independently, choosing your own texts for wider reading and devising your own comparison question. Many non-fiction prose texts provide suitable material for this kind of work, as this suggested essay question shows:

Brian Keenan *An Evil Cradling*, 1993
Primo Levi *If This is a Man*, 1987

Each of these writers found himself removed from his familiar world and forced into a situation which was not just physically dangerous, but which threatened to destroy his identity. Compare how each writer presents the experience of imprisonment and how each attempts to cope and preserve some sense of self.

(*If This is a Man* is Levi's intensely moving account of his experiences in a Nazi concentration camp. It was originally written in Italian, but it is usually permissible to study one text in translation.)

Activity

> 1 Research and read two prose texts on a theme of your own choice.
> 2 Devise an essay title which focuses your ideas on the topic which links the texts. When writing your question, bear in mind that it is vital to draw out how the authors use language to present their ideas. (See Unit 17 page 243, for more on devising coursework essay titles.)

Special Feature: Jonathan Swift

Jonathan Swift was one of the finest proponents of satire in the Eighteenth Century. In this special feature we are going to look in detail at his satirical essay, *A Modest Proposal*. This will be a way of studying a complete prose work but also of looking at the notion of satire. Both areas of study will be good preparation for tackling unseen non-fiction texts or for using a longer prose work as the basis for coursework.

The concept of satire

Authors usually write about the society in which they live, and often they feel motivated to criticize what they see. So it is not surprising that they sometimes choose to satirize or 'send up' the foolishness of society's customs, beliefs, and politics. Writers of satire may mock trivial things, the foibles and weaknesses of individuals, but they may also make serious points about politics or use their wit angrily to attack cruelty or injustice, in the hope of stirring people to make changes. The latter is true of Swift's *A Modest Proposal*.

A great deal of powerful satirical writing was produced in the late Seventeenth and early Eighteenth Centuries, after the restoration of the monarchy, during the reign of Queen Anne. John Dryden, Alexander Pope, and Jonathan Swift were all important writers of this period. Dryden and Pope wrote most of their satires in verse, but Swift wrote his greatest works in prose. You probably know the story of Gulliver's adventures in Lilliput, which is often presented, in simplified form, as a children's story. *Gulliver's Travels* is, in fact, a large-scale work of biting satire which Swift hoped would 'vex the world rather than divert' it.

All three of these writers liked to draw attention to hypocrisy and artificiality; to show up things or people which were not what they seemed or pretended to be – those hiding behind grandiose facades and behaving in unnatural ways. This can be seen in works such as Pope's *The Rape of the Lock* and Dryden's *Absalom and Achitophel*. Dryden's own definition from his *An Essay Upon Satire* (1679) is perhaps as good as any:

'...the boldest way...
To tell men freely of their foulest faults;
To laugh at their vain deeds and vainer thoughts.'

Activity

> **1** Without any further background, read the first part of *A Modest Proposal*. Take the first three paragraphs and then discuss the following points with a partner:
> - What kind of person or character writes or speaks these words?
> - What do you think his purpose is?
>
> **2** Now read the next six paragraphs up to the end of this extract.
> - How do your views of the writer and his purpose change?
> - At what point do you begin to suspect that his intentions are different from what you first thought?

A Modest Proposal

FOR

Preventing the Children of poor People in Ireland, from being a Burden to their Parents or Country; and for making them beneficial to the Publick.
Written in the Year 1729

(1) IT is a melancholly Object to those, who walk through this great Town, or travel in the Country; when they see the *Streets*, the *Roads*, and *Cabbin-doors* crowded with *Beggars* of the Female Sex, followed by three, four, or six Children, *all in Rags*, and importuning every Passenger for an Alms. These *Mothers*, instead of being able to work for their honest Livelyhood, are forced to employ all their Time in stroling to beg Sustenance for their *helpless Infants*; who, as they grow up, either turn Thieves for want of Work; or leave their *dear Native Country, to fight for the Pretender* in Spain, or sell themselves to the *Barbadoes*.

(2) I THINK it is agreed by all Parties, that this prodigious Number of Children in the Arms, or on the Backs, or at the *Heels* of their *Mothers*, and frequently of their *Fathers*, is *in the present deplorable State of the Kingdom*, a very great additional Grievance; and therefore, whoever could find out a fair, cheap, and easy Method of making these Children sound and useful Members of the Commonwealth would deserve so well of the Publick, as to have his Statue set up for a Preserver of the Nation.

(3) BUT my Intention is very far from being confined to provide only for the *Children of professed Beggars*: It is of a much greater Extent, and shall take in the whole Number of Infants at a certain Age, who are born of Parents, in effect as little able to support them, as those who demand our Charity in the Streets.

(4) As to my own Part, having turned my Thoughts for many Years, upon this important Subject, and maturely weighed the several *Schemes of other Projectors*, I have always found them grosly mistaken in their Computation. It is true a Child, *just dropt from its Dam*, may be supported by her Milk, for a Solar Year with little other Nourishment; at most not above the Value of two Shillings; which the Mother may certainly get or the Value in *Scraps*, by her lawful Occupation of *Begging*: And, it is exactly at one Year old, that I propose to provide for them in such a Manner, as, instead of being a Charge upon their *Parents*, or the *Parish*, or *wanting Food or Raiment* for the rest of their Lives; they shall, on the contrary, contribute to the Feeding, and partly the Cloathing, of many Thousands.

(5) THERE is likewise another great Advantage in my *Scheme*, that it will prevent those *voluntary Abortions*, and that horrid Practice of *Women murdering their Bastard*

Children; alas! too frequent among us; sacrificing the *poor innocent Babes*, I doubt, more to avoid the Expence than the Shame; which would move Tears and Pity in the most Savage and inhuman Breast.

(6) THE Number of Souls in *Ireland* being usually reckoned one Million and a half; of these I calculate there may be about Two hundred Thousand Couple whose Wives are Breeders; from which Number I subtract thirty thousand Couples, who are able to maintain their own Children; although I apprehend there cannot be so many, under *the present Distresses of the Kingdom*; but this being granted, there will remain an Hundred and Seventy Thousand Breeders. I again subtract Fifty Thousand, for those Women who miscarry, or whose Children die by Accident, or Disease, within the Year. There only remain an Hundred and Twenty Thousand Children of poor Parents, annually born: The Question therefore is, How this Number shall be reared, and provided for? Which, as I have already said, under the present Situation of Affairs, is utterly impossible, by all Methods hitherto proposed: For we can *neither employ them in Handicraft or Agriculture*; we neither build Houses, (I mean in the Country) nor cultivate Land: They can very seldom pick up a Livelyhood *by Stealing* until they arrive at six Years old; except where they are of towardly Parts; although, I confess, they learn the Rudiments much earlier; during which Time, they can, however, be properly looked upon only as *Probationers*; as I have been informed by principal Gentleman in the County of *Cavan*, who protested to me, that he never knew above one or two Instances under the Age of six, even in a Part of the Kingdom *so renowned for the quickest Proficiency in that Art*.

(7) I AM assured by our Merchants, that a Boy or a Girl before twelve Years old, is no saleable Commodity; and even when they come to this Age, they will not yield above Three Pounds, or Three Pounds and half a Crown at most, on the Exchange; which cannot turn to Account either to the Parents or the Kingdom; the Charge of Nutriment and Rags, having been at least four Times that Value.

(8) I SHALL therefore humbly propose my own Thoughts which I hope will not be liable to the least Objection.

(9) I HAVE been assured by a very knowing *American* of my Acquaintance in *London*; that a young healthy Child, well nursed, is, at a Year old, a most delicious, nourishing, and wholesome Food; whether, *Stewed, Roasted, Baked*, or *Boiled*; and I make no doubt, that it will equally serve in a *Fricasie* or *Ragoust*.

Filling in the background

Now that you have a flavour of the text, we will consider the background to *A Modest Proposal*. Swift was born in Ireland in 1667 and educated there. He was a clergyman, rising to become Dean of St Patrick's Cathedral in Dublin, but he was also very much involved in politics which held a lifelong fascination for him. The state of Ireland and its relationship with England was his central concern. At this time, Ireland was an English colony and the country as a whole, and its poorer citizens in particular, suffered exploitation at the hands of absentee English landlords. In addition, those Irish people who were wealthy spent their money on English goods which were considered more fashionable than Irish products, draining the Irish economy even more. As a result, poverty and starvation were rife.

Swift, as a clergyman, did his best to help the people in his care in practical ways, but also wrote tracts and pamphlets to influence people politically and to suggest remedies for these problems. His writings had some influence for a while, but by the time he wrote *A Modest Proposal* in 1729, he was full of anger and despair that so little had changed. It seemed that the English and the wealthy Irish saw the majority of Ireland's people only as material to be used and exploited.

Activity | Now read the rest of the text, paying careful attention to how Swift presents his subject.

A Modest Proposal

(10) I DO therefore humbly offer it to *publick Consideration*, that of the Hundred and Twenty Thousand Children, already computed, Twenty thousand may be reserved for Breed; whereof only one Fourth Part to be Males; which is more than we allow to *Sheep, black Cattle*, or *Swine*; and my Reason is, that these Children are seldom the Fruits of Marriage, *a Circumstance not much regarded by our Savages*; therefore, *one Male* will be sufficient to serve *four Females*. That the remaining Hundred thousand, may, at a Year old, be offered in Sale to the *Persons of Quality* and *Fortune*, through the Kingdom; always advising the Mother to them suck plentifully in the last Month, so as to render them plump, and fat for a good Table. A child will make two Dishes at an Entertainment for Friends; and when the Family dines alone, the fore or hind Quarter will make a reasonable Dish; and seasoned with a little Pepper or Salt, will be very good Boiled on the fourth Day, especially in *Winter*.

(11) I HAVE reckoned on a Medium, that a Child just born will weigh Twelve Pounds; and in a solar Year, if tolerably nursed, encreaseth to twenty-eight Pounds.

(12) I GRANT this Food may be somewhat dear, and therefore very *proper for Landlords*; who, as they have already devoured most of the Parents, seem to have the best Title to the Children.

(13) INFANTS Flesh will be in Season throughout the Year; but more plentiful in *March*, and a little before and after: For we are told by a grave* Author, an eminent *French* Physician, that *Fish being a prolifick Dyet*, there are more Children born in *Roman Catholick Countries* about Nine Months after Lent, than at any other Season: Therefore reckoning a Year after *Lent*, the Markets will be more glutted than usual; because the Number of *Popish Infants*, is, at least, three to one in this Kingdom; and therefore it will have one other Collateral Advantage, by lessening the Number of *Papists* among us.

(14) I HAVE already computed the Charge of nursing a Beggar's Child (in which List I reckon all *Cottagers, Labourers*, and Four-fifths of *Farmers*) to be about two Shillings per Annum, Rags included; and I believe, no Gentleman would repine to give Ten Shillings for the *Carcase of a good fat Child*; which, as I have said, will make four Dishes of excellent nutritive Meat, when he hath only some particular Friend, or his own Family, to dine with him. Thus the Squire will learn to be a good Landlord, and grow popular among his Tenants; the Mother will have Eight

*Rabelais [Swift's footnote]

Shillings net Profit, and be fit for Work until she produceth another Child.

(15) THOSE who are more thrifty (*as I must confess the Times require*) may flay the Carcase; the Skin of which, artificially dressed, will make admirable *Gloves for Ladies*, and *Summer Boots for fine Gentlemen*.

(16) As to our City of *Dublin*; Shambles may be appointed for this Purpose, in the most convenient Parts of it; and Butchers we may be assured will not be wanting; although I rather recommend buying the Children alive, and dressing them hot from the Knife, as we do *roasting Pigs*.

(17) A VERY worthy Person, *a true Lover of his Country*, and whose Virtues I highly esteem, was lately pleased, in discoursing on this Matter, to offer a Refinement upon my Scheme. He said, that many Gentlemen of this Kingdom, having of late destroyed their Deer; he conceived, that the Want of Venison might be well supplied by the Bodies of young Lads and Maidens, not exceeding fourteen Years of Age nor under twelve; so great a Number of both Sexes in every Country being now ready to starve, for Want of Work and Service: And these to be disposed of by their Parents, if alive, or otherwise by their nearest Relations. But with due Deference to so excellent a Friend, and so deserving a Patriot, I cannot be altogether in his Sentiments. For as to the Males, my *American* Acquaintance assured me from frequent Experience, that their Flesh was generally tough and lean, like that of our School-boys, by continual Exercise, and their Taste disagreeable; and to fatten them would not answer to the Charge. Then, as the Females, it would, I think, with humble Submission, *be a Loss to the Publick*, because they would soon become Breeders themselves; And besides it is not improbable, that some scrupulous People might be apt to censure such a Practice (although indeed very unjustly) as a little bordering on Cruelty; which, I confess, hath always been with me the strongest Objection against any Project, how well soever intended.

(18) BUT in order to justify my Friend; he confessed, that this Expedient was put into his Head by the famous *Salmanaazor*, a Native of the Island of *Formosa*, who came from thence to *London*, above twenty Years ago, and in Conversation told my Friend, that in his Country, when any young Person happened to be put to Death, the Executioner sold the Carcase to *Persons of Quality*, as a prime Dainty; and that, in his Time, the Body of a plump Girl of fifteen, who was crucified for an Attempt to poison the Emperor, was sold to his Imperial *Majesty's prime Minister of State*, and other great Mandarins of the Court, *in Joints from the Gibbet*, at Four hundred Crowns. Neither indeed can I deny, that if the same Use were made of several plump young girls in this Town, who, without one single Groat to their Fortunes cannot stir Abroad without a chair, and appear in the *Play-house*, and *Assemblies* in foreign Fineries, which they never will pay for; the Kingdom would not be the worse.

(19) SOME Persons of a desponding Spirit are in great Concern about that vast Number of poor People, who are Aged, Diseased, or Maimed; and I have been desired to employ my Thoughts what Course may be taken, to ease the Nation of so grievous and Incumbrance. But I am not in the least Pain upon the Matter; because it is very well known, that they are every Day *dying*, and *rotting*, by *Cold* and *Famine*, and *Filth*, and *Vermin*, as fast as can be reasonably expected. And as to the younger Labourers, they are now in almost as hopeful a Condition:

They cannot get Work, and consequently pine away for Want of Nourishment, to a Degree, that if at any Time they are accidentally hired to common Labour, they have not Strength to perform it; and thus the Country, and themselves, are in a fair Way of being soon delivered from the Evils to come.

(20) I HAVE too long digressed; and therefore shall return to my Subject. I think the Advantages by the Proposal which I have made, are obvious, and many, as well as of the highest Importance.

(21) FOR, *First*, as I have already observed, it would greatly lessen the *Number of Papists*, with whom we are yearly overrun; being the principal Breeders of the Nation, as well as most dangerous Enemies; and who stay at home on Purpose, with a Design to *deliver the Kingdom to the Pretender*; hoping to take their Advantage by the Absence of *so many good Protestants*, who have chosen rather to leave their Country, than stay at home, and pay Tithes against their Conscience, to an idolatrous *Episcopal Curate*.

(22) SECONDLY, The poorer Tenants will have something valuable of their own, which, by Law, may be made liable to Distress, and help to pay their Landlords Rent; their Corn and Cattle being already seized, and *Money a Thing unknown*.

(23) THIRDLY, Whereas the Maintenance of an Hundred Thousand Children, from two Years old, and upwards, cannot be computed at less than ten Shillings a Piece *per Annum*, the Nation's Stock will be thereby encreased Fifty Thousand Pounds *per Annum*; besides Profit of a new Dish, introduced to the Tables of all *Gentlemen of Fortune* in the Kingdom, who have any Refinement of Taste; and the Money will circulate among ourselves, the Goods being entirely of our own Growth and Manufacture.

(24) FOURTHLY, The constant Breeders, besides the Gain of Eight Shillings *Sterling per Annum*, by the Sale of their Children, will be rid of the Charge of maintaining them after the first Year.

(25) FIFTHLY, This Food would likewise bring great *Custom to Taverns*, where the Vintners will certainly be so prudent, as to procure the best Receipts for dressing it to Perfection; and consequently, have their Houses frequented by all the *fine Gentlemen*, who justly value themselves upon their Knowledge in good Eating; and a skilful Cook, who understands how to oblige his Guests, will contrive to make it as expensive as they please.

(26) SIXTHLY, This would be a great Inducement to Marriage, which all wise nations have either encouraged by Rewards, or enforced by Laws and Penalties. It would encrease the Care and Tenderness of Mothers towards their Children, when they were sure of a Settlement for Life, to the poor Babes, provided in some Sort by the Publick, to their annual Profit instead of Expence. We should soon see an honest Emulation among the married Women, *which of them could bring the fattest Child to the Market*. Men would become as fond of their Wives, during the Time of their Pregnancy, as they are now of their *Mares* in Foal, their *Cows* in Calf or *Sows* when they are ready to farrow; nor offer to beat of kick them, (as it is too *frequent* a Practice) for fear of a Miscarriage.

(27) MANY other Advantages might be enumerated. For instance, the Addition of some Thousand Carcases in our Exportation of barrelled beef: The Propagation of *Swines Flesh*, and Improvement in the Art of making good Bacon; so much wanted among us by the Destruction of *Pigs*, too frequent at our Tables, and are

no way comparable in Taste, or Magnificence, to a well-grown fat yearling Child; which, roasted whole, will make a considerable Figure at a *Lord Mayor's Feast*, or any other publick Entertainment. But this, and many others I omit, being studious of Brevity.

(28) SUPPOSING that one Thousand Families in this City, would be constant Customers for Infants Flesh; besides others who might have it at *merry Meetings*, particularly *Weddings* and *Christenings*; I compute that *Dublin* would take off, annually, about Twenty Thousand Carcasses; and the rest of the Kingdom (where probably they will be sold somewhat cheaper) the remaining Eighty Thousand.

(29) I CAN think of no one Objection, that will possibly be raised against this Proposal; unless it should be urged, that the Number of People will be thereby much lessened in the Kingdom. This I freely own; and it was indeed one principal Design in offering it to the World. I desire the Reader will observe, that I calculate my Remedy *for this one individual Kingdom of* IRELAND, *and for no other that ever was, is, or I think ever can be upon Earth*. Threrefore, let no man talk to me of other Expedients: *Of taxing our Absentees at five Shillings a Pound: Of using neither Cloaths, nor Houshold Furniture except what is of our own Growth and Manufacture: Of utterly rejecting the Materials and Instruments that promote foreign Luxury: Of curing the Expensiveness of Pride, Vanity, Idleness, and Gaming in our Women: Of introducing a Vein of Parsimony, Prudence and Temperance. Of learning to love our Country, wherein we differ from* LAPLANDERS, *and the Inhabitants of* TOPINAMBOO: *Of quitting our animosities, and Factions; nor act any longer like the* Jews, *who were murdering one another at the very Moment their City was being taken: Of being a little cautious not to sell our Country and Consciences for nothing: Of teaching Landlords to have, at least one Degree of Mercy towards their Tenants*. Lastly, *Of putting a Spirit of Honesty, Industry, and Skill into our Shop-keepers; who, if a Resolution could now be taken to buy only our native Goods, would immediately unite to cheat and exact upon us in the Price, the Measure, and the Goodness; nor could ever yet be brought to make one fair Proposal of just Dealing, though often and earnestly invited to it.*

(30) THEREFORE I repeat, let no Man talk to me of these and the like Expedients; till he hath, at least, a Glimpse of Hope, that there will be some hearty and sincere Attempt to put *them in Practice*.

(31) BUT, as to my self; having been wearied out for many Years with offering vain, idle, visionary Thoughts; and at length utterly despairing of Success, I fortunately fell upon this Proposal; which, as it is wholly new, so it hath something *solid* and *real*, of no Expence, and little Trouble, full in our own Power; and whereby we can incur no Danger in *disobliging* ENGLAND: For, this Kind of Commodity will not bear Exportation; the Flesh being of too tender a Consistence, to admit a long Continuance in Salt; *although, perhaps, I could name a Country, which would be glad to eat up our whole Nation without it.*

(32) AFTER all, I am not so violently bent upon my own Opinion, as to reject any Offer proposed by wise Men, which shall be found equally innocent, cheap, easy, and effectual. But before something of that Kind shall be advanced, in Contradiction to my Scheme, and offering a better; I desire the Author, or Authors, will be pleased maturely to consider two Points. *First*, As Things now stand, how they

will be able to find Food and Raiment, for a Hundred Thousand useless Mouths and Backs? And *secondly*, There being a round Million of Creatures in human Figure, throughout this Kingdom; whose whole Subsistence, put into a common Stock, would leave them in Debt two Millions of Pounds *Sterling*; adding those, who are Beggars by Profession, to the Bulk of Farmers, Cottagers, and Labourers, with their Wives and Children, who are Beggars in Effect; I desire those Politicians, who dislike my Overture, and may perhaps be so bold to attempt an Answer, that they will first ask the Parents of these Mortals, Whether they would not, at this Day, think it a great Happiness to have been sold for Food at a Year old, in the Manner I prescribe; and thereby have avoided such a perpetual Scene of Misfortunes, as they have since gone through; by the *Oppression of the Landlords*; The Impossibility of paying Rent, without Money or Trade; the Want of common Sustenance, with neither House nor Cloaths, to cover them from the Inclemencies of the Weather; and the most inevitable Prospect of intailing the like, or greater Miseries upon their Breed for ever.

 I PROFESS, in the Sincerity of my Heart, that I have not the least personal Interest, in endeavouring to promote this necessary Work; having no other Motive than the *publick Good of my Country, by advancing our Trade, providing for Infants, relieving the Poor, and giving some Pleasure to the Rich*. I have no Children, by which I propose to get a single Penny; the youngest being nine Years old, and my Wife past Child-bearing.

The writer's voice and the use of a persona

We have already begun to consider the type of person who is 'speaking' in the text and have realized that Swift's intentions are not quite straightforward. He is not using his own voice, but is adopting a persona – or a front character – in order to add an extra dimension to his writing. In this case Swift chooses an apparently well-meaning politician so that, as well as making his points about Irish poverty, he can simultaneously criticize politicians, who may be uncomfortably like his persona, without directly mentioning names.

Using a persona in this way means that there is a split between the surface meaning of the text and the deeper meaning which usually carries the writer's real message. Satire often involves this kind of use of heavy irony – saying the opposite of what is really meant. For more on irony see page 258.

Activity

> Now take a closer look at the character or persona Swift has chosen to adopt.
> 1 Note down everything you can find out about this persona's background, family, education, position, personality, and especially his political ideas. What does this man want his readers to think of him? Indeed, who are his supposed readers?
> 2 Now write down what you think Swift himself believes and thinks. Can you pinpoint any places where Swift makes his own views clear to us?
> 3 Finally, assess what Swift thinks of people like his persona? What qualities of his 'politician' does he want to 'send up'?

The structure of the proposal

A Modest Proposal is carefully constructed to imitate a real political speech or pamphlet of Swift's time. The chosen form itself might persuade its readers that this 'politician' knows what he is talking about! Making a study of its structure will help to clarify Swift's intentions and also reveal how he uses certain techniques and ruses that politicians use when they want to influence us.

Activity

> **1** Working with a partner, divide the text into between seven and ten sections. In each you should find the 'politician' has a particular aim or intention. Explain what he is saying and what effect he hopes to have on his readers. Can you show why his efforts are sometimes counter-productive?
>
> **2** Compare your ideas with other pairs in your group and then with the suggested analysis of the text given below.

Summary

Here is one way of dividing the text.

1 (Paragraphs 1–5) The persona introduces the problem of poverty, drawing people in by saying anyone may witness these things in the streets of Dublin, and suggests that if someone can solve this problem, he will be a great benefactor and hints that he might just have the solution. He holds our interest and builds on it by telling us what the benefits of his idea will be, while keeping it, so far, a secret. He criticizes other politicians whose ideas are useless because they get their sums wrong!

2 (Paragraphs 6–7) He lays before us a lot of figures and calculations, to show us that he has done his research properly and knows what he is talking about. As in modern political speeches statistics help to give the argument credibility.

3 (Paragraphs 8–16) He presents his idea with mock humility. He backs it up with evidence from a 'knowing American' to show he has consulted the authorities, and includes plenty of little asides to show that he has considered every possible argument. The practice of using authorities to give weight to one's argument is a feature of classical rhetoric. This is also the point where Swift reveals the true nature of his persona. His argument has hidden under cover of reason thus far. Now it is out in the open.

4 (Paragraphs 17–19) A digression. This is someone else's idea which he puts down in a patronizing way. He wants us to think he is fair minded and has listened to others. Digressions (straying from the main subject) were fashionable in literature of the time and are another figure of classical rhetoric. They do also tend to be a natural feature of political speeches!

5 (Paragraphs 20–28) He presents us with a formal list of the advantages of his idea, using 'First,... Secondly...' etc. He wants to impress us with his 'well-reasoned' argument.

6 (Paragraphs 29–30) He can think of no objections to his idea. Instead he lists other peoples' silly ideas, so as to deflate any opposition to his plans. However, at this point, it is impossible for Swift to hide his own anger any longer. The 'silly' ideas here are all the sensible and humane suggestions Swift himself had proposed seriously in earlier writings and which had been ignored.

7 (Paragraphs 31–33)   He sums up, reiterating his idea, stressing the newness of it, and reminding us of his own humility. Of course, he would listen if anyone had a better idea! He points out that he cannot stand to gain anything from his idea, as he has no children. He wants us to see him as honest and disinterested.

In his use of a measured introduction, setting out of the reasoning behind his plans, debunking opposing ideas, and his final summation, Swift echoes the structure of a political speech. The inclusion of rhetorical devices, such as supportive facts and figures, referring to authorities to give credibility, and the use of digression, reinforces the chosen form and underline the satire.

Analysing the language

In the process of examining the conflicting purposes of Swift and his persona, you may have begun to notice some features of the language he uses. Now we shall look at these more closely. Remember that when you are talking and writing about literature, it is vital to focus on *how* writers use language to convey ideas and *why* they choose particular devices, styles, or vocabulary.

Activity

> **1** Look again at the text, and make notes, this time focusing on how Swift (or his persona) uses language. What do you notice about:
> - the 'style' he uses
> - the way he constructs sentences
> - his vocabulary
> - phrases or ideas which are repeated
>
> Also note that the original spellings and capitalizations have been adhered to in this text.
>
> **2** Think carefully about why he has written in this way. (Referring back to your notes from page 134 about what the persona wants us to think of him will help here.)

Swift's politician wants to impress his readers and these are the ways in which his language reflects this.

1 He uses the elaborate style of a political speech or of the law, with many long, rolling sentences consisting of several clauses. Look at his opening sentence and where he lists the advantages of his scheme in a highly formal way. Sometimes his language is quite high-flown:

'…a Preserver of the Nation.'

'A VERY worthy person, *a true Lover of his Country*, and whose Virtues I highly esteem, was lately pleased, in discoursing on this Matter, to offer a Refinement upon my Scheme.'

2 He often chooses a long word, e.g. discoursing, where a short one would do.

3 There are also touches of bathos in his speech (when language suddenly descends to a lower, basic level), as when he mentions the methods of cooking a child for food:

'...the fore or hind Quarter will make a reasonable Dish; and seasoned with a little Pepper or Salt, will be very good Boiled on the fourth Day...'

This, of course, reveals him as a man who enjoys his food and who is unlikely to have any real understanding of those who are starving. It also proves him to be coarser than he pretends to be.

4 He presents himself as business-like and matter-of-fact, giving us many facts and figures and using the language of calculation:

'...I calculate there may be about Two hundred Thousand Couple whose Wives are Breeders; from which Number I subtract thirty thousand Couples, who are able to maintain their own Children...'

This, though, shows he is calculating, in more than one sense. He sees the poor not as real individuals but only as figures on a balance sheet. This impression is strengthened when he applies dehumanizing language to them. The poor are discussed in animal terms. Mothers are referred to as 'Breeders' and a new-born baby as '...a Child just dropt from its Dam'.

5 This politician also wants people to think he is caring and soft-hearted, so he also uses language which is emotive and sentimental. For example, he uses the phrase 'sacrificing the *poor innocent Babes*' when he talks of mothers killing their children because they cannot feed them. His plan is oddly similar but so much worse because it will turn the killing to profit. Such language is double-edged, revealing his hypocrisy.

6 From behind his persona Swift makes numerous black jokes. Babies are proposed as a prime dish for Christening celebrations; he proposes that men will stop beating and kicking their wives because they will need to take care of them, as they do with other breeding animals which bring in a profit.

7 Language also illustrates the backwards logic of the argument in places. For example, where the politician talks about the plight of the old and disabled, the people who are concerned about their situation are 'of a desponding spirit', while younger labourers who may themselves die imminently are in a 'hopeful condition'.

Activity

1 Write a detailed study of *A Modest Proposal*, referring to the notes you have collected in this unit. You will need to write about:
   • the purpose of the text
   • Swift's use of a persona
   • the surface and deeper meanings and the tension between these
   • the way the text is structured and why
   • how Swift uses language (sentence structures, vocabulary, style) to achieve his purpose

2 Using *A Modest Proposal* as a model, choose a topic which interests or concerns you and write a satirical 'proposal' of your own, with a detailed commentary.

- Make your ideas and solutions for your chosen problems as ridiculous as you can but keep your language as precise and formal as possible. Some contemporary topics which work well are:

Unemployment
Lack of resources in schools
Overcrowding in prisons
Homework

- Choose an appropriate persona. Hypocrisy needs to be their strongest characteristic!
- Model your work on Swift's, closely imitating the structure and devices used in the original.

Then write a detailed commentary on your piece in which you demonstrate your understanding of Swift's work and explain how you used it to construct your own piece.

3 According to Dryden, satire '...is the boldest way.../To tell men freely of their foulest faults.' How does Swift achieve this in *A Modest Proposal*?

Section II
Developing Your Language of Criticism

7 Preparing for Writing

Objectives
- To introduce strategies for planning writing
- To practice using different strategies
- To settle on the best planning methods for own writing

Applying the rules

In Willy Russell's play *Educating Rita*, Rita – a young woman from a working-class background – begins to study English Literature through the Open University. She decides that an 'education' will give her more choices in life. After her first unsuccessful attempts at essays, her tutor Frank explains:

Frank: There is a way of answering examination questions that is expected. It's a sort of accepted ritual, it's a game, with rules. And you must observe those rules.

Later, the play suggests that in order to write according to the rules, Rita will have to give up some aspects of herself and her own natural, emotional responses to what she reads. Frank does not believe this will be altogether a good thing. Similarly, the challenge of writing about literature at A-level is to learn the 'rules of the game' so as to write in the appropriate way for examination questions without losing the ability to respond in a personal way.

Through the units in Section II, we will consider those 'rules' and identify strategies for developing your language of criticism. As we work through these, we will look at some examples of planning and writing activities based on a scene from the play *A Streetcar Named Desire* by Tennessee Williams, which is often set for A-level study.

Planning strategies

Whether you are writing an essay for classwork, in an examination, or beginning a major piece of coursework, it can often be difficult to get started. However, there are several measures you can take to make this easier. There are also ways of thinking and planning beforehand that can help you feel more confident and secure about essay writing.

Many students find it best to develop their own preparing and planning methods which feel familiar and which can be used in examinations as well as for less formal pieces of writing. However, it is a good idea to try out several different methods and then choose those that work best for you. Your choice will depend on your 'learning style'. For example, some people naturally find it easier to grasp information when it is presented using pictures and diagrams, while others are more comfortable with words, and prefer information written in list or note form. The remainder of this unit presents some strategies for planning your work. Experiment to find which ones are most helpful to you.

Analysing the question

After reading the text or passage at least twice, consider the question you plan to answer very carefully. Check that you understand it fully. (If you do not, ask for help or if possible choose a question that you feel more confident about.) What are its key words and ideas? Underline them, like this:

Chaucer: *The Miller's Tale*
Someone once described *The Miller's Tale* as a <u>rude story</u> told with <u>speed</u> and <u>wit</u>. To what extent do you agree?
or this:
Toni Morrison: *Beloved*
What <u>features</u> of this novel did you find <u>disturbing</u>?

The underlined words represent the ideas that you will need to keep in mind while you plan and write your answer. In addition to identifying these specific points, do not forget that the 'hidden message' in almost all questions is that you need to write about *how* the writer has used language to create effects. For more on analysing question types see Unit 13, pages 205–210.

Activity

> Look at the following question on Scene 3 of *A Streetcar Named Desire* and decide which key words you would underline:
>
> Write as fully as you can about Scene 3 *The Poker Night*, focusing on the way the male and female characters are presented.

Annotating the text

When you are preparing to write an essay, annotating your text can help highlight the main points that you will want to make. This is true whether the text is a poem or a passage set for unseen practical criticism, or a complete novel or play. (There is more guidance about annotation of texts for the Open Book Exam in Unit 14, pages 217–219.) If you already have an essay question or a topic to focus on when you read and annotate, it will be easier to recognize the information, lines, and phrases from the text which are relevant for you to underline or highlight.

The following annotations on the opening stage directions for Scene 3 of *A Streetcar Named Desire*, and a brief excerpt from later in the scene, have been made with the above question in mind.

To set the scene, Blanche Dubois, a complex woman with much to hide, is staying with her sister Stella and her husband Stanley in New Orleans. Their life is very different from the unrealistic expectations she carries from her girlhood as a 'Southern Belle'. Here, she and Stella return from an evening out to find Stanley playing poker with his friends.

A Streetcar Named Desire

Scene 3
The Poker Night

(*There is a picture of Van Gogh's of a billiard-parlour at night. The kitchen now suggests that sort of* <u>lurid nocturnal brilliance,</u> *the* <u>raw</u> *colours of childhood's spectrum. Over the* <u>yellow</u> *linoleum of the kitchen table hangs an electric bulb with a* <u>vivid green glass shade.</u> *The poker players –* **Stanley**, **Steve**, **Mitch**, *and* **Pablo** *– wear coloured shirts, solid blues, a purple, a red-and-white check, a light green, and they are men* <u>at the peak of their physical manhood, as coarse and direct and powerful as the primary colours.</u> *There are* <u>vivid slices of watermelon</u> *on the table, whisky bottles, and glasses.*

Colours bold, bright, simple, modern

'Raw' suggests uncultivated

(Brilliant light where the men are)

Colour of watermelon could suggest raw flesh

The *bedroom is relatively dim* with only the light that spills between the portières and through the wide window on the street. The sisters appear around the corner of the building.) ...

(Where the women will be is 'dim': only light from outside)

Stella: The game is still going on.

Blanche: How do I look?

Blanche concerned with her appearance. Stella gives the answers she needs to hear

Stella: Lovely, Blanche. ←

Blanche: I feel so hot and frazzled. Wait till I powder before you open the door. Do I look done in?

Stella: Why no. You are as fresh as a daisy.

(**Stella** *opens the door and they enter.*)

Stella: Well, well, well. I see you boys are still at it!

Stanley: Where you been?

Stella: Blanche and I took in a show. Blanche, this is Mr Gonzales and Mr Hubbel.

Blanche: Please don't get up.   *Old-fashioned – she expects courtesy*

Stanley: Nobody's going to get up, so don't be worried.   *She doesn't get it!*

Stella: How much longer is this game going to continue?   *Stan takes no account of Stella's wishes. His responses to both women are abrupt, rude.*

Stanley: Till we get ready to quit.

Trying to get 'in' with the men

Blanche: Poker is so fascinating. Could I kibitz?   *= Look over someone's shoulder and sit in on their hand of cards*

Stanley: You could not. Why don't you women go up and sit with Eunice?   *He wants them out of the way – poker is a man's world. Women excluded*

Stan will have none of it

Stella: Because it is nearly two-thirty.   *Derogatory tone*

(**Blanche** *crosses into the bedroom and partially closes the portières.*)

Stella trying to be reasonable

Stella: Couldn't you call it quits after one more hand?   *'loud whack' – Stanley is solid, boisterousness*

(*A chair scrapes.* **Stanley** *gives a loud whack of his hand on* **Stella's** *thigh.*)   *Chauvinistic reaction – treats Stella roughly, disrespectfully, as his possession*

Stella: (*Sharply*) That's not fun, Stanley.

(*The men laugh.* **Stella** *goes into the bedroom.*)

Tennessee Williams

She dislikes this; at least she expresses her anger – but she gets no support – the men think her annoyance is funny. All she can do is walk out

Listing key points

Quickly make a list of 4 to 6 points which you would need to cover in order to answer the different aspects of the question posed on page 141. Try to arrange them in a logical order, so that you can move easily from one to another as you write. Often, it is best to begin with the most general point, and then move on to more specific ones. If you are answering an examination question, 4 to 6 points should be sufficient. (If you are writing a larger-scale essay for coursework, you will probably need a longer list.)

Taking our question on *A Streetcar Named Desire*, here is a possible list of topics, jotted down quickly.

> MEN: dominant, forceful, violent
>
> POKER: a man's world – women excluded
>
> WOMEN: feminine – much less powerful
>
> BLANCHE: nervous, flirtatious
>
> SETTING: men – 'lurid' kitchen; women – 'dim' bedroom
>
> COLOURS: men – bold; women – white, delicate

An answer which included a paragraph on each of these would cover the main points appropriate to the essay question.

Using diagrams

Try writing your key words or topic headings in the middle of a blank sheet of paper. Write phrases for related ideas around them, working outwards towards more detailed points, as shown in the spider diagram below, Link the words in as many ways as possible and circle or highlight ideas of most importance. Some people who use these say that you can begin your essay with any point on your diagram and find a way to work through all your ideas. Others prefer to start from one of the topic headings, for example, 'Men' or 'Women' in this case.

A Streetcar Named Desire: Scene 3

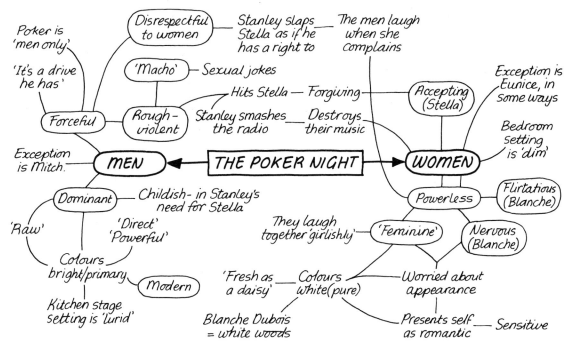

Charting information

Devise your own ways of arranging information in diagram form. For example, family trees can help sort out complex relationships, or you could use a graph to plot the ups and downs of a character's life.

If the essay question asks you to consider two 'sides' argumentatively, or involves a comparison, listing the opposing ideas like this in a table can help.

Male characters	Female characters
Dominant; powerful.	Powerless; can't change the men.
Rough, violent, macho.	'Feminine'; Blanche presents an image of herself as sensitive and well-bred.
Disrespectful to women; see them as objects, don't take them seriously and are amused when they are annoyed.	Blanche flirtatious with men; Stella accepts violence as 'normal' and continues to love Stanley; strong sexual bond holds them together.

Arranging ideas on cards

Write important points and related quotations, or notes for the individual paragraphs you want to include on cards. You can then arrange these, like jigsaw pieces, in different ways until you work out the best order in which to write about them. An example, taking characters from *A Streetcar Named Desire* is shown below.

Blanche – wants to appear respectable, thoughtful, sensitive to Mitch.

'I can't stand a naked light bulb, any more than a rude remark or a vulgar action.'

'I am not accustomed to having more than one drink.'

Uses sentimental, clichéd expressions – 'Sorrow makes for sincerity, I think.'

to tease Mitch about other – embarrass him.

...ck and we'll fix you – tit.'

...is spineless, mean, not mother's boy.

...get ants when they win.'
...when he goes home he'll deposit them one by one in a piggy bank his mother give him.'

This technique is not suitable for examination situations! It is most useful when you are working on a long text and need to collect notes and examples on a theme or character as you read. An alternative is to use a reading log for each text you study, as suggested in Unit 4, page 66.

Finding your own strategies

Activity

> Having seen the various planning strategies in action in this unit, try out at least three using an extract from one of your set texts.
>
> As you work on each technique decide how successful it is for you and which methods you find most fruitful in your interpretation of the text.

We do need to remember, however, that sometimes the process of writing is in itself an exploration. At times we need to throw away all our plans and plunge into the writing before we can find out exactly what our ideas are; some arguments and ideas only take shape when we have worked through them in writing. Some writers always work this way and are not comfortable with planning in advance.

The most important thing is that you discover planning strategies that work for *you*, and use them so that they become a natural part of your writing process. Then you will have a familiar starting point when faced with the pressure of exam conditions. (For more on planning exam essays see Unit 16, pages 237–239.)

8 Formulating Views in Writing

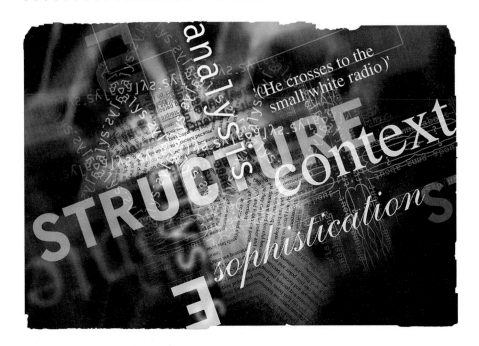

Objectives

- To consider the features of clear structure in literary essays
- To use a student's written response as a model for learning
- To study the effective use of quotation in essays

Writing a considered essay

Another moment from Willy Russell's, *Educating Rita*, will get us thinking about what is meant by a considered essay.

Frank: In response to the question, 'Suggest how you would resolve the staging difficulties inherent in a production of Ibsen's *Peer Gynt*, you have written, quote, 'Do it on the radio', unquote.

Rita: Precisely.

Frank: Well?

Rita: Well what?

Frank: Well I know it's probably quite naïve of me but I did think you might let me have a considered essay.

Rita's answer is not wrong, but as Frank tells her, she has not yet learned the rules she needs to follow in order to write a 'considered essay'.

Activity   Your understanding of essay writing will be far more sophisticated than Rita's is at this stage! Working in a small group, create an advice sheet for her about the dos and don'ts of writing literary criticism.

Using evidence from the text effectively

Once you have done some thinking and planning for the question you will be writing about, you will have established the main points that you want to convey in your essay, and perhaps even feel you have an 'answer', as Rita does. However, as you write, it is essential that you provide some good reasons and evidence to support what you say. Evidence in this sense means examples and quotations from the text. It is not very useful, for example, to write that a poet 'uses a great deal of alliteration' in a poem. That would be to make an assertion without giving any grounds for it. All it would demonstrate is that you can recognize alliteration and that you know the technical term for it. You need to follow this statement with some quotations from the poem which contain alliteration. From there you will need to go on and analyse the quotation and comment on the effect created by the alliteration.

So, broadly speaking, the process of literary comment has three stages.
1 State the point you wish to make.
2 Follow this with your quotation, making sure the context of the quotation is clear, by briefly explaining the situation, or who is speaking and to whom. Quotations should be presented in speech marks or clearly differentiated from the rest of your writing.
3 Analyse the quotation in detail, commenting on individual words or phrases and explaining how and why they are used and with what effect.

For example, *The Laboratory* by Robert Browning is a poem, in the form of a monologue, spoken by a jealous woman who plans to murder the woman who is her rival. At the time she speaks she is in the laboratory of an alchemist who is mixing some arsenic for her to use, and her words are addressed to him. (Apparently this situation was not that uncommon in Renaissance France and Italy!)
1/ In stanza three, as the alchemist works on preparing the poison, she
2 comments on his actions, and seems to be enjoying the process. Her words include some alliteration which heightens this effect:
'Grind away, moisten and mash up thy paste,
Pound at thy powder – I am not in haste.'
3 The repeated 'm' sounds of 'moisten' and 'mash' suggest her almost chewing these words with relish, while the 'p' sounds not only suggest the actual sound of the pestle and mortar, but, because of their explosive quality, express her spiteful pleasure at the thought of her rival's death.

Of course, you will not want to keep rigidly to this three-stage process of Statement, Quotation, Analysis; that would produce rather mechanical essays. However, it is useful to bear it in mind until it becomes integrated into your writing.

These are two of the most common difficulties that students have with essay-writing.

- **Context:** not providing enough information to make sense of quotations, i.e. sprinkling quotations in essays without providing crucial details about the situation. However do not fall into the trap of spending all your time paraphrasing the text. It is a fine balance to achieve.
- **Analysis:** students usually find this third stage of the process the most challenging. However, its importance is shown in the A-level marking criteria where it is the ability to be analytical to a high degree that gains candidates higher grades.

In any case, you will no doubt find your study of literature more rewarding when you know how to recognize and comment on the important details of how writers use language. It will also help you to become more aware of the language choices you make when you are writing.

Structuring an essay

There is no one structure that will work for every essay. Each question will demand a slightly different approach as the following guidelines, using a basic framework, illustrate.

1 Introduction
Briefly outline the subject of the essay; it can be useful to refer to the question and its key words and ideas.

Sometimes in coursework it can be useful to give a very concise introduction to the text(s) you are writing about. This might include one or two sentences to establish the context of the question, for example, in terms of plot or character. It is vital that you do not tell the story at length. All your time and effort should be devoted to answering the question.

2 Main section
This could take several different forms, depending on the type of question that you are answering.

- If the question has several key words or ideas, or asks you to explore more than one aspect of the text, you may be able to see a ready-made structure for the main part of your essay.
- If you have already thought about the question and made a plan, in one of the ways suggested in Unit 7 (pages 140–145), you can then set about working through the topics in your list or diagram, presenting them in an order which allows you to move easily from one to another.
- If the question requires you to consider two sides of an argument before concluding with your own views, you can organize your writing in one of two ways:

  Present all the arguments on one side first, making sure you always support your ideas with evidence. Then repeat the process for the other side of the argument.

  or

Make a table showing the arguments on each side of the question, then work through them 'zig-zag' fashion, presenting an argument from one side followed by one from the other side, and so on until you have covered all the points you wish to make. This may seem harder to do, but can often have more impact.

3 Conclusion

Once you have explored all the ideas or arguments you want to mention, finish by explaining the conclusion you have reached and/or briefly summing up the most important points you have made. Sometimes it is useful to restate the key words and ideas from the question in your conclusion. Try to express your conclusion clearly. An otherwise good essay can be marred by a weak ending, and you want to leave your reader with a good impression!

Adding more sophistication

The above essay structure is quite straightforward. You will often find, however, that in following a line of argument, it is necessary to explore a side issue or a related topic before returning to your central theme. It is vital that you can do this without becoming sidetracked and never returning to the main path, or jumping jarringly from one idea to another.

Let us look again at the question on *A Streetcar Named Desire* which featured in Unit 7:

> Write as fully as you can about Scene 3 *The Poker Night*, focusing on the way the male and female characters are presented.

We know from the planning activities that the central theme for discussion is the contrast between the male characters – presented as dominant, hard, and forceful – and the female characters – portrayed as gentler and less powerful. Yet, in the course of the essay, we are likely to explore several side issues, some of which will contribute to the main argument while others offer exceptions to it or alternative views. It is important to find ways of incorporating these while maintaining a strong sense of direction and flow in the writing. Using connecting devices like the ones shown in the following examples can help achieve this successfully.

A

One aspect of Williams' presentation in the scene, which contributes to our sense that the men are more powerful than the women, is the way in which he uses colours...
[...discussion of the use of colour and its effect...]
Having examined the use of colours in the scene, we can see that it reinforces the impression that the men are dominant here.

B

The relative powerlessness of the female characters is demonstrated by the fact that neither Blanche nor Stella commands any respect from the poker players.

However, the two women are different in the ways in which they respond to the men...

[...comparison of the behaviour of Blanche and Stella...]

Although the female characters differ in the ways they react to the situation, they are presented in general as less forceful than the male characters.

C

Although we have seen that for the most part the men are harder and more forceful than the women, there are some exceptions...

[...First... discussion of Mitch's character...

Second...examine how Stanley becomes like a pathetic small boy in his need for Stella once she has left...

Third...example of Eunice shouting roughly and angrily...]

There are, therefore, some occasions when male characters seem weaker. On the whole, however, they are presented as powerful.

In each of these examples the writer moves temporarily away from the central line of argument to discuss a side issue, but each time returns to the central question, pointing out how the side issue relates to it. This leaves the writer back on track, ready either to continue the main argument or to explore another 'by way'.

If you are tackling an unseen text for practical criticism, these structures may still be useful. We will look in more detail at ways of organizing your ideas for practical criticism in Unit 10, pages 160–161.

Activity | With a partner, look at how one student answers the question on Scene 3 *The Poker Night*. As you read, take note of the annotations given and discuss how this student has structured his work.

Write as fully as you can about *Scene 3 The Poker Night*, focusing on the way the male and female characters are presented.

A fair introductory paragraph which refers to the question and leads into his discussion of the characters

It has been said that Scene 3, which is the poker scene, actually represents the whole play and acts as a miniature version of the play. *The Poker Night* is an important scene because it shows how the male and female characters are presented by Tennessee Williams.

An interesting point in this opening sentence which could do with more explanation

The male characters as a group are presented as dominant and forceful because they have ordered the women out for the night so they can play poker and enjoy themselves. The group of men, Stanley, Steve, Mitch, and Pablo are presented as strong, powerful, and coarse. This is said in the stage directions:

'They are men at the peak of their physical manhood, as coarse and direct as the primary colours.'

'The primary colours' are the colours of the shirts the men are wearing. The colours are 'solid blues, a purple, a red-and-white check, a light green'. Also from these colours and the shirts being worn these are modern men unlike the type Stella and Blanche would have been used to in their past.

The group of men are seen as brutes of men as they sit around the poker table. Here the men start to 'argue hotly':

'I didn't hear you name it.'

Several good points about the men as a group, including some discussion of the significance of the colours they wear. Next Ian focuses on individual male characters, which makes good sense

'Didn't I name it, Mitch?'

The group of men argue over a simple game of cards. This is almost like a children's squabble.

Stanley is the prime example of a forceful modern man in a world where Stella and Blanche must do as he says. He is the most dominating male character in the group of four. Here, Stella comes in and complains to Stanley about the time they are still playing poker at. Stanley shows he isn't respectful of Stella's wishes.

'A chair scrapes. Stanley gives a loud whack of his hand on her thigh.'

Structure works quite well here. Ian conveys a sense of how the men behave as a group and also draws a contrast between them

Stanley shows his masculinity and authority over Stella by slapping her thigh in a manly way. Stanley is showing off around his friends, proving how much of a man he is. Stanley again shows his dominance over the females when he demands Blanche turns the radio off and when she doesn't do so on his word he becomes fierce.

'Stanley stalks fiercely through the portières into the bedroom. He crosses to the small white radio and snatches it off the table. With a shouted oath, he tosses the instrument out of the window.'

He uses appropriate quotations and attempts more detailed analysis in places (for example, where he comments on the significance of individual words such as 'stalks')

Even the way Stanley approaches the radio before he acts presents him in a fierce and forceful light. The words 'stalks', as if he was a primitive caveman stalking his prey, and 'fiercely', which is his anger, show how Stanley is going to act before he acts. Stanley acts more like a modern barbarian around women than a modern gentleman. Mitch is the only exception to the group. Mitch is sympathetic and much more considerate to what Blanche and Stella want than Stanley. Mitch shows he is more gentle in these stage directions: '..coughing a little shyly. He realizes he still has the towel in his hands and with an embarrassed laugh hands it to Stella.'

This is the first time we see Mitch around females and he shows he is different to the other men around him by the way he embarrassedly laughs at his little mistake. This shows a kinder and gentler side to the male populace and is a contrast to Stanley's hard, rough and ready nature. Mitch is presented as a fine character who is more suitable to Blanche and Stella and is more like the men they once knew. Here Blanche waltzes to the music with romantic gestures to Mitch.

'Mitch is delighted and moves in awkward imitation like a dancing bear.'

The point here is although Mitch didn't know how to waltz he gladly made a fool of himself dancing strangely just to please Blanche. Stanley, from what we know of him, would have laughed and walked away.

The female characters are quite similar in the way they are presented. Stella is presented as strong by the way she stands up to Stanley over the card game:

'Drunk – drunk – animal thing you! All of you – please go home! If any of you have one spark of decency in you...'

Stella confronts the group of males playing poker and challenges them. Also, Stella is shown as wanting to be treated with respect. Stanley slaps Stella's thigh and she reacts sharply and then tells Blanche:

'It makes me so mad when he does that in front of people.'

Stella is showing how she wants to look as if she is respected in front of people.

Marginal notes:

Quotations usually introduced quite neatly, providing enough information to place them in context but Ian fails to do this when he quotes Mitch's moment of embarrassment. To make the situation fully clear to the reader, he needs to say: '...in these stage directions when he comes out of the bathroom and has to pass the women, who are in the bedroom...'

Ian also slightly misreads Mitch's character here, not picking up that, although he is relatively gentle, he is also rather naïve and undignified in the way he responds to Blanche's flirtation

This section is less successful: the first sentence is ambiguous. Does he mean that the women are similar to each other, or to the men? He needs to round off his discussion of the men and then lead into his discussion of the women, like this: 'Although Mitch seems different from Stanley and the others, on the whole the men are strong and rough and form a powerful group. On the other hand, the women, although different from each other, seem much less forceful...'

Stella may be presented as strong and brave and trying to gain respect, but she is also weak when it comes down to what Stanley wants. After Stanley hits her and she and Blanche go up to Eunice's, when Stanley stands downstairs crying, she gives in and goes to Stanley, showing she needs him no matter what he's done.

Blanche shows or presents another image of the female which is provocative, flirty and deceitful...

Ian's essay continues with a discussion of Blanche's character and actions and concludes like this...

This is rather disappointing. The essay just stops, without a conclusion to draw the ideas together. The mention of the previous scene is a red herring – not relevant to the question here

...Blanche is easily older than Stella and has blatantly lied about her age so that Mitch will become more interested in her. Blanche always tries to present herself in a better light:

'I can't stand a naked light bulb, any more than I can a rude remark or a vulgar action.'

Blanche is trying to sound much more refined than she actually is. She is being provocative and flirtatious, exactly as she was in the previous scene when she was alone with Stanley.

Ian

Ian has not really made use of opportunities to analyse details in his later paragraphs. For example, Blanche's statement that she 'can't stand a naked light bulb' deserves much more attention. As Ian has pointed out, she is deceitful. The naked light bulb would reveal too much literally – she lies about her age – and metaphorically – it also represents the fact that she has a lot more to hide

Activity

1 Swap answers to a recent essay with a partner. Assess the structure of your partner's essay. Annotate it to show where the structure is clear and informative and where it could be improved. (Use the notes around Ian's essay as models for your own.)

2 Hand back the annotated essay and discuss your comments on it with your partner.

9 Getting Tone and Style Right

Objectives
- To develop personal writing style
- To implement formal and objective elements of style
- To look at style in literary criticism

Being 'objective'

Until you are familiar with the conventions for writing literary criticism, it may be difficult to grasp exactly what kind of tone or style is appropriate. One way to approach this is to read some good critical writing to get the 'feel' of it. Collections of critical writing which contain essays and reviews relating to a particular author or to specific texts can be useful in this respect. These often illustrate widely differing points of view and so serve as good reminders that there is rarely only one way to interpret a text. As well as introducing you to some different ways of thinking about the texts you are studying, they will help you to develop your awareness of the accepted language of criticism.

Some of these points are brought out in this extract from *Educating Rita*.

Educating Rita

Frank: Now the piece you wrote for me on – what was it called...?
Rita: *Rubyfruit Jungle.*
Frank: Yes, it was – erm...

Rita: Crap?

Frank: No. Erm – the thing is, it was an appreciation, a descriptive piece. What you have to learn is criticism.

Rita: What's the difference?

Frank: Well. You must try to remember that criticism is purely objective. It should be approached almost as a science. It must be supported by reference to established literary critique. Criticism is never subjective and should not be confused with partisan interpretation. In criticism sentiment has no place. (*He picks up the copy of* Howards End) Tell me, what did you think of *Howards End*?

Rita: It was crap.

Frank: What?

Rita: I thought it was crap!

Frank: Crap? And who are you citing in support of your thesis, F. R. Leavis?

Rita: No. Me!

Frank: What have I just said? 'Me' is subjective.

Rita: Well it's what I think.

Willy Russell

Perhaps Frank's assertion that literary criticism is 'purely objective' and like a science, is going too far. In studying A-level Literature there should be opportunities for you to express your own responses to texts as well as writing objectively about them. However, the more objective approach always needs to form the backbone of your critical writing, and when you do express your opinions or feelings about the effectiveness of a piece of writing, you still need to support them with reasoned evidence. Usually this evidence will take the form of quotations from the text, as was shown in Unit 8. Beware of writing statements like 'The imagery in stanza 2 is extremely evocative and effective.' or 'I found this chapter very moving.' – and leaving it at that. You need to provide specific examples or quotations and explain how the lines are effective and why.

In the extract, Frank also suggests that Rita should make 'reference to established literary critique'. In other words, she should refer to the views held by well-known academics who have already written about the text. A word of warning here. Reading the work of experienced literary critics can be useful in developing your awareness of style and also in introducing you to some different ways of approaching your text. However, it is very important that you do not write about other critics' ideas at the expense of expressing your own ideas about the text.

Examiners will always look for well-supported ideas and interpretations that you have worked out for yourself. They will also look for your understanding of other readings of the text. However, if you do want to include the views of other critics, these need to be presented as quotations and acknowledged. Otherwise you run the risk of plagiarizing: 'borrowing', or even stealing, someone else's ideas and presenting them as your own. For more on other critical views see Unit 19, page 252–255.

Here is an example of critical writing to give a sense of an appropriate tone and style. This extract also illustrates the ways in which quotations from the text can be introduced and analysed. It is from an essay on Dickens's *Great Expectations*, by G. Robert Stange. Here he discusses some patterns of imagery and symbolism in the novel.

On Great Expectations

On his way to visit Miss Havisham for the first time, Pip spends the night with Mr Pumblechook, the corn-chandler, in his lodgings behind his shop. The contrast between the aridity of this old hypocrite's spirit and the viability of his wares is a type of the conflict between natural growth and social form. Pip looks at all the shopkeeper's little drawers filled with bulbs and seed packets and wonders 'whether the flower-seeds and bulbs ever wanted of a fine day to break out of those jails and bloom.' The imagery of life repressed is developed further in the descriptions of Miss Havisham and Satis House. The first detail Pip notices is the abandoned brewery where the once active ferment has ceased; no germ of life is to be found in Satis House or in its occupants:

'...there were no pigeons in the dove-cot, no horses in the stable, no pigs in the sty, no malt in the storehouse, no smells of grains and beer in the copper or the vat. All the uses and scents of the brewery might have evaporated with its last reek of smoke. In a by-yard, there was a wilderness of empty casks...'

On top of these casks Estella dances with solitary concentration, and behind her, in a dark corner of the building, Pip fancies that he sees a figure hanging by the neck from a wooden beam, 'a figure all in yellow white, with but one shoe to the feet; and it hung so, that I could see that the faded trimmings of the dress were like earthy paper, and that the face was Miss Havisham's.'

Miss Havisham is death. From his visits to Satis House Pip acquires his false admiration for the genteel; he falls in love with Estella and fails to see that she is the cold instrument of Miss Havisham's revenge on human passion and on life itself. When Pip learns he may expect a large inheritance from an unknown source he immediately assumes (incorrectly) that Miss Havisham is his benefactor; she does not undeceive him. Money, which is also death, is appropriately connected with the old lady rotting away in her darkened room. Conflicting values in Pip's life are also expressed by the opposed imagery of stars and fire. Estella is by name a star, and throughout the novel stars are conceived as pitiless: 'And then I looked at the stars, and considered how awful it would be for a man to turn his face up to them as he froze to death, and see no help or pity in all the glittering multitude.' Estella and her light are described as coming down the dark passage of Satis House 'like a star,' and when she has become a woman she is constantly surrounded by the bright glitter of jewelry.

Joe Gargery, on the other hand, is associated with the warm fire of the hearth or forge. It was his habit to sit and rake the fire between the lower bars of the kitchen grate, and his workday was spent at the forge.

G. Robert Stange

Formality of style

As well as being more objective, Frank hints that Rita needs to develop a more formal style of writing before her essays will be acceptable (see page 155). This can be difficult to define, but there are some things to avoid.

Summary

- **The first person**   Generally, avoid *over-using* the first person in your responses. For example, rather than saying 'I think Louisa is imaginative because', try to use expressions like 'It appears that Louisa has a vivid imagination, because...' or 'Louisa seems to be imaginative because...' Having said that, the occasional use of 'I' or 'me' in a piece of critical commentary to reinforce an important point can be most effective.
- **Slang**   Avoid using slang expressions (unless, of course, they appear in quotations from your text!). Colloquial language is the language of informal speech. Try to develop your awareness of the differences between spoken English and written English.
- **Dialect and local usage**   Some words or expressions may be used only in some parts of the country; these are appropriate in some forms of writing, but in a formal essay Standard English is preferable. Try to develop your awareness of your local dialect and, if you can, substitute Standard English equivalents in your essays. This will also avoid confusions in meaning. For example, 'to get wrong' (North-east England) = 'to get into trouble' (Standard English).
- **Abbreviations**   It is better not to use abbreviated forms in formal writing. For example, write 'did not' rather than 'didn't'; and avoid using 'etc.'.
- **Numbers**   These should be written in word form, for example, 'thirty-seven' rather than '37', unless the figure is very large.

However, do use:
- **The present tense**   Most literary criticism is written in the present tense. This is because the text, whether a novel or a poem, always exists in the same way, even though the narrative may be in the past tense. Aim to keep your writing in the present tense. For example, 'The opening scenes of the play take place in...' not '...took place in...'. It is even more important to be consistent: whether you use present or past tense, make sure you use the same one throughout. There are many examples of critical responses written in the present tense throughout this book.

Activity

Here is part of a draft student essay where the style needs quite a lot of attention. Redraft it, improving the style in as many ways as possible. Compare your version to that of another student in your group.

In the scene of the poker night the men and women were presented very differently. Stanley seems to me to be presented in a very macho style character. This is shown in the way that Stanley gets very drunk and this is seen to be the manly thing to do. Also the way he mocks Mitch about having to go home and see his Mam. Stanley says 'Hurry back and we'll fix you a sugar-tit'. He's also shown as a hard and nasty character when he hits Stella because she wants them to stop playing poker. This shows Stanley to be a harsh and hard character because he hits his wife because she asks them to stop playing poker.

Whereas in contrast with the other 3 men, Mitch is shown to be a very sensitive and understanding person. This is shown in the fact that he goes home early to see his Mam because she's ill. Mitch says, 'I gotta sick mother. She don't sleep until I come in at night. She says go out, so I do, but I don't enjoy it. I just keep wondering how she is.' I think this shows Mitch is sensitive and caring and thinks about his mother a lot.

Mitch also shows his sensitivity when after Stanley had hit Stella he said, 'This is terrible. Poker should not be played in a house with women.' This showed Mitch felt very sorry and awful about what had happened to Stella.

The craft in your writing

As your study of literature progresses, you will develop an awareness of the variety of ways in which writers use language. You may begin to think of writing as a 'craft', something which most writers think about and work at with great care and attention to detail, rather than something which simply happens rather haphazardly.

Try to think about your own writing in the same way.

- Make deliberate choices about the vocabulary you use, choosing the best word for the job, rather than the first one that comes to mind.
- Try out different lengths and types of sentences.
- Think about the different ideas you wish to include in your paragraphs.
- Try to weigh ideas against each other when you are writing argumentatively.

Some fortunate people – usually those who have read very widely – seem to have an innate sense of how to write appropriately for different purposes. Others only develop a sense of style with practice. The aim is to reach the point where you know you can communicate ideas clearly and that you are in complete control of your writing.

Activity

1 Reread some of your own recent essays. What are the strengths and weaknesses of your written style? Think about this carefully yourself and/or ask a teacher for feedback. Choose one weakness (for example, not putting quotations properly in context; changing tense; poor punctuation) and focus on correcting it in your next essay.

2 In a group of four, swap essays or other written work. Work in pairs to read and discuss a partner's work. Consider these points.
  - Is it easy to read and understand?
  - Has the question been answered?
  - Are quotations used effectively?
  Make a note of positive comments and advice about improvements before giving each other feedback.

10 Practical Criticism

<table>
<tr><td>Objectives</td><td>

- To establish a strategy for approaching unseen texts
- To practise practical criticism on poetry and prose texts
- To learn the skills of comparative practical criticism

</td></tr>
</table>

What makes practical criticism different?

Unseen practical criticism differs from much of the other written work that you will do during the A-level course in that it involves writing in response to a short text (or texts) which you will not have previously studied. In many ways, it is false to think that the skills needed for practical criticism are separate from the skills we use when encountering any literary text for the first time. In Section I, you will find many suggestions for analysing poems and extracts which would work equally well if they were set for practical criticism.

However, when you write about a set text in an examination, you will have a body of information, ideas, and notes at your disposal. Your memory is being tested as well as your ability to organize what you already know in response to particular questions. This is not the case when you are asked to tackle a text which you have not studied before. Then you are being asked to demonstrate different qualities and skills. These abilities can be summarized as follows:

- To read and make sense of a text and recognize its most important features quickly – a sort of instant 'research'

- To apply your own literary understanding rather than ideas you have read or been taught
- To know about 'how writers write', in terms of style and structure
- To organize your ideas in writing quickly

Practical criticism draws on the 'raw' skills of literary study. You cannot revise texts or rely on your memory. You are being asked to 'think on your feet'. Even so, there are some methods and ways of planning your approach to an unseen text which can be helpful, and getting as much practice as possible will help you be prepared for any text you might meet.

Developing your skills

First, it is important not to be daunted by the poem or prose extract you are given to analyse. There will be good reasons why a particular piece has been chosen, and with close reading you will be able to discover them. Texts about which there is nothing to say are not usually chosen for examination papers! You are most likely to be presented with either one poem or extract, or two shorter texts which are linked in some way, usually by their theme.

Once you have the text in front of you, it is helpful to have a strategy which will allow you to examine it in detail. Here is a possible checklist of the things you need to consider as you read it. As this list suggests, it is a good idea to begin with a general point, such as the theme of the text, and go on to look at the details. Your written answer will probably be structured in this way too.

Summary

1 **Subject or theme**   What is the text about? (This may seem too obvious, but it is a good broad starting point.) What other information do you have, for example the poet's name or a date?

2 **Speaker and/or situation**   Whose 'voice' do you hear in the text? Is it in the third- person or the first-person? If it is first-person writing, is it the voice of the author, or are they taking on a role? In poems, in particular, writers sometimes write with the voice of an object (for example a mountain/the wind), an animal, or even a god, as well as with the voices of people or characters.
Next ascertain to whom the text is addressed, and the situation in which it is set. (For example, Thomas Hardy's poem *God-forgotten* is written from the point of view of a messenger sent from Earth to ask God to help the human race, only to discover He has forgotten He ever created the planet. The poem consists of the messenger's dialogue with God.)

3 **Form**   What is the overall structure of the piece? Is it in a recognizable poetic form? Are there any obvious ways in which it could be divided into sections, either by its layout, its meaning, or by changes in the way language is presented at different points?

4 **Ideas and messages**   Look for ideas which are embedded 'below the surface' of the text. Think about the author's aims and purposes. Are there any signs of irony or satire. (See Unit 6 pages 127–138 for examples.)

5 **Tone and atmosphere** How would you describe the writer's 'tone of voice'? Is there an atmosphere or feeling which pervades the poem, such as sadness, gloom, or joy? If so, what is it about the writing that creates this effect? (For example, long sentences, with soft consonant sounds and repeated use of 'oo' and 'o' vowels, tend to create a sombre effect.)

6 **Imagery** What kinds of visual images or 'word-pictures' does the text present? How does the writer use simile or metaphor? Comment on both individual examples and on patterns of images which you notice. Be careful to explain and analyse these examples in terms of their contribution to the overall meaning of the text.

7 **Vocabulary** What do you notice about the individual words and phrases which the writer has chosen? Are there types of words which recur? (For example, there may be several words relating to death, or fire, or childhood.) Are there words which seem unexpected or out of place? What effect do they create?

8 **Rhyme, rhythm, and sound effects** If the text is a poem has it got a rhyme-scheme and what is its effect? (Beware of simply describing a rhyme-scheme without going on to say why you think the poet has chosen it and how far this aim is achieved.) Rhythm can be important in prose as well as in poetry. Are the lines/sentences flowing or short and jerky? Does the rhythm change at key points in the text? Other sound effects or aural images are created through the use of devices like alliteration. Remember to comment on the effect of these. If you cannot see any particular effect, it is better not to mention these features at all.

9 **Conclusion** Finally, return to an overview of the text. Sum up how the effects and details of style you have analysed come together to create a 'whole' piece of writing. What has your reading of it contributed to your understanding of the subject that it deals with? Does it offer a way of looking at things which you had not considered before? If the question invites you to give a personal response to the text, this is the place for it.

Not every unseen text requires detailed analysis of every one of these points but this checklist can act as a starting point and you can easily omit any aspects which are not relevant. If you develop your skills using this strategy, you should be able to approach unseen practical criticism with confidence.

Poetry

First, let us consider a single poem using this practical criticism strategy.

Activity

1 Working alone or with a partner, read the question and *Swifts* carefully, making notes under each of the headings 1–9 given above. The poet Ted Hughes said that his aim in some of his poems was 'capturing animals' in words. How does he set about doing so in the following poem?

> **2** Then compare your notes with those that follow on from the poem.
> What are the main similarities and differences in interpretation? You
> will no doubt have noticed different effects and meanings.

Swifts

Fifteenth of May. Cherry blossom. The swifts
Materialize at the tip of a long scream
Of needle. 'Look! They're back! Look!' And they're gone
On a steep

Controlled scream of skid
Round the house-end and away under the cherries. Gone.
Suddenly flickering in sky summit, three or four together,
Gnat-whisp frail, and hover-searching, and listening

For air-chills – are they too early? With a bowing
Power-thrust to left, then to right, then a flicker they
Tilt into a slide, a tremble for balance,
Then a lashing down disappearance

Behind elms.
They've made it again,
Which means the globe's still working, the Creation's
Still waking refreshed, our summer's
Still all to come –
And here they are, here they are again
Erupting across yard stones
Schrapnel-scatter terror. Frog-gapers,
Speedway goggles, international mobsters –

A bolas of three or four wire screams
Jockeying across each other
On their switchback wheel of death.
They swat past, hard fletched,

Veer on the hard air, toss up over the roof,
And are gone again. Their mole-dark labouring,
Their lunatic limber scramming frenzy
And their whirling blades
Sparkle out into blue –
Not ours any more.
Rats ransacked their nests so now they shun us.
Round luckier houses now
They crowd their evening dirt-track meetings,

Racing their discords, screaming as if speed-burned,
Head-height, clipping the doorway
With their leaden velocity and their butterfly lightness,
Their too much power, their arrow-thwack into the eaves.

Every year a first-fling, nearly-flying
Misfit flopped in our yard,
Groggily somersaulting to get airborne.
He bat-crawled on his tiny useless feet, tangling his flails

Like a broken toy, and shrieking thinly
Till I tossed him up – then suddenly he flowed away under
His bowed shoulders of enormous swimming power,
Slid away along levels wobbling

On the fine wire they have reduced life to,
And crashed among the raspberries.
Then followed fiery hospital hours
In a kitchen. The moustached goblin savage

Nested in a scarf. The bright blank
Blind, like an angel, to my meat-crumbs and flies.
Then eyelids resting. Wasted clingers curled.
The inevitable balsa death.
Finally burial
For the husk
Of my little Apollo -

The charred scream
Folded in its huge power.

Ted Hughes

One interpretation

1 **Subject or theme**   As the title tells us, the poem is almost entirely devoted
   to describing and 'capturing' in writing the appearance, movements, and
   behaviour of the swifts. (Fast-moving, forked-tailed birds related to
   swallows and martens, they are summer visitors to Britain.)
2 **Speaker and/or situation**   The poem is written in the first person. There is
   no reason to question that the poet is writing in his own voice and that he
   is addressing the reader directly. Although his chief purpose is to convey
   the characteristics of the birds in words, there are also elements of a 'story'
   in the poem. Watching and describing the punctual arrival of the swifts in
   May, Hughes reacts with excitement:
   'Look! They're back! Look!'
   For him, they signal the beginning of summer. As he puts it:
   '...our summer's
   Still all to come – '
   Placing 'Still all to come' on a separate line seems to convey his pleasure in
   anticipating the summer that lies ahead.
   Later in the poem, Hughes reminisces about previous seasons and tells the
   story of how each year a young bird would fail to manage its first flight, be

rescued and cared for, wrapped in a scarf and offered 'meat-crumbs and flies', only to die later and be buried.

3 **Form**   For the most part, four-line stanzas are used, but rather freely. Line lengths vary. Lines are quite frequently broken or interrupted, or run on to the next line, suggesting the fast, erratic flight of the birds.

4 **Ideas and messages**   This poem does not seem to carry a hidden message but it does hold some thought-provoking ideas. For Ted Hughes, the annual arrival of the swifts is a reminder that life goes in cycles; they are a signal that the seasons continue to change and spring and summer will follow winter.

'They've made it again,
Which means the globe's still working, the Creation's
Still waking refreshed...'

The phrase 'Which means the globe's still working' contains a touch of humour, suggesting, perhaps, that he had begun to doubt whether summer would come again.

In his description of his vain attempts to keep the helpless small birds alive each year and his tone of resignation as they reach 'The inevitable balsa death', he may be reminding us that there is little point in trying to interfere with the inexorable course of nature. The rule of the survival of the fittest would ensure that the weak bird did not live long.

5 **Tone and atmosphere**   Most of the poem has a tone of excitement, and haste. The swifts move with such speed that

'...they're gone
On a steep
Controlled scream of skid
Round the house-end and away under the cherries. Gone.'

almost before you have seen them. The way in which they dart in and out of sight is reflected in these short, broken lines. They give the poem an almost breathless quality, enforced by repetitions of '...gone' and '...here they are again...'

The second half of the poem is slightly more subdued, but the feeling of great speed continues whenever Hughes focuses on the movements of the birds. Many lines run into each other without punctuation, adding to the effect of fast, perpetual motion.

6 **Imagery**   As you might expect in a poem whose main aim is descriptive, the use of imagery is particularly powerful here. Most noticeable is the repeated use of metaphors likening the birds to machines (a device typical of Hughes). Many words and phrases suggest the flight of planes – fast fighter-planes in particular – or speedway driving. For example:

'On a steep
Controlled scream of skid'

and

'...With a bowing
Power-thrust to left, then to right, then a flicker they
Tilt into a slide...'

would not be out of place in an account of an air display. Words like 'Power-thrust', 'Erupting', and 'Schrapnel-scatter terror' suggest something violent and frightening.

However, there is a contradictory quality to the swifts. As well as making them sound powerful and dangerous, Hughes also draws attention to their delicacy: they 'flicker' and 'tremble' and are 'Gnat-whisp frail'. He repeatedly uses paradox to contrast their speed, which seems blundering and uncontrolled, a 'lunatic, limber scramming frenzy', with their tiny size and grace which is very much under control. They have 'leaden velocity' and 'butterfly lightness'.

Another aspect which Hughes captures is the swifts' cry – a high-pitched screaming sound. Somehow he manages to combine their sound with their movement. It is as if the birds are faster than their sounds, which they leave trailing behind them like wires:

'A bolas of three or four wire screams'

When they come into view they:

'Materialize at the tip of a long scream
Of needle...'

So conversely sometimes they are heard first and then seen. The word 'needle' conveys the sharp, piercing quality of their cry and their movement.

7 **Vocabulary**   In addition to these metaphors, there are other interesting choices of words. When Hughes describes the injured young bird, he emphasizes its mysterious, wild, and rather awe-inspiring qualities by referring to it as a 'moustached goblin savage' and as 'my little Apollo'. This suggests that he worships it like a little god. Apollo, the sun god, was one of the more powerful gods of Greek mythology; 'goblin' also suggests something supernatural, but rather mischievous too. Hughes refers to the bird's 'balsa death'. Balsa wood is very light and brittle, so this word encapsulates the feel of the bird's corpse, little more than feathers and bones.

8 **Rhyme, rhythm, and sound effects**   Formal rhyme does not feature in this poem. As we have noted, some lines and sentences run on fluently, while others are abrupt and broken. The rhythmic pattern emulates the darting movements of the swifts.

Hughes does also use some sound effects to contribute to his imagery. In particular, when he describes the young bird which fails to fly, it is a 'first-fling, nearly flying misfit' which 'flopped' in the yard. The alliterative repetition of the soft 'f', 'l' and 's' sounds creates an aural image which helps to suggest the bird's floundering as well as representing the fluttering sound of its wings.

9 **Conclusion**   To sum up, Hughes's main concern here is to 'capture' and convey as clearly as possible his impressions of the swifts. Through his use of metaphor and choice of words he gives an impression both of their incredible speed, power, and vivacity and of their tiny lightness of touch.

If you were to omit the headings from these notes and adapt them slightly, you would have a reasonable analysis of the poem in essay form. Of course, not every detail of the poem has been examined here; probably you noted other ideas or other examples of imagery that you would include in an answer. However, with a poem of this length, it is advisable to be selective in the details you choose to analyse.

Activity

> Working alone or with a partner, now look at the following student response to *Swifts* and compare it with your own notes and the ideas given above.
> - Which aspects of the poem has James covered thoroughly and which need more attention?
> - Has he supported his ideas by quoting details from the text?
> - Has he analysed details of the text closely? Can you find places where he needs to do more of this?
> - Is his written style clear and appropriate?

The poet Ted Hughes said that his aim in some of his poems was 'capturing animals' in words. How does he set about doing this in the following poem?

Ted Hughes begins the poem by describing the time and one aspect of the natural surroundings associated with that time when the birds return.
'Fifteenth of May. Cherry blossom.'
The poet also shows how excited he is to see the returning swifts. This is shown by the use of exclamation marks and the repetition of the word 'Look!' Almost immediately the poet goes on to discuss the speed of the swifts. He does this by saying that by the time a step has been taken the swifts are out of sight. This is a sign of the tone of the poem, the most striking feature is that of the way the poet describes the speed with which the swifts fly. The speed of the swifts are also shown by the poet by the way the different stanzas are written. The sentences are fragmented as they use exclamation marks, dashes, commas, and question marks. This gives the poem a sense of pace which is reflected by the way the swifts fly. The use of language the poet uses in the first stanza shows how the swifts use power and agility to fly. This is best described in the line
'Power-thrust to left, then to right, then a flicker they
Tilt into a slide'.
The swifts manage to use both power and agility to fly, which is something that man-made machines fail to achieve. A rocket has power but agility is reserved for machines such as gliders.
The poet also uses metaphors of nature to explain how the swifts arrived.
'They've made it again. Which means the globe's
still working'.
This gives the connotation that the arrival of the swifts signifies that nature will continue to develop as long as they arrive after their winter break.
In the next few stanzas sporting metaphors are used and this helps again to highlight the speed at which the swifts fly. Examples of these are 'Speedway goggles', 'Jockeying', and 'Veer on the hard air.' These are used because of the speed associated with them, speedway for fast motorbikes, jockeying as for jockeying for a position in a race, and veering hard as in some other form of

motor sport. These all help to give a sense of realism to the reader who may be unfamiliar with the sight of a swift flying.

The poet feels saddened when they have gone. He tries to find something to blame. In this case it is the rats who have destroyed their nests. The poet seems jealous that the swifts have gone, this is shown in the line that says they are 'Round luckier houses now'.

This also shows the fondness which the poet has for the birds.

The next stanza best highlights the speed of the swifts. Again dashes are used in the sentence structure which adds to the sense of speed. The way the poet describes how the swifts are

'clipping the doorway'

shows that the birds are flying so quickly that there is hardly any margin for error. They try to take short-cuts to reach their destination quicker and this could prove fatal.

The final few stanzas show the youth of the swift and how frail and vulnerable they can be. This is in great contrast to the agility and power with which they are described early in the poem.

The poet describes how in the early days, swifts, like any other birds, find it hard to fly. He uses language which again is in contrast to the language used earlier. Words such as 'crawled', 'useless feet', and 'tangling' are in vast contrast with the sure and certain movements such as 'erupting' and veering. These also show the power the young swift has to come.

The poet also describes how he once found a swift that had 'crashed among the raspberries', he attempted to care for it in his kitchen but the bird died. The poet describes the death of the swift as

'The inevitable balsa death'.

This shows both the benefits and drawbacks of being, as balsa wood is when used for model planes it is swift and light through the air but also frail.

The life the swifts lead is best described by

'the fine wire'.

This shows that they live on the edge risking their life by flying so quickly through the air.

James

Activity

> Now try applying the same procedure to Hughes' poem, *Second Glance at a Jaguar* on page 168. Again, his main purpose is to 'capture' the characteristics of an animal in words. Make notes under each of the nine headings before writing a short critical essay to answer the same question that was asked on *Swifts*:
>
> > The poet Ted Hughes said that his aim in some of his poems was 'capturing animals' in words. How does he set about doing so in the following poem?
>
> For Ted Hughes' commentary on writing to 'capture' his subjects see Unit 11, page 186.

Second Glance at a Jaguar

Skinful of bowls he bowls them
The hip going in and out of joint, dropping the spine
With the urgency of his hurry
Like a cat going along under thrown stones, under cover,
Glancing sideways, running
Under his spine. A terrible, stump-legged waddle
Like a thick Aztec disemboweller,
Club-swinging, trying to grind some square
Socket between his hind legs round,
Carrying his head like a brazier of spilling embers
And the black bit of his mouth, he takes it
Between his back teeth, he has to wear his skin out,
He swipes a lap at the water-trough as he turns,
Swivelling the ball of his heel on the polished spot,
Showing his belly like a butterfly.
At every stride he has to turn a corner
In himself and correct it. His head
Is like the worn down stump of another whole jaguar,
His body is just the engine shoving it forward,
Lifting the air up and shoving on under,
The weight of his fangs hanging the mouth open,
Bottom jaw combing the ground. A gorged look,
Gangster, club-tail lumped along behind gracelessly,
He's wearing himself to heavy ovals,
Muttering some mantrah, some drum-song of murder
To keep his rage brightening, making his skin
Intolerable, spurred by the rosettes, the Cain-brands,
Wearing the spots off from the inside,
Bounding some revenge. Going like a prayer-wheel,
The head dragging forward, the body keeping up,
The hind legs lagging. He coils, he flourishes
The blackjack tail as if looking for a target,
Hurrying through the underworld, soundless.

Ted Hughes

Now that we have looked at some poems where the emphasis is on using language descriptively, let us move to one where the poet, Louis MacNeice, is more concerned with conveying some thought-provoking ideas about what it means to be human and with the form of the poem.

Activity

> **1** Read the poem on page 169, making notes as outlined in the practical criticism strategy on pages 160–161. Pay particular attention to:
> - the messages MacNeice conveys about his view of human life
> - the shape and form of the poem, including the length of the stanzas
> - the use of repetition, rhythm, rhyme, and unusual choices of words
> **2** Then compare your ideas to the analysis which follows the poem.

Prayer before Birth

I am not yet born; O hear me.
Let not the bloodsucking bat or the rat or the stoat or the
   clubfooted ghoul come near me.

I am not yet born; console me.
I fear that the human race may with tall walls wall me.
   with strong drugs dope me, with wise lies lure me,
      on black racks rack me, in blood-baths roll me.

I am not yet born; provide me
With water to dandle me, grass to grow for me, trees to talk
   to me, sky to sing to me, birds and a white light
      in the back of my mind to guide me.

I am not yet born; forgive me
For the sins that in me the world shall commit, my words
   when they speak me, my thoughts when they think me,
      my treason engendered by traitors beyond me,
         my life when they murder by means of my
            hands, my death when they live me.

I am not yet born; rehearse me
In the parts I must play and the cues I must take when
   old men lecture me, bureaucrats hector me, mountains
      frown at me, lovers laugh at me, the white
         waves call me to folly and the desert calls
            me to doom and the beggar refuses
               my gift and my children curse me.

I am not yet born; O hear me
Let not the man who is beast or who thinks he is God
   come near me.

I am not yet born; O fill me
With strength against those who would freeze my
   humanity, would dragoon me into a lethal automaton,
      would make me a cog in a machine, a thing with
         one face, a thing, and against all those
            who would dissipate my entirety, would
               blow me like thistledown hither and
                  thither or hither and thither
                    like water held in the
                      hands would spill me.

Let them not make me a stone and let them not spill me.
Otherwise kill me.

Louis MacNeice

One possible commentary

1 **Subject or theme**   As the title reveals, this poem takes the form of the prayer of an unborn child, expressing hopes and fears about its life which is yet to begin.

2 **Speaker and/or situation**   The 'voice' we hear in the poem is that of the unborn baby. Its words are addressed, perhaps, to God, or to those who have the power to protect and nurture it in life, or to the Universe in general.

3 **Form**   The form is important here. The poem echoes the form of a prayer from a formal church ritual, with its petitions, intercessions and requests for forgiveness – 'O hear me', 'console me', 'forgive me'. It is also rhythmic and repetitive. The poem also has a 'shape'. For the most part, the stanzas increase in length, suggesting the growth of the child and the increasing complexity of the different stages of human life.

4 **Ideas and messages**   The poem is a series of pleas for safety from the dangers which might befall the child in its lifetime. The first stanza begins with babyhood, when the child's chief need is to be heard – it asks 'O hear me' – and when the dangers it faces are physical threats or the fearful fantasies of a small child:

'Let not the bloodsucking bat or the rat or the stoat or the
    clubfooted ghoul come near me.'

As we move through the stanzas, the dangers become more sophisticated, suggesting that the child is becoming gradually older and more responsible. By the fourth stanza it is asking 'forgive me', and finally the request is for 'strength against those who would freeze my humanity'. This is mirrored by the generally increasing length of the stanzas.

The second and third stanzas seem to be concerned with childhood and adolescence, and the danger that the young person will be deceived and exploited by 'the human race', used in wars and 'blood-baths', tortured on 'black racks' or doped with 'strong drugs'. The phrase 'with tall walls wall me' suggests a fear of being hemmed in and deprived of freedom and opportunity. The child also asks to be supported and provided with the good things the world has to offer. These are presented simply: water, grass, trees, sky, birds, as we might find in a child's painting. The request for a 'white light in the back of my mind to guide me' suggests a need for something pure and clear, a spiritual presence to direct the child through life. The child is a passive recipient of both the good and bad that the world has to offer.

In the fourth stanza, the child becomes more involved in the adult world, but is not yet fully responsible. It is as if the child is a channel which the world and others in it use to transmit ideas or commit evil deeds. We see this in the unusual way in which these lines are constructed, placing the expected objects of the phrases ('thoughts'; 'words') as their subjects. The child asks to be forgiven

'For the sins that in me the world shall commit, my words
when they speak me, my thoughts when they think me.'

This also suggests that the child is very impressionable – almost made up of the thoughts, ideas, and actions of others.

Next, the child looks forward to a time when it must be far more active, and asks for guidance about how to fulfil the many roles life will require. It sees adult life as a series of parts to be played and acts to be performed. The child needs to learn how to 'act' and deal with experiences which are painful or frightening, to cope when

'old men lecture me, bureaucrats hector me, mountains

frown at me, lovers laugh at me...'

The brief sixth stanza echoes the first, with its plea to be protected from what is most dangerous. MacNeice seems to suggest this time that two types of human beings pose the biggest threat to the child: ' the man who is beast' – presumably one who is no more aware of the consequences of his actions than an animal – and the man 'who thinks he is God' and so has lost touch with reality, seeing himself as all-powerful.

Finally, there are the complex dangers that arise for the now fully responsible adult. These are threats to mental health, to freedom of choice, and sense of self. The child prays for the strength to resist those things that can destroy its individuality, by turning it into a 'cog in a machine', or a 'lethal automaton' – things which do not think and make decisions for themselves. The final line

'Otherwise kill me.'

tell us that for MacNeice, life without consciousness and choice is not worth having.

Altogether, the poem is a plea that the child be allowed to grow and develop to its full potential, physically, mentally, and spiritually.

5 **Tone and atmosphere**   The use of the prayer form, with its repetitions and traditional patterns creates a rather subdued or perhaps hypnotic effect like an incantation.

6 **Imagery**   There are many powerful images here, from the childlike ideas of 'trees to talk to me, sky to sing to me' which suggest simplicity and innocence, through the threat of the mountains that 'frown', to the horrific possibility that the child will become a 'thing with one face', or a 'stone', something inhuman which is unable to respond to things in more than one way.

7 **Vocabulary**   Much of the vocabulary is strong, and often suggests violence. The dangers which await the child are forcefully expressed. Adjectives such as 'clubfooted', bloodsucking', 'lethal', and verbs like 'dope', 'rack', 'freeze' and 'dragoon' suggest a harsh world. The strength of these words and images is thrown into relief by the mesmerizing effect of the prayer form.

8 **Rhyme, rhythm, and sound effects**   Within the repetitive and rhythmic prayer structure, many sound effects contribute to the poem's ritualistic style. Alliteration and half-line or internal rhymes attract attention to and intensify the meaning in many lines:

'I fear that the human race may with tall walls wall me,

with strong drugs dope me, with wise lies lure me,

on black racks rack me, in blood-baths roll me.'

Different combinations of repeated consonants and vowels create different effects in each of these phrases. The hard sounds of 'b' and 'ck' with short 'a' suggest the violent torture of the rack; in contrast, the 'l', 's' and 'i' sounds need to be spoken slowly, with relish, and hint at the attractiveness of the 'wise lies'. The poem is full of such devices.

9 Conclusion   Many complexities lie behind the ritualized form of this poem, which could be read, perhaps, in the unthinking, mechanical manner of a congregation 'going through the motions' of a liturgical service. In that case, we fall into one of the traps MacNeice fears: that of ceasing to be an individual who thinks and is aware, and becoming a mere 'automaton'. His choice of form and language deliberately tests us in that way. In fact, we need to stop and question the significance of every line.

Activity

> **1** Norman Nicholson's poem below also deals with the subject of life before and after birth. Read it carefully and write your own analysis of it, using as many aspects of the practical criticism strategy as seem relevant.
>
> **2** Later, you may wish to return to and write a comparison of the MacNeice and Nicholson poems.
> For another comparison of two poems see Unit 15, pages 224–228.

To a Child before Birth

This summer is your perfect summer. Never will the skies
So stretched and strident be with blue
As these you do not see; never will the birds surprise
With such light flukes the ferns and fences
As these you do not hear. This year the may
Smells like rum-butter, and day by day
The petals slip from the cups like lover's hands,
Tender and tired and satisfied. This year the haws
Will form as your fingers form, and when in August
The sun first stings your eyes,
The fruit will be red as brick and free to the throstles.
Oh but next year the May
Will have its old smell of plague about it; next year
The songs of the birds be selfish, the skies have rain;
Next year the apples will be tart again.
But do not always grieve
For the unseen summer. Perfection is not the land you leave,
It is the pole you measure from; it gives
Geography to your ways and wanderings.
What is your perfection is another's pain;
And because she in impossible season loves
So in her blood for you the bright bird sings.

Norman Nicholson

Prose extracts

The strategy for approaching unseen criticism can also be applied to prose passages, although you may find you need to focus on different aspects of the texts. You will be examining many of the same literary techniques, such as imagery, choice of vocabulary, and rhythm, but these will probably be more 'dilute' in prose writings than in poetry. This may mean you need to concentrate even harder, when studying prose passages, noticing how the writer uses language as well as commenting on the ideas that are expressed.

For the most part, prose passages will be extracts from longer works rather than complete texts, although occasionally very short essays or short stories are set. Again, you are likely to be asked to work on one passage or to compare two which are connected. The next piece we will look at is the opening of a novel, *The Crow Road*, by Iain Banks.

Activity | First, read the following extract carefully. Working with a partner, make notes in preparation for answering this question.
Write an assessment of the beginning of *The Crow Road* by Iain Banks, commenting on its effectiveness as the opening of a novel.

The Crow Road

It was the day my grandmother exploded. I sat in the crematorium, listening to my Uncle Hamish quietly snoring in harmony to Bach's Mass in B Minor, and I reflected that it always seemed to be death that drew me back to Gallanach. I looked at my father, sitting two rows away in the front line of seats in the cold, echoing chapel. His broad, greying-brown head was massive above his tweed jacket (a black arm-band was his concession to the solemnity of the occasion). His ears were moving in a slow oscillatory manner, rather in the way John Wayne's shoulders moved when he walked; my father was grinding his teeth. Probably he was annoyed that my grandmother had chosen religious music for her funeral ceremony. I didn't think she had done it to upset him; doubtless she had simply liked the tune, and had not anticipated the effect its non-secular nature might have on her eldest son.
My younger brother, James, sat to my father's left. It was the first time in years I'd seen him without his Walkman, and he looked distinctly uncomfortable, fiddling with his single earring. To my father's right my mother sat, upright and trim, neatly filling a black coat and sporting a dramatic black hat shaped like a flying saucer. The UFO dipped briefly to one side as she whispered something to my father. In that movement and that moment, I felt a pang of loss that did not entirely belong to my recently departed grandmother, yet was connected with her memory. How her moles would be itching today if she was somehow suddenly reborn!
'Prentice!' My Aunt Antonia, sitting next to me, with Uncle Hamish snoring mellifluously on her other side, tapped my sleeve and pointed at my feet as she murmured my name. I looked down.

I had dressed in black that morning, in the cold high room of my aunt and uncle's house. The floorboards had creaked and my breath had smoked. There had been ice inside the small dormer window, obscuring the view over Gallanach in a crystalline mist. I'd pulled on a pair of black underpants I'd brought especially from Glasgow, a white shirt (fresh from Marks and Sparks, the pack-lines still ridging the cold, crisp cotton) and my black 501s. I'd shivered, and sat on the bed, looking at two pairs of socks; one black, one white. I'd intended to wear the black pair under my nine-eye Docs with the twin ankle buckles, but suddenly I had felt that the boots were wrong. Maybe it was because they were matt finish...

The last funeral I'd been to here – also the first funeral I'd ever been to – this gear had all seemed pretty appropriate, but now I was pondering the propriety of the Docs, the 501s, and the black biker's jacket. I'd hauled my white trainers out of the bag, tried one Nike on and one boot (unlaced); I'd stood in front of the tilted full-length mirror, shivering, my breath going out in clouds, while the floorboards creaked and a smell of cooking bacon and burned toast insinuated its way up from the kitchen.

The trainers, I'd decided.

So I peered down at them in the crematorium; they looked crumpled and tea-stained on the severe black granite of the chapel floor. Oh-oh; one black sock, one white. I wriggled in my seat, pulled my jeans down to cover my oddly-packaged ankles. 'Hell's teeth,' I whispered. 'Sorry, Aunt Tone.'

My Aunt Antonia – a ball of pink-rinse hair above the bulk of her black coat, like candy floss stuck upon a hearse – patted my leather jacket. 'Never mind, dear,' she sighed. 'I doubt old Margot would have minded.'

'No,' I nodded. My gaze fell back to the trainers. It struck me that on the toe of the right one there was still discernible the tyre mark from Grandma Margot's wheelchair. I lifted the left trainer onto the right, and rubbed without enthusiasm at the black herring-bone pattern the oily wheel had left. I remembered the day, six months earlier, when I had pushed old Margot out of the house and through the courtyard, past the outhouses and down the drive under the trees towards the loch and the sea.

Iain Banks

Activity	Read this student's response to the question and then study the comments on its strengths and weaknesses which follow.

Write an assessment of the beginning of *The Crow Road*, by Iain Banks, commenting on its effectiveness as the opening of a novel.

The extract from the novel, 'The Crow Road' by Iain Banks is rather unusual. The passage describes his family at his grandmother's cremation in his home town of Gallanach. The piece is unusual as it is written in a jovial style which is not often connected with death except in Black comedy. However, this is not a comedy so is unusual. The opening sentence, 'It was the day my grandmother exploded.' is so surprising when put in context with the rest of the passage.

The narrator does not dwell on the grief of losing a member of his family, but more so on his isolation from his parents. In a movement his mother makes to his father he feels 'a pang of loss that did not entirely belong to my recently departed grandmother'.

The fact he has had to stay at his aunt and uncle's house and is sitting with them shows his isolation from his parents. The narrator does not seem to 'fit in' with the rest of his family. His clothes are different and his whole attitude towards the funeral is distracted.

This distraction of the narrator is shown in his digressions from the funeral. How he notices his father's ears move, as he grinds his teeth, like 'John Wayne's shoulders when he walks'. He notices his brother James is not wearing his Walkman for the first time in years and that his mother's dramatic hat is shaped like a UFO. There does not seem to be many emotions shown by the narrator, nor any of the other characters. He remarks how his father is probably angry his grandmother had chosen religious music for her funeral ceremony instead of secular, as he would have wanted. His Uncle Hamish has fallen asleep and is snoring 'In harmony to Bach's Mass in B Minor'; he is obviously oblivious or uncaring of the situation around him.

The narrator tries to create a cold atmosphere, one traditionally associated with death. They are sitting in the cold 'echoing chapel' which emulates a feeling of emptiness and loss. The cold temperature of his bedroom, however, which the author embellishes upon, seems to be more related to his isolation from his family. The fact he is not in his parents' home shows how they have excluded him from their lives. Also that they do not sit with him at the chapel. The atmosphere is not maintained as the author makes comical asides which are more light-hearted, for example the references to John Wayne and the UFO and the fact his boots didn't look right because they had a matt finish. Also, how he has odd socks on and his description of his Aunt Antonia being like 'a candy floss stuck upon a hearse'.

From this passage, the narrator shows himself to be a young man who has moved away from his home town, possibly without his parents' blessing as they have become disassociated. The narrator shows that he did love his grandmother Margot as he describes a fond memory of her at the end of the passage, yet shows no real signs of grief.

This passage is quite effective as the opening of a novel as it makes me want to read on. It provides details of what are, presumably, the main characters (his family) and it would be interesting to find out what happens next. His jovial style is easy to read and understand, it being quite light-hearted.

Julia

Comments on the strengths and weaknesses of Julia's response.

Julia provides a clear introductory paragraph, giving enough information to put the passage in context without wasting time on paraphrasing. She could say more to make it clear that the narrator is a fictional character.

She describes the style as 'jovial'. This may be a good way to describe it, but she will need to clarify what she means by explaining fully later in the essay.

The reference to black comedy is very useful. Again she needs to pick out examples of this later, even though she has stated that the passage as a whole is not comedy.

She comments on the surprising first sentence in relation to the rest of the passage. A fuller analysis would improve this. For example, she could point out the strangely matter-of-fact tone of the sentence and the shocking effect of the word 'exploded' when applied to a 'grandmother'!

Julia's point in paragraph 3 about the narrator seeming isolated from his parents is a good one. We have to be careful, though, not to speculate too far. From this extract, we do not know that the whole family were not staying with the aunt and uncle! Its best to keep to points for which you can find evidence in the passage. However, within the extract, there is a sense of his distance from his parents.

Julia has pointed out that his clothes are different, but could expand on this. What do the details of his clothes tell us about him? They could suggest an image or stereotype: 'Nine-eye Docs, 501s and the black biker's jacket'?

She makes a good point about the narrator's 'digressions' in paragraph 4, giving examples of how his attention wanders to dwell on the people around him. Again, she could comment more analytically about these, on what they tell us about the members of his family and also, through his choice of words, about himself. For example, the similes he uses, referring to John Wayne and UFOs, suggest the popular culture of film stars and science fiction, which contrasts with the sombre music his grandmother has chosen. It seems that his brother, too, with his earring, but without his Walkman, has made concessions for the occasion.

In paragraph 5, Julia's remarks on atmosphere are apt, the quotation is helpful, and she has added some further comment. She could also go on to say something about the use of colour in the passage. Repeated 'black' and 'white' are appropriate for cold and death. Having mentioned the aunt's pink hair, she could go on to explain why this is humorous: its inappropriateness among all the black, which is captured by the candy-floss/hearse image.

The penultimate paragraph is disappointing. Julia is rather too concerned with inventing theories about the young man's background at the expense of paying close attention to the details that are provided.

This highlights a broader point. If you are familiar with the whole text from which the extract has been set, this will have advantages and disadvantages. You will be able to relate key points from the extract to your wider knowledge of the text, but will need to make it clear that you have read the full text. However, you will need to beware of your wider knowledge distracting you from focusing on and making deductions from the details of the passage itself. Julia does begin to explore the narrator's reference to his grandmother at the end; however, we are not given any evidence in the extract that the memory is a 'fond' one.

There is more to notice about the young man in relation to his family and the scene at the crematorium:

- his outward 'style' and image, which suggest rebellious youth, could lead to his being labelled uncaring. It contrasts with the conventional dress of his older relatives. As Julia points out, he does not overtly declare his emotions or much sense of loss, although we do not detect much emotion in the other characters either.
- in opposition to this, his painful preoccupation with 'getting it right'. He is very concerned that his dress should be appropriate, so he does care. In a strange sense, what seemed inappropriate is in fact fitting: the white trainers his aunt objects to carry the mark of his grandmother's wheelchair, and serve as a record of their last meeting, and of his having shown his care of her. The 'adults', on the other hand, may be dressed more conventionally, but seem, if anything, less involved in the proceedings.

The passage has obviously captured Julia's interest, and her final paragraph provides a fair summing up of her response. The length of Julia's answer is about what you can expect to write in the short time available for analysing an extract in an unseen criticism examination paper (45 minutes–1 hour). So you can see that you need to write very succinctly and that there is no time for writing anything which does not contribute directly to answering the question.

Activity

> Now look at Richard's answer, which has different qualities. Read this carefully, noting its strengths and suggesting some ways in which his work could be improved. In particular, look at:
> - major points he has noticed about the passage
> - how well his ideas are supported with evidence
> - appropriateness of quotations from the text
> - his analysis of the writer's style
> - clarity of expression: is it easy to follow? Is the writing well organized or chaotic?
> - technical accuracy: punctuation, paragraphing, and spelling

Write an assessment of the beginning of *The Crow Road*, by Iain Banks, commenting on its effectiveness as the opening of a novel.

This passage is an effective opening to the novel, as the first sentence 'It was the day my grandmother exploded' grabs the reader's attention instantly. This opening line also establishes the mood of the piece, a quite darkly humorous style – the various family members present at the crematorium are described in a lot of detail – the images created of them are expanded upon (the narrator's mother is said to be wearing a hat that looks like a flying saucer – this is furthered when we are given the image of it 'dipping' to the side when she talks). There is a very sarcastic tone to the passage in places, such as when the narrator tells us his father is probably 'annoyed that my grandmother had chosen religious music for her funeral ceremony', and the constant references to Uncle Hamish snoring in the background – this style of humor fits in quite well with the proceedings as it isn't (for want of a better term) 'Har-de-har-har' humor – it is subtle, and certain points about it are written in such a way, that they could just be taken as extra description of the events (the flashback to the narrator getting dressed is a good example – with him rattling off precise descriptions of his clothes, and where they are from). The atmosphere, despite the humor, is retained: the formal mood is (kind of) still there, and there are references to the cold atmosphere to add to this (although this refers to the morning, it still has an effect on the scene at hand) also, a lot of the comments from the narrator (who seems to be taking the event as a sort of 'family reunion' – or a freak show, depending) are linked with death, even if in an obscure way such as referring to somebody as looking like candy floss stuck on a hearse – which in itself, is mixing something associated with fun & something associated with death – much like the whole passage.

PS – is the 'smell of cooking bacon & burned toast' line a really sick reference to the cremation taking place?

Richard

Comparing texts

Often, practical criticism questions will give you the option of comparing two texts. Usually these will show how two writers approach the same topic or theme, although they may have other connections. In your written answer your focus will first be on

Connections   Establish the links between the texts first, and make clear any similarities in theme, approach, or style

and then

Contrasts   Concentrate on what makes the texts different. You may notice differences in:

- attitude shown to the subject
- writer's point of view or role
- formal/informal structure
- tone
- use of imagery
- choice of vocabulary
- other stylistic features

In preparing and planning an answer for a comparative study, it is often useful to lay out your ideas in a table or diagram to help make these similarities and differences clear. For an example of this technique see Unit 7, pages 143–144.

Activity

1 Read these two poems on the theme of anger, making notes using the strategy on page 160. Combine your findings in a table.
2 Compare your ideas with the table which follows the poems.
3 Use your notes to write a short essay to answer this question:
   Examine the similarities and the differences in the ways Elizabeth Daryush and William Blake describe feelings of anger in the following poems. (AEB 1994)

'Anger lay by me all night long'

Anger lay by me all night long,
   His breath was hot upon my brow,
He told me of my burning wrong,
   All night he talked and would not go.

He stood by me all through the day,
   Struck from my hand the book, the pen;
He said: 'Hear first what I've to say,
   And sing, if you've the heart to, then.'

And can I cast him from my couch?
   And can I lock him from my room?
Ah no, his honest words are such
   That he's my true-lord, and my doom.

Elizabeth Daryush

A Poison Tree

I was angry with my friend:
I told my wrath, my wrath did end.
I was angry with my foe:
I told it not, my wrath did grow.

And I watered it in fears,
Night & morning with my tears;
And I sunned it with smiles,
And with soft deceitful wiles.

And it grew both day and night,
Till it bore an apple bright.
And my foe beheld it shine,
And he knew that it was mine.

And into my garden stole,
When the night had veiled the pole:
In the morning glad I see
My foe outstretched beneath the tree.

William Blake

	Daryush	**Blake**
Subject	The experience of anger and its effects	The effects of anger; the results of expressing or suppressing anger.
Speaker/ Situation	First person; poet describes being overpowered by anger, which is personified as a male character. She resists her anger at first, then seems to accept it as justified, though still threatening ('doom').	First person; poet tells of being angry, with a friend, and then an enemy. The symbol of a tree represents unexpressed anger, which, nurtured, grows and bears the fruit of revenge. The story is fable-like, and the speaker is more an archetype or representative human being than an individual.
Form	3 rhyming, 4-line stanzas which convey the point neatly in few words.	4 x 4-line stanzas with simple rhythm and rhyme, like a nursery rhyme; the simplicity is deceptive.
Ideas/Messages	Anger can take hold of a person and dominate life. The poet lives, works, and sleeps with anger which she cannot release: 'And can I lock him from my room? Ah no...' Describing it as a separate person suggests her inability to control the anger. If we dwell on angry thoughts and words this only increases our rage. Her mind is full of a sense of being a victim of some wrongdoing: 'He told me of my burning wrong, All night he talked and would not go.'	Anger which is openly expressed quickly passes, while hidden anger grows. Nursing a grudge can make one vengeful and destructive. The poet's anger is nurtured, becomes poisonous and eventually destroys the enemy, leaving him jubilant: 'In the morning glad I see/My foe outstretched beneath the tree.'
Tone/ Atmosphere	Sense of urgency, being swept along by the anger; punctuation pushes each stanza on towards its last line, especially the last, making her 'doom' seem inevitable.	Simple language gives an unemotional quality; rather cold, distanced from the anger, with a sense that his revenge is deliberate, premeditated, and enjoyed ('soft deceitful wiles'; 'glad').

	Daryush	Blake
Imagery	Personification of anger extends throughout; image of powerful, violent man who is persistent and demands attention. 'Hear first what I've to say, And sing, if you've the heart to, then.'	Symbolic image of hidden anger as the destructive 'Poison Tree' throughout. He nurtures anger like a gardener with a favourite plant ('watered'; 'sunned'). Image of tree/apple is biblical, suggesting Adam and Eve; the Tree of Knowledge of good and evil, with overtones of loss of innocence, and betrayal.
Vocabulary	Words like 'hot' and 'burning' suggest, perhaps, a devilish quality; also a feverishness, adding to the sense of urgency. 'Honest' and 'true-lord' are a surprise: as if she now accepts her anger as genuine and justifiable.	Mainly simple; words reminiscent of the Bible (in older translations): 'foe' 'wrath'; 'bore'; these enhance the timeless, fable-like quality.
Rhyme, Rhythm, and Sound Effects	Strong rhythmic movement; 4 stressed 'beats' in each line, driving poem forward to its conclusion and emphasizing rhymes – they seem unavoidable, like the anger. Use of hard consonant sounds, sometimes alliteratively, suggests her struggle, (breath/brow/burning; cast/couch; struck/lock/book) while the repeated 'oo' sound in the final line (true/doom) slows the pace, suggesting resignation.	Simple 4-beat lines; rhyming couplets with final words stressed emphasizing contrasting ideas. (friend/foe/end/grow; smiles/wiles; night/bright) Some alliteration and sound patterns. Deceit is emphasized by repeated soft 's' sounds (sunned/smiles/soft/deceitful); many lines begin with 'I' while others echo its sound, also giving a 'sly' quality – or revealing the self-absorption of the speaker.

For a student response that compares two different poems see Unit 15, page 224–228.

Before attempting the next activity which provides a chance to compare prose extracts, refer back to the comments about working with prose texts on pages 173–177.

Activity

> Read the two extracts carefully several times, and then write about the ways that the writers present:
> • the nature of the city
> • the relationship of the man with the city

A

City of the Mind

Driving through the city, he is both here and now, there and then. He carries yesterday with him, but pushes forward into today, and tomorrow, skipping as he will from one to the other. He is in London, on a May morning of the late Twentieth Century, but is also in many other places, and at other times. He twitches the knob of his radio: New York speaks to him, five hours ago, is superseded by Australia tomorrow and presently by India this evening. He learns of events that have not yet taken place, of deaths that have not yet occurred. He is Matthew Halland, an English architect stuck in a traffic jam, a person of no great significance, and yet omniscient. For him, the world no longer turns; there is no day or night, everything and everywhere are instantaneous. He forges his way along Euston Road, in fits and starts, speeding up, then clogged again between panting taxis and a lorry with a churning wasp-striped cement mixer. He is both trapped, and ranging free. He fiddles again with the radio, runs through a lexicon of French song, Arab exhortation, invective in some language he cannot identify. Halted once more, he looks sideways and meets the thoughtful gaze of Jane Austen (1775–1817), ten feet high on a poster, improbably teamed with Isambard Kingdom Brunel and George Frederick Handel, all of them dead, gone, but doing well – live and kicking in his head and up there guarding the building site that will become the British Library. And then another car cuts in ahead of his, he hoots, accelerates, is channelled on in another licensed burst of speed. Jane Austen is replaced by St Pancras.

Thus he coasts through the city, his body in one world and his head in many. He is told so much, and from so many sources, that he has learned to disregard, to let information filter through the mind, and vanish, leaving impressions – a phrase, a fact, an image. He knows much, and very little. He knows more than he can confront; his wisdoms have blunted his sensibility. He is an intelligent man, and a man of compassion, but he can hear of a massacre on the other side of the globe and wonder as he listens if he remembered to switch on his answering machine. He is aware of this, and is disturbed.

The city, too, bombards him. He sees decades and centuries, poverty and wealth, grace and vulgarity. He sees a kaleidoscope of time and mood: buildings that ape Gothic cathedrals, that remember Greek temples, that parade symbols and images. He sees columns, pediments, and porticos. He sees Victorian stucco, twentieth-century concrete, a snatch of Georgian brick. He notes the resilience and tenacity of the city, and its indifference.

Penelope Lively

B
Hawksmoor

Hawksmoor could have produced a survey of the area between the two churches of Wapping and Limehouse, and given at the same time a precise account of the crimes which each quarter harboured. This had been the district of the CID to which he had been attached for some years, before he was assigned to the Murder Squad, and he had come to know it well: he knew where the thieves lived, where the prostitutes gathered, and where the vagrants came. He grew to understand that most criminals tend to remain in the same districts, continuing with their activities until they were arrested, and he sometimes speculated that these same areas had been used with similar intent for centuries past: even murderers, who rapidly became Hawksmoor's speciality, rarely moved from the same spot but killed again and again until they were discovered. And sometimes he speculated, also, that they were drawn to those places where murders had occurred before. In his own time in this district, there had been a house in Red Maiden Lane in which three separate murders had been perpetrated over a period of eight years, and the building itself gave such an impression to those who entered it that it had stayed unoccupied since the last killing. In Swedenborg Gardens Robert Haynes had murdered his wife and child, and it was Hawksmoor who was called when the remains were found beneath the floorboards; in Commercial Road there had been the ritual slaying of one Catherine Hayes, and then only last year a certain Thomas Berry had been stabbed and then mutilated in the alley beside St George's-in-the-East. It had been in this district, as Hawksmoor knew, that the Marr murders of 1812 had occurred – the perpetrator being a certain John Williams, who, according to De Quincey whose account Hawksmoor avidly read, 'asserted his own supremacy above all the children of Cain'. He killed four in a house by Ratcliffe Highway – a man, wife, servant, and child – by shattering their skulls with a mallet and then gratuitously cutting their throats as they lay dying. Then, twelve days later and in the same quarter, he repeated his acts upon another family. He was transformed, again according to De Quincey, into a 'mighty murderer' and until his execution he remained an object of awe and mystery to those who lived in the shadow of the Wapping church. The mob tried to dismember his body when eventually it was brought in a cart to the place of burial – at the conflux of four roads in front of the church, where he was interred and a stake driven through his heart. And, as far as Hawksmoor knew, he lay there still: it was the spot where he had this morning seen the crowd pressing against the cordon set up by the police.

Peter Ackroyd

(AEB Specimen Paper issued 1993)

11 The Process of Writing

Objectives	• To learn about the process of writing from authors' own words
	• To study writers' drafts to see the process in action

Gaining an insight

In Unit 9 we commented that for many people writing is a craft, a process which requires much thought and attention to detail. In your English studies you will probably have been encouraged to draft and redraft your own original, creative writing and critical essays. You may have assumed that this is something that only students have to do, and that published authors, fuelled by inspiration, produce a finished work of art at the first attempt. This is, of course, not true. Most writers produce draft versions of their work, or spend time amending and changing what they write as they go along.

We can gain further insight into how writers' minds work and what their aims are by examining and comparing draft versions of their work alongside the final published text. We can see where a writer has exchanged one word or phrase for another, altered the structure of a sentence, or deleted a paragraph entirely, and we can pose questions like these about why this has been done.

• Why does the writer consider the new version to be more effective?
• What qualities in the new word or phrase attract the writer?

- Do you agree with the choices made, or do you think the original version is preferable? If so why?

If a line, phrase, or word has been changed several times, we will understand that the writer has struggled to create just the right effect, and has compromised when an ideal solution was not forthcoming.

We can also see how writers set about their task by reading their own words on the subject, in autobiography, letters, or other personal writings. Before we move on to look at examples of writers' drafts, here are some comments from a novelist and a poet about the process of writing.

The Victorian novelist Anthony Trollope was a prolific and energetic author who, despite working full time in the Post Office, disciplined himself to wake at 5.30 each morning to write and to complete a daily quota of words. Here, he is journeying on a long sea-voyage to Alexandria but keeps to his resolve to write every day.

Autobiography

There was no day on which it was my positive duty to write for the publishers, as it was my duty to write reports for the Post Office. I was free to be idle if I pleased. But as I had made up my mind to undertake this second profession, I found it to be expedient to bind myself by certain self-imposed laws. When I have commenced a new book, I have always prepared a diary, divided into weeks, and carried on for the period which I have allowed myself for the completion of the work. In this I have entered, day by day, the number of pages I have written, so that if at any time I have slipped into idleness for a day or two, the record of that idleness has been there, staring me in the face, and demanding of me increased labour, so that the deficiency might be supplied.

[He goes on to give some advice to writers of fiction.]

I have from the first felt sure that the writer, when he sits down to commence his novel, should do so, not because he has to tell a story, but because he has a story to tell...
But the novelist has other aims than the elucidation of his plot. He desires to make his readers so intimately acquainted with his characters that the creations of his brain should be to them speaking, moving, living, human creatures. This he can never do unless he knows those fictitious personages himself, and he can never know them well unless he can live with them in the full reality of established intimacy. They must be with him as he lies down to sleep, and as he wakes from his dreams. He must learn to hate them and to love them. He must argue with them, quarrel with them, forgive them, and even submit to them. He must know of them whether they be cold-blooded or passionate, whether true or false, and how far true, and how far false. The depth and the breadth, and the narrowness and the shallowness of each should be clear to him. And as, here in our outer world, we know that men and women change, – become worse or better as temptation or conscience may guide them, – so should these creations of his change, and every change should be noted by him. ...If the would-be

novelist have aptitudes that way, all this will come to him without much struggling; – but if it do not come, I think he can only make novels of wood. ...The language in which the novelist is to put forth his story, the colours with which he is to paint his picture, must of course be to him matter of much consideration. Let him have all other possible gifts, – imagination, observation, erudition, and industry, – they will avail him nothing for his purpose, unless he can put forth his work in pleasant words. If he be confused, tedious, harsh, or unharmonious, readers will certainly reject him. ...To do this, much more is necessary than to write correctly. He may indeed be pleasant without being correct, – as I think can be proved by the works of more than one distinguished novelist. But he must be intelligible, – intelligible without trouble; and he must be harmonious. ...The language used should be as ready and as efficient a conductor of the mind of the writer to the mind of the reader as is the electric spark which passes from one battery to [another] battery. ...The habit of writing clearly soon comes to the writer who is a severe critic to himself.

Anthony Trollope

Ted Hughes has spoken of his poetry as a process of 'capturing' his subject (see Unit 10, page 162 for a poem that does just this). In the following extract, aimed at younger writers, he writes in detail about what that process entails.

Poetry in the Making

...as a poet, you have to make sure that all those parts over which you have control, the words and rhythms and images, are alive. That is where the difficulties begin. Yet the rules, to begin with, are very simple. Words that live are those which we hear, like 'click' or 'chuckle', or which we see, like 'freckled' or 'veined', or which we taste, like 'vinegar' or 'sugar', or touch, like 'prickle' or 'oily', or smell, like 'tar' or 'onion'. Words which belong directly to one of the five senses. Or words which act and seem to use their muscles, like 'flick' or 'balance'.

But immediately things become more difficult. 'Click' not only gives you a sound, it gives you the motion of a sharp movement ...such as your tongue makes in saying 'click'. It also gives you the feel of something light and brittle, like a snapping twig. Heavy things do not click, nor do soft bendable ones. In the same way, tar not only smells strongly. It is sticky to touch, with a particular thick and choking stickiness. Also it moves, when it is soft, like a black snake and has a beautiful black gloss. So it is with most words. They belong to several of the senses at once, as if each one had eyes, ears, and tongue, or ears and fingers and a body to move with. It is this little goblin in a word which is its life and its poetry, and it is this goblin which the poet has to have under control.

Well, you will say, this is hopeless. How do you control all that? When the words are pouring out how can you be sure that you do not have one of these side meanings of the word 'feathers' getting all stuck up with one of the side meanings of the word 'treacle', a few words later. In bad poetry this is exactly what happens, the words kill each other. Luckily you do not have to bother about it so long as you do one thing.

That one thing is, imagine what you are writing about. See it and live it. Do not think it out laboriously, as if you were working out mental arithmetic. Just look at it, touch it, smell it, listen to it, turn yourself into it. When you do this, the words look after themselves, like magic. If you do this you do not have to bother about commas or full stops or that sort of thing. You do not look at the words either. You keep your eyes, your ears, your nose, your taste, your touch, your whole being on the thing you are turning into words. The minute you flinch, and take your mind off this thing, and begin to look at the words and worry about them... then your worry goes into them and they set about killing each other.

Ted Hughes

Activity

> Compare the words of Trollope and Hughes. What aspects of writing do they seem to agree about, and in what ways do their ideas differ? Do their ideas reveal anything about the different priorities of a nineteenth-century author and a twentieth-century one?

Examining drafts

Sometimes it is possible to examine different versions of a writer's work. Though draft versions are not often readily available, you can sometimes examine writers' original notebooks or drafts in their original form, in museums or at exhibitions. There are also editions of writers' work where examples of alternative wording, lines, stanzas, or paragraphs, or other changes made in the drafting are included alongside the final version.

Let us look at one such example through Wilfred Owen's poem, *The Send-off*. This deals with the subject of young men newly drafted into the army setting off for the killing fields of France during the First World War.
First, here is the finished poem in its entirety.

The Send-off

Down the close, darkening lanes they sang their way
To the siding-shed.
And lined the train with faces grimly gay.

Their breasts were stuck all white with wreath and spray
As men's are, dead.

Dull porters watched them, and a casual tramp
Stood staring hard,
Sorry to miss them from the upland camp.
Then, unmoved, signals nodded, and a lamp
Winked to the guard.

So secretly, like wrongs hushed-up, they went.
They were not ours:
We never heard to which front these were sent.

Nor there if they yet mock what women meant
Who gave them flowers.

Shall they return to beatings of great bells
In wild train-loads?
A few, a few, too few for drums and yells,
May creep back, silent, to still village wells
Up half-known roads.

Wilfred Owen

Now, here are four draft versions of the first stanza:

1

Softly down darkening lanes they sang their way
And no word said.
They filled the train with faces vaguely gay
And shoulders covered all white with wreath and spray
As men's are, dead.

2

Low-voiced through darkening lanes they sang their way to
    the cattle shed.
And filled the train with faces grimly gay.
Their breasts were stuck all white with wreath and spray, as
    men's are, dead.

3

Down the wet darkening lanes they sang their way to the
    cattle-shed
And lined the train with faces grimly gay.
Their breasts were stuck all white with wreath and spray
As men's are, dead.

4

Down the deep, darkening lanes they sang their way
    To the waiting train,
And filled its doors with faces grimly gay,
And heads and shoulders white with wreath and spray,
As men's are, slain.

Activity

> **1** Examine all five versions of the stanza. Look closely at all the
> amendments Owen has made, considering each change carefully.
> What is gained or lost by each of these? For example:
> - You may think the alliteration of 'Down the deep, darkening lanes...'
>   is effective as an opening line, but what extra shades of meaning are
>   added by starting the line with 'Softly...' or 'Low-voiced..'?
> - What is suggested by 'siding–shed', 'cattle–shed', 'waiting train'?

> **2** In the final stanza, do the alterations in layout and line lengths affect the emphasis on particular words, or cause any changes in meaning? Here are Owen's alterations presented together for comparison.

Shall
    } they return to beatings of great bells
Will

In wild train-loads?

A few, a few, too few for drums and yells,

May { creep / walk } back, silent, to { still / their / strange } village wells,

Up half-known roads.

We asked the poet, U. A. Fanthorpe, whose work is often studied at A-level, if she would let us study an example of her work through the drafts. A feature of her work is that she often writes 'in role'. Taking on the characters of famous characters from literature or mythology, or of people she has encountered in life, she presents them to us in a new, thought-provoking, and sometimes humorous light.

Waiting Gentlewoman is one of four poems titled *Only Here for the Bier* in which she explores how minor characters from Shakespeare plays might have experienced the world they lived in. In this case, Lady Macbeth's lady-in-waiting reflects on the happenings at Dunsinane Castle.

What follows is a commentary from U. A. Fanthorpe on how she wrote the poem and how generally she sets about writing.

Waiting Gentlewoman revisited, or *Very Poor Legs for a Kilt*

Digging these rough drafts out of their retirement in plastic bags in the attic reminded me sharply of my early days as a writer. They are written on the backs of hospital lists, which it was my job to type. There was never a question of piles of fresh gleaming paper. I felt what I was doing was provisional, and it seemed right to work on paper that had been used already. In the same way, I wrote in pencil, because pencil can always be rubbed out. Biro, pen or whatever commits you. Nowadays I use a notebook, because stray bits of paper are so easily lost. And I've given up pencils; for one thing, they're so tiresome, always having to be sharpened. In one way I've changed, in that there are far more rough drafts. When I began, the world was full of subjects; now, 18 years later, I've written about some of them and am no longer in such a hurry. Ways in which I've remained the same: I'm still unable to write at all until I've got at least the first three lines quite clearly in my head; and I won't go near the typewriter until I'm absolutely sure that the thing is as right as it can be.

How I set about writing a poem: it generally sits around inside my head for a long time, as if it were bread waiting to rise. I think about it when walking the dog, waking up in the morning – these are both good times for writing in one's head. Eventually there's a point when I can't put off the writing any longer, but it's still a long process. One poem took four years, and that's not abnormal. The set of poems in *Only Here for the Bier* was quicker because it was based on two simple ideas: (1) what was it like to be a woman in the male world of Shakespearian tragedy? (one would be a minor character, unlikely to last until Act V) and (2) could I use the tones of voice of people I knew for these women? I had not to invent the voices, but remember them, which made things quicker, but I couldn't get them completely consistent at first. I enjoy writing in someone else's voice, working out the limits of their vocabulary, the way the mouth moves, and so on. I like to think that I can write better than this; but I must confess to enjoying the view from a minor character, and seeing how much I can suggest through the words of someone not very articulate.

Here is the finished version of the poem.

Waiting Gentlewoman

If Daddy had known the setup,
I'm absolutely positive, he'd never
Have let me come. Honestly,
The whole thing's too gruesome
For words. There's nobody here to talk to
At all. Well, nobody under about ninety,
I mean. All the possible men have buggered
Off to the other side, and the rest,
Poor old dears, they'd have buggered off
Too, if their poor old legs would have
Carried them. HM's a super person, of course,
But she's a bit seedy just now,
Quite different from how marvellous she was
At the Coronation. And this doctor they've got in –
Well, he's only an ordinary little GP,
With a very odd accent, and even I
Can see that what HM needs is
A real psychiatrist. I mean, all this
About *blood* and *washing*. Definitely Freudian.
As for Himself, well, definitely
Not my type. Daddy's got this thing
About selfmade men, of course, that's why
He was keen for me to come. But I think
He's gruesome. What HM sees in him
I cannot imagine. *And* he talks to himself.
That's so rude, I always think.
I hope Daddy comes for me soon.

U. A. Fanthorpe

Before we go on to look at some draft versions of the poem, it may be useful to think about some of its important features and about what U. A. Fanthorpe's aims are. As she tells us, choosing to write in the roles of minor characters from Shakespearian tragedy offers the opportunity to look at a famous situation from a rather different perspective. The waiting gentlewoman in *Macbeth* makes only one significant appearance. This is in Act V Scene 1, where she watches with the doctor as Lady Macbeth demonstrates her madness and guilt by trying obsessively to wash from her hands the blood of the murdered King Duncan. This is the 'seedy' HM of the poem, while 'Himself' is, of course, Macbeth.

The poet also uses the 'tones of voice of people she knew'. These are superimposed on the Shakespearian characters in an interesting and sometimes amusing way. As a result, the 'waiting gentlewoman' is not only Shakespeare's character, but also a 'type' – a character from the modern world. We gain an impression of her from her manner of speaking. She refers to 'Daddy' although she is an adult, uses extreme phrases like 'absolutely positive' and ' too gruesome', calls the queen a 'super person', and informs us that she is 'a bit seedy just now'. All of these contribute to an impression of a rather well-bred, opinionated, but not terribly bright débutante. She likes to be 'in' with the 'right' sort of people and to demonstrate her familiarity with royalty by referring to the queen as 'HM'. The poem works best if we can almost hear her tone of voice and recognize her 'type', while acknowledging the references to *Macbeth*.

This combination of the old and the new provides scope for clever humour. Macbeth's famous soliloquies, for example, are reduced to 'And he talks to himself', while describing him as a 'selfmade man' is rather a comical understatement considering his bloodthirsty rise to power. As you look at the two draft versions of the poem which follow, you need to study how the different choices of words or lines that the poet has made contribute to realizing her aims: to comment on *Macbeth* from a different viewpoint and to create a character.

First draft

I'm ~~absolutely~~ quite positive if Daddy
Had known what it was going to be like
He would never have let me come. Honestly,
The whole setup's too gruesome for words.
Nobody here to talk to at all! Well,
Nobody under ninety, I mean.

All the really attractive ~~ones~~ men have oozed
Off to the other side, ~~and you can see~~ the ones who're left,
Poor old dears, they'd have gone too,
If their legs would have carried them.
HM's a super person of course but there's no doubt
She's feeling a bit seedy just now.
Quite different from how, marvellous she was
At the Coronation. And this doctor they've got in –
Well, my dear, he's only an ordinary little GP
With a very odd accent, and even I
Can see that what HM needs is
A ~~proper~~ real psychiatrist. I mean all this
About *soap*, and *washing*. Definitely Freudian.
So I ~~said~~ muttered ~~something about a second opinion~~
~~But you know how bossy these little men are,~~
~~Absolutely no chance.~~ As for Himself, well,
Definitely/not my type. Daddy's got this thing
About selfmade men, of course, that's why
He was keen for me to come ~~here~~. But I think
~~Think~~ He's gruesome. What HM sees in him
I ~~can't~~ cannot imagine. ~~And very poor legs for a kilt.~~
And he talks to himself. // I always think
That's so rude. // I hope Daddy comes for me soon.

There is also a second draft in which she is much closer to her final version.
It begins:

Waiting Gentlewoman

~~I'm quite positive if Daddy had known~~
If Daddy had known ~~all this~~ the set up,
I'm absolutely positive, he'd never
Have let me come. Honestly,
The whole ~~setup's~~ thing's too gruesome
For words.

Activity

1 With a partner, compare and discuss the changes U. A. Fanthorpe makes in the draft versions of her poem. Again, look at each word she has changed and at the lines she has omitted, considering carefully the effects of each option.

Here are some specific points to discuss.

- Why do you think she tried out 'quite positive' and 'absolutely positive' in the opening lines? Why did she opt for 'absolutely'? How is it more apt for the character she is creating?

- She talks about how all the younger men have defected 'to the other side' (an ironic reference to how Macbeth has alienated every decent citizen in Scotland). In draft 1, they are 'All the really attractive ones/men', while in the final version they are 'All the possible men'. What does this line tell us about the waiting gentlewoman's preoccupations? What difference does the change make?

- In the first draft, the men have 'oozed' off to the other side, but this has been amended to 'buggered off'. What are the effects of each of these word choices? ('Oozed' perhaps tells us more about what the character thinks of the men's behaviour, while 'buggered off' may be more in keeping with our character's manner of speaking.)

- In the same sentence, why do you think she has chosen to repeat 'poor old' in the final version?

- What is the effect of adding 'marvellous' (line 13) and of omitting 'my dear' (line 15)?

- In line 19, 'soap and washing' appears in both drafts, while in the final version 'soap' has been replaced by 'blood'. Do you agree that this is the better choice? Why?

- In the first draft, there are three lines of further comment about doctors (lines 20–22). Has anything been lost by omitting these? Why do you think she made this decision?

- What difference is made by using 'cannot' and not 'can't' in line 27?

- Why do you think she decided to leave out 'And very poor legs for a kilt' (in line 27)?

- The sentence 'I always think that's so rude.' is inverted in the final version: 'That's so rude, I always think.' How does this alter the emphasis and slightly change our sense of the character?

  The effect of most of the amendments seems to be a slight modification or 'fine tuning' of the characterization. In the first version she seems just slightly 'nicer'; a little softer in her approach, perhaps, when she says 'my dear', and a little less definite when she says 'I always think that's so rude.' In the finished version she is more abrasive. Repeating 'poor old...' takes away its sympathetic quality and makes it into just a formula – a habit of speech. 'That's so rude, I always think' sounds more self-righteous, and leaves no room for disagreement.

2 Using your notes from the questions above, write a detailed commentary on the different versions of the poem.

12 Examining Writers' Styles

Objectives
- To look closely at what makes a distinctive style
- To use parody to highlight aspects of writers' styles

What makes a style?

Throughout this book you are being asked to think not only about what writers are saying – the content of their work – but also about *how* they write. This means examining the particular combination of literary devices, structures, and vocabulary which a writer uses and which go together to form that writer's individual 'style'. From your own reading you will know that some writers' work is easy to recognize immediately because they have a distinctive 'style'. However, it can be more difficult to explain exactly which characteristics make a writer's style recognizable.

As a student of A-level Literature, you will need to develop the ability to analyse and write about style. One shortcoming noted by examiners is that students fail to take account of this and do not engage in enough detailed analysis of how texts are written. It is easier to concentrate on the writer's use of language when studying poetry, but it can be tempting, when writing about novels or other longer prose works, to focus on the plot or the ideas and neglect to examine the features that make up the author's style.

Try thinking of 'style' as the product of many choices the writer makes about these elements.

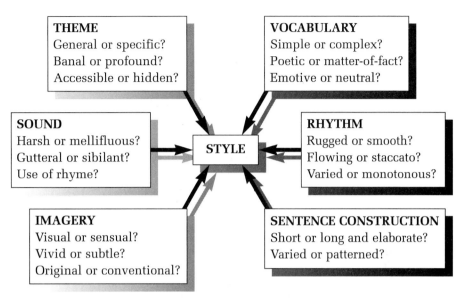

These are only some examples of the choices writers make, but they are a helpful reminder of the questions we need to ask when considering style.

Thinking or feeling

'Style' can also be viewed as the expression of a writer's personality and preoccupations. The way in which a writer experiences the world and the things which are most important to them are bound to affect how and what they write.

The psychologist Carl Jung puts forward the theory that people tend towards being **introverted** (more concerned with the 'inner' world of thought or imagination) or **extraverted** (more grounded in the external world of physical reality and other people). Stemming from this, he maintains that some people are thinking types, most at home with thoughts and ideas and perhaps less comfortable with the experience and expression of emotions; others use their intuition. A third group are feeling types, relying on their feelings more than their thoughts to guide them through life and a final group are sensation types, experiencing the world via their physical senses.

This is a partial and simplistic explanation of Jung's ideas, and many other people have created models to try and understand the human personality. However, factors like these are bound to influence the choices authors make when they write, in terms of content and style. They may also account for the fact that most of us respond or 'relate' better to some writers than others. We naturally feel more at home with the work of a writer who experiences the world as we do, while reading the work of a writer who experiences it very differently may feel like struggling to understand a foreign culture.

Of course, most writing – the act of putting ideas and experiences into words – involves a rather cerebral or 'thinking' activity. Most writers 'craft' their work carefully (for an extreme example see *Of Studies*, the essay by Francis Bacon in Unit 6, page 119), even if their aim is to use words to convey emotional or sensual experiences. Although there are some who use more intuitive or free-writing techniques, allowing their words to flow without judging or altering them.

Now let us consider how these ideas might help us in gaining a sense of an author's personal 'style'.

First, read the following passage from *The Rainbow*. This novel by D. H. Lawrence, traces the patterns of love and relationships through three generations of the Brangwens, a family of farmers in the East Midlands. Here, in the early part of the book, Tom Brangwen struggles with his sense of being both close to and distant from the woman he will marry.

The Rainbow

Chapter 1

Then, as he sat there, all mused and wondering, she came near to him, looking at him with wide, grey eyes that almost smiled with a low light. But her ugly-beautiful mouth was unmoved and sad. He was afraid.

His eyes, strained and roused with unusedness, quailed a little before her, he felt himself quailing and yet he rose, as if obedient to her, he bent and kissed her heavy, sad, wide mouth, that was kissed, and did not alter. Fear was too strong in him. Again he had not got her.

She turned away. The vicarage kitchen was untidy, and yet to him beautiful with the untidiness of her and her child. Such a wonderful remoteness there was about her, and then something in touch with him, that made his heart knock in his chest. He stood there and waited, suspended.

Again she came to him, as he stood in his black clothes, with blue eyes very bright and puzzled for her, his face tensely alive, his hair dishevelled. She came close up to him, to his intent, black-clothed body, and laid her hand on his arm. He remained unmoved. Her eyes, with a blackness of memory struggling with passion, primitive and electric away at the back of them, rejected him and absorbed him at once. But he remained himself. He breathed with difficulty, and sweat came out at the roots of his hair, on his forehead.

'Do you want to marry me?' she asked slowly, always uncertain.

He was afraid lest he could not speak. He drew breath hard, saying:

'I do.'

Then again, what was agony to him, with one hand lightly resting on his arm, she leaned forward a little, and with a strange, primeval suggestion of embrace, held him her mouth. It was ugly-beautiful, and he could not bear it. He put his mouth on hers, and slowly, slowly the response came, gathering force and passion, till it seemed to him she was thundering at him till he could bear no more. He drew away, white, unbreathing. Only, in his blue eyes was something of himself concentrated. And in her eyes was a little smile upon a black void.

She was drifting away from him again. And he wanted to go away. It was intolerable. He could bear no more. He must go. Yet he was irresolute. But she turned away from him.

With a little pang of anguish, of denial, it was decided.

'I'll come an' speak to the vicar to-morrow,' he said, taking his hat.

She looked at him, her eyes expressionless and full of darkness. He could see no answer.

'That'll do, won't it?' he said.

'Yes,' she answered, mere echo without body or meaning.

'Good night,' he said.

'Good night.'

He left her standing there, expressionless and void as she was. Then she went on laying the tray for the vicar. Needing the table, she put the daffodils aside on the dresser without noticing them. Only their coolness, touching her hand, remained echoing there a long while.

They were such strangers, they must for ever be such strangers, that his passion was a clanging torment to him. Such intimacy of embrace, and such utter foreignness of contact! It was unbearable. He could not bear to be near her, and know the utter foreignness between them, know how entirely they were strangers to each other. He went out into the wind. Big holes were blown into the sky, the moonlight blew about. Sometimes a high moon, liquid-brilliant, scudded across a hollow space and took cover under electric, brown-irridescent cloud-edges. Then there was a blot of cloud and shadow. Then somewhere in the night a radiance again, like a vapour. And all the sky was teeming and tearing along, a vast disorder of flying shapes and darkness and ragged fumes of light and a great brown circling halo, then the terror of a moon running liquid-brilliant into the open for a moment, hurting the eyes before she plunged under cover of cloud again.

D. H. Lawrence

Activity

> Having read the passage carefully, make notes on the following questions.
>
> **1** To what extent is Lawrence concerned with:
> - his character's thoughts and ideas
> - his character's feelings and emotions
> - his character's experience of the physical world around him
> - relationships?
>
> **2** What choices does Lawrence make relating to:
> - theme
> - vocabulary
> - sentence structures
> - rhythm
> - sound?

Lawrence is a writer deeply concerned with human relationships, particularly those between men and women. He tries to articulate the effect people have on each other and presents an ambivalent view of close relationships, which can bring great happiness, but may also be very threatening or destructive.

You will probably have noticed in this extract that he seems to be chiefly aiming to convey Brangwen's feelings, both in a physical and in an emotional sense. Brangwen feels sexual desire for the woman, but is also fearful of losing himself in love, of being 'absorbed' by it. Lawrence sometimes describes this in terms of the actual physical sensations in his body:

'He breathed with difficulty, and sweat came out at the roots of his hair, on his forehead.'

However, when he describes their kiss, he can no longer be quite so concrete. To convey the emotional and physical sensations Brangwen feels here, Lawrence uses the image of her seeming to be 'thundering' at him, which suggests something both powerful and threatening, but is much less direct. It is the nearest he can get to an impression of his character's feelings.

Some of Lawrence's work was originally banned for being too sexually explicit, but often, as he tries to convey his characters' experiences of love and sex, his descriptions have this rather impressionistic quality. Powerful images and metaphors from nature are used to portray emotional and sexual needs as something almost mystical. Something of this is present in the final paragraph of the extract above, where his description of the stormy night sky mirrors Brangwen's experience with the woman. The moon, which scuds behind the clouds appears intermittently, 'hurting the eyes' and causing 'terror', reminds us of the moments when he fully feels the presence of the woman and their mutual desire, or looks into her eyes and sees 'a little smile upon a black void'. Both are elusive, beautiful, and frightening.

Having recognized that Lawrence's 'style' has its basis in the emotional, physical, and sensual exploration of life, we can go on to examine in detail some of the choices he makes in using language. You may have noticed some of these.

- Predictably, perhaps, he uses 'feeling' words in almost every sentence: 'unmoved and sad', 'afraid', 'fear', 'agony', and 'anguish' are just a few.
- Although this is a third-person narrative, everything is filtered through Brangwen's emotional responses.
- Colours, and other adjectives, are sometimes used repeatedly, reinforcing their effect, creating patterns, or even giving a ritualistic effect. His eyes are blue and very bright, while hers are grey, black, or 'full of darkness' and her 'sad, wide' mouth is 'ugly-beautiful'.
- Sentence lengths are varied. This too contributes to the portrayal of Brangwen's feelings. Moments of tension and uncertainty are made up of short or incomplete sentences, which give a sense of pain, urgency, and indecision:
  'She was drifting away from him again. And he wanted to go away. It was intolerable. He could bear no more. He must go. Yet he was irresolute.'

- The description of the ragged sky is similarly broken up, but there are other moments when the sentences flow more freely, usually when the two characters seem more connected. The use of sentence patterns to enhance a sense of drama is typical of Lawrence.
- The sound qualities of the words are fairly varied, with a few alliterative patterns. Hard consonants are used and, in the case of the image of the disordered sky 'teeming and tearing along', add to the sense of confusion.

Exaggerating style

One interesting – and amusing – way of becoming more aware of a writer's style is to look at a pastiche or parody. The parodist usually takes the most obvious features of a writer's style and exaggerates them, as a cartoonist exaggerates physical features in visual images. A successful parody can make it obvious what a writer's stylistic 'habits' are and help you to recognize them when you return to the original. Writing parody yourself encourages you to concentrate hard on the features which make a writer's style distinctive.

Activity | What features of Lawrence's writing do you recognize in this short parody? |

Sons and Aztecs

She lay, motionless, in the burning heat. She gave herself to the sun in an act of supreme worship. Her body was the sacrament.
He watched and was thrilled to the soul. A dark primeval shout resounded through his whole being. To him, she was the true female spirituality. Not the whimpering, cloying, tendrilled feminine grasp of demand and duty, not the empty ache of sentiment, but the pure lambent flame of passion. He warmed to her flame. She basked in his primitive mooncold light. She was the sun, and he the moon.
He lay down beside her. Then he climbed on top of her and did it to her.

Richard Curtis

A 'thinking' style

Now we will look at how a very different writer, Henry James, presents a scene of courtship. In his novel *Washington Square*, Catherine Sloper, a likeable, but rather plain and naïve young woman who is heiress to a great fortune, receives a visit from her 'lover' Morris Townsend, of whom her father disapproves. Mrs Penniman is her sentimental, meddling aunt.

Washington Square

Chapter 10
Catherine received the young man the next day on the ground she had chosen – amidst the chaste upholstery of a New York drawing-room furnished in the fashion of fifty years ago. Morris had swallowed his pride, and made the effort

necessary to cross the threshold of her too derisive parent – an act of magnanimity which could not fail to render him doubly interesting.

'We must settle something – we must take a line,' he declared, passing his hand through his hair and giving a glance at the long narrow mirror which adorned the space between the two windows... If Morris had been pleased to describe the master of the house as a heartless scoffer, it is because he thought him too much on his guard, and this was the easiest way to express his own dissatisfaction – a dissatisfaction which he had made a point of concealing from the Doctor. It will probably seem to the reader, however, that the Doctor's vigilance was by no means excessive, and that these two young people had an open field. Their intimacy was now considerable, and it may appear that, for a shrinking and retiring person, our heroine had been liberal of her favours. The young man, within a few days, had made her listen to things for which she had not supposed that she was prepared; having a lively foreboding of difficulties, he proceeded to gain as much ground as possible in the present. He remembered that fortune favours the brave, and even if he had forgotten it, Mrs Penniman would have remembered it for him. Mrs Penniman delighted of all things in a drama, and she flattered herself that a drama would now be enacted. Combining as she did the zeal of the prompter with the impatience of the spectator, she had long since done her utmost to pull up the curtain. She, too, expected to figure in the performance – to be the confidante, the Chorus, to speak the epilogue. It may even be said that there were times when she lost sight altogether of the modest heroine of the play in the contemplation of certain great scenes which would naturally occur between the hero and herself.

What Morris had told Catherine at last was simply that he loved her, or rather adored her. Virtually, he had made known as much already – his visits had been a series of eloquent intimations of it. But now he had affirmed it in lover's vows, and, as a memorable sign of it, he had passed his arm round the girl's waist and taken a kiss. This happy certitude had come sooner than Catherine expected, and she had regarded it, very naturally, as a priceless treasure. It may even be doubted whether she had ever definitely expected to possess it; she had not been waiting for it, and she had never said to herself that at a given moment it must come. As I have tried to explain, she was not eager and exacting; she took what was given her from day to day; and if the delightful custom of her lover's visits, which yielded her a happiness in which confidence and timidity were strangely blended, had suddenly come to an end, she would not only not have spoken of herself as one of the forsaken, but she would not have thought of herself as one of the disappointed. After Morris had kissed her the last time he was with her, as a ripe assurance of his devotion, she begged him to go away, to leave her alone, to let her think. Morris went away, taking another kiss first. But Catherine's meditations had lacked a certain coherence. She felt his kisses on her lips and on her cheeks for a long time afterward; the sensation was rather an obstacle than an aid to reflection. She would have liked to see her situation all clearly before her, to make up her mind what she should do if, as she feared, her father should tell her that he disapproved of Morris Townsend.

Henry James

Activity

> Now ask yourself these questions about the style of this extract.
> 1 To what extent, would you say, is James concerned with:
>   • his characters' thoughts and ideas
>   • his characters' feelings and emotions?
> 2 Where do you think he stands in relation to his characters? What is his attitude towards them?

Probably you will have noticed the enormous difference between this extract and the one from *The Rainbow* on page 196. Both depict an encounter between a man and a woman where marriage is in question, yet the writers are poles apart in the ways they approach this subject. Where Lawrence is so intent on conveying a sense of his characters' emotions and sensations, James is much more concerned with what they are thinking, or with analysing what is going on.

The effect is that reading Lawrence can be a powerful emotional experience: we are presented with such a close view of the characters that it can almost feel as if we are 'inside' their skins. Reading James, however, is often more of an intellectual challenge. It is not that his characters do not have feelings, but that they stop and think about them – or James does – for several pages sometimes. Situations are weighed up and the rights and wrongs of their responses pondered. James maintains a good distance between himself and his characters, leaving himself space to comment and judge, to use irony, or to gently mock. (It is almost impossible, incidentally, to imagine Lawrence being ironic or mocking his characters.) As a result, we as readers also feel more remote from James' characters.

There are other factors in James' writing which contribute to this very different 'style'. Asking some further questions about the details of how he uses language should reveal these.

Activity

> Look again at the passage from *Washington Square*.
> 1 What are James' choices with respect to:
>   • vocabulary
>   • imagery
>   • sentence structures
>   • sound?
>   What do these choices contribute to his 'style'?
> 2 What words would you use to describe his 'style'?

These are some of the points you may have noted.

• James' vocabulary tends to be demanding or 'inflated': he often deliberately chooses words which are complex or latinate (derived from Latin), when simpler words would convey his meaning equally well. Morris is not 'worried', for example, but has 'a lively foreboding of difficulties' (and this extract is a relatively straightforward example!) This gives a sense of formality, and adds to the feeling of distance mentioned earlier: only someone who steps back and weighs his words would make these choices. Also, James' tone becomes ironic or mocking as he uses long words when his characters and subjects do not really merit them. They may be foolish, like Mrs Penniman, or dishonest or ordinary, but think themselves grander than they really are.

- There is little imagery in the extract, but what there is is deliberately clever. For example, the extended metaphor which describes Mrs Penniman's propensity for acting as if life is a stage drama ('Combining as she did the zeal of the prompter... between the hero and herself.') goes on a bit, as we may imagine Mrs Penniman herself does.
- On the whole, James' sentence structures also tend to be complex. (More extreme examples can be found elsewhere in his work.) He is renowned for producing sentences with multiple clauses which temporarily digress from their subject. These require us to hold several ideas in mind simultaneously which demands concentration. You will find this aspect of his style particularly noticeable if you try to read the passage aloud.
- There is no evidence that James chooses words in order to create deliberate sound effects. However, the complex and latinate vocabulary does perhaps give a rather dry, crisp effect to his style, but precision in meaning is his chief aim.
- There can be little doubt that James' main purpose is to present us with something to think about. It is the meanings and ideas contained in his long, precisely constructed sentences, carefully chosen vocabulary, and clever metaphors which are important, never sensual effects like alliteration or visual imagery. It is as difficult to imagine James writing to appeal to the senses as it is to imagine Lawrence being ironic.

To conclude, here is another example of parody, this time of Henry James. It tells of two children awakening on Christmas morning.

The Mote in the Middle Distance

It was with the sense of a, for him, very memorable something that he peered now into the immediate future, and tried, not without compunction, to take that period up where he had, prospectively, left it. But just where the deuce had he left it? The consciousness of dubiety was, for our friend, not this morning, quite yet clean-cut enough to outline the figures on what she had called his 'horizon', between which and himself the twilight was indeed of a quality somewhat intimidating. He had run up, in the course of time, against a good number of 'teasers'; and the function of teasing them back – of, as it were, giving them, every now and then, 'what for' – was in him so much a habit that he would have been at a loss had there been, on the face of it, nothing to lose. Oh, he always had offered rewards, of course – had ever so liberally pasted the windows of his soul with staring appeals, minute descriptions, promises that knew no bounds. But the actual recovery of the article – the business of drawing and crossing the cheque, blotched though this were with tears of joy – had blankly appeared to him rather in the light of sacrilege, casting, he sometimes felt, a palpable chill on the quest. It was just this fervour that was threatened as, raising himself on his elbow, he stared at the foot of his bed. That his eyes refused to rest there for more than the fraction of an instant, may be taken – was, even then, taken by Keith Tantalus – as a hint of his recollection that after all the phenomenon wasn't to be singular. Thus the exact repetition, at the foot of Eva's bed, of the shape pendulous at the foot of his was hardly enough to account for the fixity with which he envisaged it, and for which he was to find, some years later, a motive in the (as it turned out) hardly generous fear that Eva had already made the great investigation 'on her own'. Her very regular breathing presently reassured him that, if she had peeped into 'her' stocking, she must have done so in sleep. Whether he should wake her now, or wait for their nurse to wake them both in due course, was a problem presently solved by a new development. It was plain that his sister was now watching him between her eyelashes. He had half expected that. She really was – he had often told her that she really was – magnificent; and her magnificence was never more obvious than in the pause that elapsed before she all of a sudden remarked, 'They so very indubitably are, you know!'

Max Beerbohm

Activity

1 What features of James' style are being exaggerated here? (If you have read *The Turn of the Screw*, this parody may have a familiar ring.)
2 Look at other texts you are reading where the author has a distinctive style. Analyse the details which create this style and use your findings to write your own parody.

Section III
Approaching Revision and Assessment
13 Different Types of Response

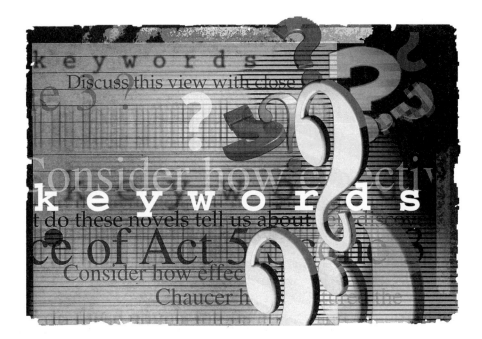

Objectives

- To understand the different question types to be found on A-level English Literature examination papers
- To think about appropriate ways of responding to these question types

Range of question types

In A-level English Literature exams various types of questions are used. These require different approaches and different kinds of responses but ultimately their objective is the same – to allow you to show to the best of your ability your knowledge, understanding, and personal response to the particular text in question.

One way in which you can prepare yourself for the exam is to be fully aware of the various kinds of questions you can be asked to respond to. Exactly what question types you will encounter on your course and in what combination will depend on the syllabus you are studying. Options do vary considerably from board to board. Here are the question types commonly found on A-level Literature papers. Find out from your teacher which of these you need to concentrate on.

- Context questions
- Generic questions
- Comparison questions
- Thematic questions
- 'Unseen' questions

Some Exam Boards offer a choice between an 'Open Book' exam and a 'Closed Text' format where you are not allowed to take the texts into the exam. All of the above question types can occur in the Open Book or the Closed Text exam. If you are studying a syllabus that offers an option, it is likely that this decision will have been made for you by your teacher, your school, or college.

We will look at the unseen question in more detail in Unit 15. Remember, though, that all exam questions are designed to test your ability to show an informed personal response and that a key element in your success will be developing the ability to read the question and understand what it is asking you to do. Whatever part of the exam you are preparing for, it is essential that you spend time looking at past papers to become familiar with the format and phrasing that are commonly used in the questions. Your teacher will probably be able to provide you with specimen and past-paper questions or you can obtain these from the examination board.

Approaching questions

When presented with any question that you have not seen before it is vital that you read it carefully and are totally clear what it is asking of you. One useful way of doing this is to identify the key words and the focus of the question. Circle or underline the key words or phrases and then jot down in a few words what the question is asking you to focus on. For example:

Shakespeare: *The Winter's Tale*
In the last scene of the play Hermione steps down from her pedestal. What is your response as Leontes, Perdita, Polixenes, and Camillo wonder at Hermione's statue and then see it come to life? Consider the language they use and how Shakespeare creates a dramatic atmosphere. What is the importance of Act 5 Scene 3 to the play as a whole?

Keywords   Your response; language; dramatic atmosphere; importance to the play as a whole.
Focus   Act 5 Scene 3; a retrospect to play

or this one:

Chaucer: *The Miller's Tale*
Lines 13–34 describe Nicholas; lines 35–47 describe the carpenter; lines 48–86 describe the carpenter's wife. How does Chaucer, through his descriptive devices in these lines, excite your anticipation for the story that is to follow?
Keywords   descriptive devices; excite; anticipation
Focus   Lines 13–86 leading to the rest of the poem
(AEB exemplars 1996)

Activity

> Now practise this technique for yourself. Look at a selection of essay questions on the texts that you have studied. You could take these from past papers or use ones supplied by your teacher. Go through them identifying clearly the key words and the focus of each. It can be useful to work in pairs on this and discuss your ideas with a partner.

Now let us have closer look at some specific question types.

Context questions

We looked at this kind of question in some detail in the Special Feature on Shakespeare in Unit 4 page 59 but context questions can be used on a whole range of other texts too. Boards vary as to just where they use context questions. It is worth remembering though that with all Open Book exams close textual analysis questions can appear anywhere.

To prepare yourself for a context question in the exam there are a number things that you need to do.

- Know the text really well. This might seem so obvious that it should not need saying but it is clear from some answers that students go into the exam still hazy about some aspects of their texts. If you want to do well you cannot afford to be unclear about any aspect of your text.
- Read the passage through carefully at least twice before you start writing. Older-style questions often asked you to 'place' the passage in context, describing where it fitted into the narrative of the text as a whole. This is rarely asked now as the emphasis is much more focused on analysis. Most students do not have a problem in identifying the passage or extract. It is, of course, worrying if you do!
- Read the questions through carefully too. Underline or circle key words just as you did with the textual questions. Make absolutely sure that you have understood every part of the question. Give each part of the question adequate coverage in your response.
- If the question requires close analysis do not confuse this with description. Examiners often comment that students include far too much woolly retelling of the 'story' in their responses rather than

specific analytical comments on language, its effects, or whatever aspect of the text that the question focuses on.

- Do not try to incorporate notes you have read or taken from elsewhere into your answer. Answer the question clearly and straightforwardly referring closely to the selected passage.
- Often the question will require you to broaden the discussion by referring to other parts of the text to reinforce the points you make. Look carefully at the wording of the question to see if you are asked to do this.

Activity

> 1 Look at some examples of context questions which are relevant to your syllabus. Examine the format and question types carefully.
> 2 Now, using a text that you have studied, select an appropriate extract and devise a set of questions using a past paper as your model.
> 3 Exchange your paper with a partner and each have a go at drafting out brief essay plans showing how you would tackle each question.
> 4 When you have finished, pass your papers back and 'mark' the work. Discuss the strengths and weaknesses of each other's questions and answers.

Thematic questions

Some exam boards offer syllabuses that involve the study of texts that are linked through a common theme. For example, it could be possible to study the theme of 'Love and Relationships' through *Jane Eyre* and *Emma* together with a third, complementary text, perhaps chosen by the centre (*Sons and Lovers* might be one suggestion).

This approach produces another style of exam question which can involve the comparison of one text with another as in this example on *Jane Eyre* and *Emma*.

> Remind yourself of Chapter 1 of *Emma*, from the section that begins with 'Mr Knightley, a sensible man about seven or eight and thirty...'
> to the end of the chapter, and of the episode in Chapter 12 (XII) of *Jane Eyre* which begins
> 'A rude noise broke out on these fine ripplings and whisperings...'
> and which ends with,
> '...it reminded me that I was late, and I hurried on.'
> Compare and contrast the ways the writers introduce Mr Knightley and Mr Rochester respectively and say how these episodes reflect what you consider to be the novels' major themes.
> (AEB 1996)

This kind of question obviously focuses you closely on particular parts of these texts, asks you to undertake a quite specific task, and then to relate the ideas you have explored to the broader idea of the novels' themes.

Other questions can be much broader as in this one:

> What do these novels have to tell us about self-discovery and love?
> (AEB 1996)

It is important to remember in this kind of question to give equal weight to both texts. A poor answer might devote a page to one text then a page to the other. A better answer might integrate comments on both texts together and give equal coverage to both. It would also be a bad idea to answer the last question by writing three sides on *Jane Eyre* without mentioning *Emma* except for a couple of brief references in the final paragraph. Keep your coverage balanced.

Sometimes a different approach is adopted where two texts are studied that are 'linked', perhaps by form, author, or period. Again the questions address both texts, as in this example using *The Duchess of Malfi* and *The Changeling*:

> 'Jacobean dramatists encourage their audience to be too fascinated by the gruesome.'
> How far does your reading of the two plays support this view?
> (NEAB)

or the Open Book paper question on the same texts:

> Look again at the opening scenes of each play. Draw out at least three ways in which the scenes echo each other and provide the reader with clues about plot development.
> (NEAB)

Generic questions

The vast majority of questions set for A-level refer to a particular text. Depending on your syllabus, though, you may encounter what are known as 'generic' questions which can be applied to whatever text you have studied rather than a particular one. This kind of question is used where a centre can choose its own text or texts for study as part of the course.

Note the wording of these examples of generic questions.

> How has the study of your Centre Chosen Text extended your understanding of the different narrative techniques employed in the writing of short stories?
> (AEB 1996)
> What methods has the writer employed to satirize the target(s) in your Centre Chosen Text?
> (AEB 1996)
> What has interested you in the way women perceive men in your Centre Chosen Text?
> (AEB 1996)
> What has particularly interested you about the representation of Black Americans in your Centre Chosen Text?
> (AEB 1996)

Obviously questions of this kind are worded so as to be applicable to whatever text has been selected. They differ from text-specific questions in several ways.

- They cannot refer you to a specific passage in a given text.
- The focus is often broader.
- You may appear to be asked to respond in a particularly personal way.

The thing to remember about generic questions is that although they may not always appear specific they are asking you quite clear things about the text. You need to know it in just as much detail as your other set texts and you need to answer with the same level of critical and analytical comment. Do not be taken in by the *apparently* general approach of questions that begin: 'What has interested you...?' An answer that simply describes part of the book and makes some general comments will not score highly. The examiner will be looking for a response to this kind of question that shows a thorough knowledge of the text revealed through analytical and well-supported comment.

'Closed Text' and 'Open Book' questions

Many syllabuses have now gone over to the 'Open Book' approach to questions and examining. We will look at this in more detail in Unit 14. However, some boards still offer 'Closed Text' exams where you are not allowed to take the books in with you. The essential difference between the two hinges on the fact that the 'Closed Text' style of question does not refer you to a particular part of the text for the good reason that you have not got the text with you in the exam. The 'Open Book' question, on the other hand, is very likely to refer you to a part of the text, or ask you to look again at a particular scene, chapter, etc. It is worth noting, though, that sometimes 'traditional' style questions can appear on 'Open Book' papers.

To exemplify these differences in approach, here are two questions on the same text. The first is a 'Closed Text' question:

Arthur Miller: *Death of a Salesman*
'Genuine tragedy, not merely social drama.'
Do you agree with this summary of *Death of a Salesman*?
(NEAB)

Here is an 'Open Book' question on the same text:

Re-read from page 42 (Penguin Edition) where Linda says to Biff 'When you write you're coming...' to Linda's speech on page 43 which ends '...nobody knows this better than me – but...'
What does this reveal about conflict and love in the family, and how does this foreshadow future events in the play?
(NEAB)

Some typical 'Closed Text' question types

Becoming familiar with the phraseology and formats that are frequently used, will help you to handle questions of different types in the exam.

Summary

Here are some examples of the more traditional question types.

- The quotation used as a springboard for the question as in:
  '*Wuthering Heights* remains a popular novel.' What particular aspects of the text make it so, in your view?
- The quotation for discussion as in:
  'Fundamentally, Marlowe is sympathetic to Faustus.' Discuss this view with close reference to the text.
- The 'Consider...' type of question as in:
  Consider how effectively Chaucer uses descriptive detail in *The Franklin's Tale*.
- The 'comparison' question as in:
  Compare the characters of Nicholas and Absolon and consider the importance of this comparison to the total effect of *The Miller's Tale*.
  (Note that this also includes a 'consider' question too – really two questions in one and you would need to deal with both parts fully.)

There are many other common ways of phrasing questions: 'To what extent...', 'Explore the ways...', 'What impression do you gain...', 'Do you think...', etc. All occur frequently.

Although these question types come under the 'traditional' heading, they can also appear within an Open Book type question. For example, the question might direct you to a passage and ask for some close analysis of it and then the second part of the question could be couched in one of the above formats.

Activity

> 1 Gather together as many questions as you can on the texts that you have studied and look carefully at the different ways in which they are worded. Draw up a table or a list to analyse the different forms that the questions take.
> 2 In note form, plan answers for as many questions as you can.

14 The Open Book Exam

Objectives	• To understand the special features of 'Open Book' questions
	• To think about ways of annotating your text
	• To consider how best to use texts in the examination and how to manage your time most effectively

Open Book issues

If you are studying a syllabus that allows texts to be taken into the exam it is worth considering how this affects the nature of the exam papers that you will be sitting. We touched on this briefly in Unit 13. Looking at some of the issues in more detail, there are a number of things that you should think about:

- 'Open Book' type questions
- The use of quotation
- Annotating texts
- Text use and time management

'Open Book' type questions

One feature of an 'Open Book' exam is that it allows Chief Examiners to set a much wider range of question types. Very often questions will direct you to a specific section or passage and will ask you about some aspect or aspects of it. These might focus on elements such as use of language, what the chosen section reveals about character, what its dramatic significance or impact might be, etc. Sometimes this kind of question will then ask you to place the passage you have examined within a broader context. For example, as in this question on *Hamlet*:

> Examine the speech of the Ghost in Act 1 Scene V which begins 'Ay, that incestuous, that adulterate beast,' and ends 'Adieu, adieu, adieu. Remember me.'

> What do you find of interest in the language used here? Go on to discuss the effect which this speech has on Hamlet, comparing his behaviour and language before his meeting with his father's ghost with the way he behaves and speaks immediately afterwards (up to the end of this scene). (AEB 1995)

You will notice that part of the focus of this question involves a detailed look at the kind of language used in the Ghost's speech but then students are asked to compare how Hamlet speaks and behaves before and after seeing his father's ghost.

This is how one second-year A-level English Literature student tackled the question. She produced her answer in one hour working under timed conditions.

Activity | Read this student's response through noting the annotations that draw attention to certain features of her work.

Sets the scene in context, perhaps a little over-long

Here the ghost of Hamlet's father has appeared for the third time on consecutive nights. Previous to this scene the ghost has not spoken, and only the guards and then Horatio have been present. However, Horatio told Hamlet of the appearance and on this third night Hamlet has accompanied the guards and Horatio. When the ghost appeared he beckoned Hamlet and this is where he speaks for the first time. The ghost reveals that since his death he has been suffering in purgatory during the day (because he did not receive absolution before his death) and that he wanders the earth at night. He also reveals and confirms Hamlet's suspicion, that he has died

Aware of the importance of this speech for the plot...

unnaturally. This marks a turning point in the plot and is also crucial in the change we see in Hamlet's character. The ghost then

...and the effect it will have on Hamlet

goes on to reveal that 'The serpent that did sting thy father's life Now wears his crown'. *Focus on the question. Quickly begins to deal with issue*

The language used by the ghost in the passage reflects the ghost's *of 'language'* feelings towards Claudius and shows Hamlet the extreme villainy and wickedness of Claudius. The ghost also refers to Claudius and Gertrude's marriage as 'incestuous' which echoes Hamlet's first

Picks up on a word that is of key significance

soliloquy and feelings. To fully expose Claudius's wicked character he tells Hamlet that Claudius 'with the witchcraft of his wit' seduced Gertrude while she was married to him. Although Hamlet's father recognizes Gertrude's guilt in the affair and is upset by her betrayal, he sees Claudius as the ultimate guilty party saying he used his witchcraft to put a spell over her and with his shameful lust he seduced her. The ghost realizes that Gertrude will suffer through her conscience for the affair 'Leave her to heaven, And to those thorns that in her bosom lodge To prick and sting her'.

Aware of the linguistic link here to the way Hamlet felt even before the appearance of the Ghost

Focus on language and effects

The language the ghost uses in describing Gertrude and Claudius's marriage reflects the disgust he feels about it. He speaks of it as 'incestuous' and that the royal bed of Denmark is now 'A couch for luxury and damned incest'. This echoes all of Hamlet's feelings seen in the previous scenes and the ghost emphasizes this point by talking about shameful lust, seduce and 'traitorous gifts'. The ghost also is very upset by Gertrude's betrayal morally and also her desertion of him, 'my most seeming virtuous Queen. What a falling off was there.'

Maintains focus on language

A little repetitive

Good specific reference to language of the text

However, the ghost's language does imply that although disappointed and hurt by Gertrude, he does not despise and hate her, he blames Claudius for all the affair. His referral to Gertrude as 'a shape of heaven', 'a radiant angel' and his contrasting reference to Claudius as 'garbage' 'adulterate beast' and as a traitor reflects his true feelings of hate for Claudius and his feelings of disappointment in Gertrude for being vulnerable enough to be seduced by the calculating Claudius.

Sustains focus on language

Good awareness of language reflecting attitude

Good point – this awareness of the contrasting attitude to Gertrude/ Claudius

Hamlet's father finally describes his death. In graphic detail he describes how Claudius poured some poison in his ear while he was asleep in the orchard and how 'The leprous distillment' affected his body and 'Thus was (he) sleeping by a brother's hand'. The ghost makes it perfectly clear that he wants Hamlet to revenge his death on Claudius but not on Gertrude.

Briefly narrative

This speech marks a crucial point where Hamlet's character changes considerably. Before this speech we see that Hamlet is deeply disturbed by his father's death. He is bitter and resentful at Claudius for taking over his father's position so quickly and at the people for accepting their new king so readily. Hamlet is also extremely grief stricken and distraught. This is shown in his first soliloquy by his fragmented language 'O God, God', 'Fie on't ah fie', 'Must I remember'. This language shows how much turmoil Hamlet feels and how distraught and alone he feels without his father. He also

Now begins to address second part of question

Addresses H's behaviour and language before meeting his father's ghost

Awareness of H's state of mind reflected in his language

now looks unfavourably on his mother, and appears cynical of all women, (Frailty, thy name is woman', because of the short space of time she has spent grieving. Just like the ghost's speech he mentions ('incestuous sheets') showing his irrational state of mind, as although closely related it is not incest, but Hamlet views it with complete disgust. As Hamlet at this point believes his father died by being poisoned by a snake, he seems more troubled by his mother's marriage and the circumstance of her marriage seems to be eating away at him more than his father's death. The isolation that Hamlet feels at this point is reflected in his soliloquy, he is very depressed and suicidal, 'Or that the Everlasting had not fixed His canon 'gainst self slaughter'. Hamlet expresses he wishes he could cease to exist. However, Hamlet's character changes after the ghost's revelations. Hamlet is more devastated and disturbed than before. His (language is fragmented again,) 'O all you host of heaven! O earth! What else' showing the deep distress and turmoil he feels. However, as well as this Hamlet displays extreme anger at Claudius and his mother (O most pernicious woman') 'damned villain' and he expresses his desire for revenge. Hamlet vows to wipe every other task from his mind and keep his mind on the ghost's 'commandment' for him to get revenge. Although Hamlet is in a more distressed and emotional state, it shows a crucial point where Hamlet forgets all thoughts of suicide and concentrates on the one thing he must obtain – revenge. Although he does not relish his task, it does give Hamlet some objective and motivation and rationalizes his state of mind so he can plan his revenge for his father's death.

The prospect of getting back at Claudius who he loathes appears to excite Hamlet as he cries 'Hillo, ho, ho, boy!'

The speech causes the turning point in Hamlet's character. Distressed, lonely and suicidal, thinking he has nothing left, because even his mother had deserted him, Hamlet is in turmoil, however, the revelations of the ghost and the task he gives him changes Hamlet's character drastically. Although still extremely upset and distressed, he becomes excited and appears anxious to start his 'commandment' – the revenge he has to exact on Claudius for his father's murder.

Louise

Margin annotations:

Attitude to his mother and the 'incestuous' link

Perceptive points

Now addresses the final part of the question

Good focus on specific detail of language

Again aware of link between language and state of mind

Good assessment of Hamlet's state of mind here

Yes, H does exhibit a kind of 'excitement'. Interesting comment with textual support

Brief summary – to the point and reflecting on the key ideas

Louise shows a great deal of insight here and a good textual grasp in her appreciation of the issues raised by the question. Her exploration of the ideas is confident and focuses well on the implications of language use and its effects using specific details to support her comments though in places these comments could be more clearly expressed. Nevertheless, she has a good overview and relates the speech effectively to what has gone before and what comes after. She rarely paraphrases and displays clear close reading skills

Activity

> 1 Choose a text that you have studied as part of your course and create a question based on that text. Your question should:
>   • refer to a specific section or passage from the text
>   • ask something quite specific which will involve looking in detail at the language used in your chosen passage
>   • require a response that relates the selected passage to another part of the text or the text as a whole
> 2 When you have finished, exchange questions with a partner and plan an answer to each other's questions. Discuss the plans you make.

Often on an exam paper you will find two questions on a set text and you will have the choice of which one to answer. Usually, one of these questions requires a detailed examination of a section of the text, while the other presents a broader topic involving a consideration of an aspect of the whole play. For example, the question paired with the previous example was this:

> Why cannot Hamlet sweep to his revenge?
> (AEB 1995)

Clearly this question is much wider in range and does not involve the same detailed examination of a passage from the play. This question addresses broader ideas and a good answer would need to be supported by close reference to the text but with references ranging widely across the whole play.

The use of quotation

The question of how much direct quotation to include in an answer is one which students often feel unsure about. In any kind of literature exam lengthy quotation is definitely not advisable. The two key points about quotation are that it should be short and it should be relevant. Only include a quotation when you use it to illustrate a comment or to act as a discussion point. It is important to choose your quotations very carefully – they should not appear to be just 'stuck in' without comment but woven in to the fabric of your writing so as to become an essential part of what you have to say.

When you have the books with you in the exam there is a danger or a temptation to over-quote to illustrate your points. Remember – time is too short to waste on simply copying out of the book. Sometimes students go into the exam having marked what they see as key quotations in their texts and seem determined to use them come what may.

Examiners also often complain that the same few quotations crop up in essay after essay from a particular centre as if students are parroting information from a common set of notes. Obviously, there will be certain quotations that are relevant to a question but it is not likely that there will only be the same three or four! Think for yourself and use the material that best suits the points that you want to make. Then you will be articulating those 'informed, independent opinions and judgements' that the objectives require.

In using quotation and textual support in the exam avoid giving the examiner some kind of instruction such as 'There is some evidence that Jane felt attracted to Rochester at this point' (see page 276) or 'You can see that this is true on page 178' or even worse 'Quote, page 71, lines 212–230'! This kind of blanket reference is of no use whatsoever and certainly will not send the examiner thumbing through the pages of the text to find the sentences you have indicated.

Very short quotations of three or four words are best worked in to the structure of your own sentence. For example:

In this soliloquy Hamlet appears deeply depressed as he considers whether it is better 'To be, or not to be...' and his mind dwells on what death might hold.

Longer quotations need setting out on a separate line but they should still be worked into the fabric of your argument to form an integrated part of it. Avoid using quotation so that it seems to be just inserted into the text of your essay and detached from the structure of your own writing, as in this example:

Hamlet thinks that people carry on even though life is painful for them because they are afraid of the unknown and what death might hold.
'But that the dread of something after death,
The undiscovered country, from whose bourn
No traveller returns, puzzles the will,
And makes us rather bear those ills we have,
Than fly to others that we know not of?'

This quotation would be more effective if it were integrated into the essay in a shortened form. As it is, it appears like a 'chunk' of text inserted with no real sense of unity with the student's own words. A more effective use of the material would be:

Hamlet thinks that people carry on even though life is painful for them because of a
'...dread of something after death,
The undiscovered country, from whose bourn
No traveller returns...'
It is this fear that '...makes us rather bear those ills we have' rather than willingly go to others that are unknown.

It is not always necessary to use direct quotation to support your ideas. 'With reference to the text' means just that and it is perfectly possible to refer to the text without quoting verbatim from it. You can explain the significance of a certain comment or draw examples from the text without using direct quotation at all. It is textual reference which supports your argument that matters, not quotation for its own sake. For example, this student makes the same point but without using direct quotation at all:

Hamlet thinks that people carry on even though life is painful for them because of the fear of what might come after death. It is this fear that drives people to continue with life no matter how hard or painful rather than go into the unknown which might be even worse.

Remember that the whole point of using quotation or textual support is to reinforce a particular point or to support close analysis: in short to add to the overall meaning or relevance of your essay. For more of the effective use of quotation see Unit 9, page 147.

Annotating texts

Annotating texts is another aspect of the 'Open Book' approach that prompts questions from students, such as: 'How much can I annotate the text?'; 'What kind of things should I write?'; 'What should I leave out?'

How much annotation can be done and what is allowed and what is not allowed is always described in exam-board syllabuses. One thing that annotations should not consist of is notes that you have filled your text with in the few weeks prior to the exam. They are meant to be notes written in the course of your exploration of the text (as shown in Unit 7). They are a part of your learning process, not information copied in the hope of it helping you to write exam essays. Annotation of texts is policed rigorously by the exam boards and by the invigilators in the exam. It is highly likely that an invigilator will want to look through your text prior to the start of the exam to check that your copy complies with the regulations. It is worth checking beforehand that you have removed any material that might not be allowed. You can do without running into problems minutes before the start of the exam!

Here is one Exam Board's instructions regarding text annotation:

> 'Candidates may take annotated editions of their set texts into these examinations. 'Annotated' refers to editorial material or textual commentary published in the editions studied and to handwritten marginal notes. Publications such as 'pass notes' or 'study guides' which do not provide the complete texts as prescribed are excluded, and no supplementary material may be taken into the examination. 'Handwritten marginal notes' may include notes written on blank pages in the editions studied, but they exclude the insertion of any additional material such as cards or markers or supplementary sheets. Candidates may take into the examination only one edition of each prescribed text studied.'
> (ULEAC)

Although this is the general pattern adopted by most boards, each board issues its own guidelines. It is worth consulting the specific instructions for the syllabus that you are studying. Seek advice from your teacher or obtain a copy of the syllabus and check it yourself.

But let us give some thought as to why you are allowed to annotate at all. Why is it considered a useful thing to do? The whole purpose of annotating a text is to help you to develop an understanding of it and to remember certain details or record responses as you work through it. It may well be that by the time you get to the exam much of what you wrote in your text, perhaps twelve or eighteen months before, will be redundant as you will have developed a deeper, more secure understanding of it. For example, all those notes you made explaining tricky lines and references when you were in the early stages of your study of a Shakespeare text will no longer be needed. Nor will that 'translation' that you wrote in your copy of Chaucer when you were first grappling with the language. By the end of the course you will probably be reading the original as fluently as if it were in modern English, and even if you do forget an individual word there is always the glossary to refer to. All these notes, which were of great use to you earlier in your studies, will no longer be needed. In fact it can be useful to rub out such original jottings and to 'clean the text up' before the exam – the last thing you need is a copy that is so cluttered with jottings that the text itself is obscured.

Here is an example of a student's preliminary annotations on Hamlet's first soliloquy. By the end of the course many of these notes would not be needed but here the student is coming to terms with the text in the early days of study.

Activity | Read the extract and its annotations. Decide which notes the student might 'rub out' prior to the exam.

Act I, Scene 2

Shows how desperate and depressed he is

Hamlet: O that this too too sullied flesh would melt,   *Flesh melts into nothing*

Thaw and resolve itself into a dew,

Wishes God had not made it a sin to commit —— Or that the Everlasting had not fix'd
suicide. Ref. to death

His cannon 'gainst self-slaughter. O God! God!   *Now I wish that suicide were not against the law of God*

View of world —— How weary, stale, flat, and unprofitable
– empty

Seem to me all the uses of this world!   *Nothing in this world seems any good*

Fie on't, ah fie, 'tis an unweeded garden   *Metaphor of the world being an unweeded garden*

That grows to seed; things rank and gross in nature

Posses it merely. That it should come to this!

✱ But two months dead – nay not so much, not two –   *Death of his father*

So excellent a king, that was to this   *Shows his father with good characteristics*

World unnatural   Hyperion to a satyr, so loving to my mother,
     Highly unnatural – half-man, half-god known for their sexual excesses
That he might not beteem the winds of heaven

Visit her face too roughly. Heaven and earth,   *Emphasizes the pain he feels*

Tortures him to remember his father and mother together

Must I remember? Why, she would hang on him   Unfavourable vision of mother

As if increase of appetite had grown

By what it fed on, and yet within a month –   Losing track of time – not thinking rationally – the more he thinks about it, the shorter the timescale becomes

Thinks unhighly of women

Let me not think on't – Frailty thy name is woman –

A little month or ere those shoes were old

With which she followed my poor father's body,

How he views his mother changes his perception of women

So many tears – everyone believed she'd never get over the death

Like Niobe all tears – why she, even she –

O God, a beast that wants discourse of reason

Sentences short, broken – have lots of exclamation marks – show a fragmented mind in turmoil

Would have mourned longer – married with my uncle,

His uncle is nothing like his father

My father's brother – but no more like my father

Than I to Hercules. Within a month,   Mentions the short space of time after his father's death – his mother married

Ere yet the salt of most unrighteous tears

Had left the flushing in her galled eyes,

His mother's marriage seems to bother him more than his father's death

Again mentions the speedy marriage of his mother and uncle

She married – O most wicked speed! To post

With such dexterity to incestuous sheets!   Sexual connotations of the relationship between his mother and uncle – almost incestuous

It is not, nor it cannot come to good,

But break, my heart, for I must hold my tongue.

Avoid cramming your text with last-minute annotations in the build-up to the exam – these will not help you. The same goes for copying chunks of prepared notes or mini essay plans into your text. Not only will they be of no help whatsoever to you in writing your answer, it is also against the regulations of the exam. It is immediately obvious to an examiner if the 'voice' of an essay is your own genuine 'voice' or if it has been 'borrowed' from a critical commentary. It is also clear if chunks or phrases taken from the Introduction of the text are used. Such discrepancies of 'voice' are always evident.

One useful way of keeping your text fairly uncluttered while at the same time being able to find the part that you want quickly is to use a system of colour-coding. Using this system you can underline or sideline references relating to different themes, topics, characters, and so on in different colours. As long as you know what the colour signifies and you do not overdo it, it can really help you to find your way around the text quickly. This can be a useful activity to carry out in the revision period.

To sum up approaches to and preparation for an 'Open Book' exam here are some points that you might find useful.

Summary Preparing the text for the exam

- Make sure that you know the 'rules' of your syllabus with regard to what you are and are not allowed to write in your text.
- Use annotations when you want to remember or note a specific point.
- Rub out annotations that are no longer needed.
- Do not put notes in your text just because you feel you must – only write something in your book if you think you really need to.
- Do not copy out chunks (or even bits) of prepared notes into your text.
- Practise doing 'Open Book' type questions as much as possible. As with any kind of examination, what is crucially important is the focus of the writing. There is no room for general introductions to the text which have no bearing on the question or for unfocused and vague comments. The question must be addressed directly and clearly.

In the exam

- Do not spend too much time looking at the text. In fact, one of the big dangers in having the books with you in the exam is that you will be tempted to spend too much time sifting through them for the bits of information that you want. When you have only forty-five minutes or so to write your answer, you do not have very much time to spend rereading the book!
- Do not use over-long quotations from the text in your answer.
- Do not use page number references in your exam answers (although in preparation essays these can be useful when it comes time to revise).
- Do not reproduce any material from your text's introduction or preface. Examiners are familiar with this material and it does not help you to produce your response anyway.
- One common fallacy about the 'Open Book' approach is that because you have the texts with you in the exam it is not so vital to have a very detailed knowledge of them. After all, so the thinking goes, you can always look up any details you might be a bit hazy about. This could not be further from the truth. You need to be so familiar with your text that you can find what you are looking for immediately without wasting valuable time flicking through the pages to find that one elusive quotation or piece of information.

15 Preparing for the Unseen

Objectives

- To consider the features of the unseen question
- To practise the skills involved in tackling unseen questions and compare your work with an annotated student response
- To discuss and write about your own responses to a variety of texts

Being prepared

In considering what you can do to help prepare for the unseen, it is useful to begin by reflecting on the whole purpose of this part of the literature exam. You will remember those core Assessment Objectives, discussed in Unit 1 (page 3). Think for a moment about which ones are tested in the unseen.

In fact, most of the following objectives are tested:

- to respond with knowledge and understanding to literary texts of different types and periods
- to communicate clearly the knowledge, understanding, and insight appropriate to literary study, using appropriate terminology and accurate written expression
- to show detailed understanding of the ways in which writers' choices of form, structure, and language shape meanings
- to articulate informed, independent opinions and judgements, showing understanding of different interpretations of literary texts

Some misconceptions

Many students feel that the unseen is the most difficult element of the A-level Literature exam to prepare for. Their argument runs: 'You can't revise for it in the same way as you can revise a text because the material that you will be asked to write about is unknown'. It is often felt that tackling the paper requires some kind of special 'literary skill' that is difficult to acquire. Indeed terms like 'Practical Criticism' or 'Critical Appreciation' can reinforce this sense that here you are dealing with something difficult to understand and very specialized.

Of course, 'criticism' or 'critical' in a literary context does not mean 'finding fault with'. It is an academic activity involving analysis, interpretation, and evaluation. If you stop and think about it, that is exactly what you have been doing in the rest of your English course, isn't it? The skills, the techniques, the whole approach to analysing and responding to literary texts that you have been applying throughout your studies are exactly the same as those that you will draw upon to respond to the unseen paper. Unseen questions should be viewed as a part of an integrated course in which the skills of literary analysis all support one another, rather than something detached from textual study. In fact, many students respond extremely well to the challenges presented by the unseen elements of their examinations and enjoy the variety of texts which they meet.

However, as you will know if you have worked through Unit 10, there are differences between writing in response to an unseen passage and writing about a text that you have studied over a period of time. For one thing, the task in the unseen is more sharply focused on you showing your under-standing of how a piece of literature actually works and on applying some of the techniques of literary critical appreciation whereas a question on a set text asks for that but may well demand a whole range of other things too.

Back to that key question then – 'How best can you prepare yourself for the unseen paper?'. To answer this let us look at the particular features that students who do well on this paper exhibit in their work. These include:

- having a solid level of background reading of a whole range of literature. This is not usually explicit in students' answers because the questions are not devised to show background reading. It often comes through implicitly, but clearly, when a student has read widely. Throughout the course of your studies you will have been gaining this invaluable experience of encountering literary texts of all kinds and it should stand you in good stead. Those students who achieve the higher grade levels are invariably those who have read well beyond the texts prescribed by the syllabus.
- having some familiarity with the techniques of literary critical appreciation.
  This does not mean learning by heart a whole battery of critical terms or a rigid formula which can be applied to whatever text you encounter.

Rather it is an awareness that texts consist of language and that writers have used this in a particular way to achieve particular effects. The ability to describe these and the means by which they are created is essential.

- recognizing that every text is individual and that there is not a 'correct' view of what a text is about but that subjective views alone are not valid. Successful students show individual and fresh responses that are firmly rooted in the text and supported by clear and detailed textual reference.

The content of the unseen paper can vary a good deal and is not necessarily restricted to a poem and a passage from a novel. Some syllabuses are clear to point out that a wide range of text types can be drawn upon including poetry, prose, drama and extracts from literary criticism, journalism, essays, and autobiography.

Just as the material itself can vary, so can the kind of questions that you are asked. You might be asked to 'write a commentary' focusing on particular aspects of the poem or extract:

> The following passage comes from Thackeray's *Vanity Fair* (1847).
> Write a commentary on it, examining in particular the author's handling of character and his control of the narrative.
> (UCLES)

Alternatively you might be asked to 'explore' a text:

> John Mortimer's play *A Voyage Round my Father* was first performed in 1970.
> Explore the dramatic presentation and effect of this passage from the play, commenting on any technical features (stage directions, for example) that seem to you significant.
> (UCLES)

Some questions make use of two passages or poems and want you to compare them in some way. In the following question students were given Thomas Hardy's *Neutral Tones* and Carol Ann Duffy's *Disgrace*:

> Explore the similarities and the differences in the ways Hardy and Duffy present the breakdown of a relationship in the two poems which follow.
> (AEB exemplars 1996)

An interesting variation to this approach is seen in a specimen question in which students were given a poem by Edward Thomas and then the prose notes on which he had based the poem:

> Passage a) is a poem by Edward Thomas (1878–1917), and passage b) presents the prose notes on which the poem is based.
> Read the passages carefully, and then:
> Write an appreciation of *Old Man* [poem a)]. You may if you wish comment on the way Thomas has incorporated his earlier notes [passage b)] into the poem.
> (UCLES)

Another approach is that which helps you to structure your response by giving a number of bullet points that you might wish to consider. The activity relating to *The Pedestrian* on page 228 is an example of this kind of question.

In Section II, you concentrated on developing your critical skills and the language of criticism. Unit 10 gave you some experience of the kinds of texts set for practical criticism. To prepare for the unseen examination you need to build on these skills and practise your strategies for handling this kind of question. Here are some points that might help you to do this.

Summary

- Begin by carefully looking at what the question(s) asks you to do and identify and highlight the key words and phrases.
- Read the piece through carefully at least twice.
- If you do not understand certain words or phrases or parts of the piece, concentrate on the rest of the text – do not get bogged down on individual words or phrases.
- Remember that whatever the poem or passage you encounter there will be many different aspects of it to comment on. (For a reminder of these see Unit 10, page 160.)
- Look for any useful information you are given about the piece, such as when it was written, who wrote it, etc.
- Do not concentrate all your efforts on content. The examiner will be much more interested in your comments on how the piece is written and the ways in which the writer has used language to create the intended effects.

Activity

> Try the following unseen question allowing yourself an hour to work under timed exam conditions.
>
> Compare and contrast poems 1 and 2, bringing out their similarities and differences.

1

Since there's no help, come let us kiss and part;
Nay, I have done, you get no more of me;
And I am glad, yea glad with all my heart
That thus so cleanly I myself can free;
Shake hands forever, cancel all our vows,
And when we meet at any time again,
Be it not seen in either of our brows
That we one jot of former love retain.
Now at the last gasp of love's latest breath,
When, his pulse failing, passion speechless lies,

When faith is kneeling by his bed of death,
And innocence is closing up his eyes;
Now if thou would'st, when all have given him over,
From death to life thou might'st him yet recover.

Michael Drayton, 1563–1631

2
Mark where the pressing wind shoots javelin-like,
Its skeleton shadow on the broad-backed wave!
Here is a fitting spot to dig Love's grave;
Here where the ponderous breakers plunge and strike,
And dart their hissing tongues high up the sand:
In hearing of the ocean, and in sight
Of those ribbed wind-streaks running into white.
If I the death of Love had deeply planned,
I never could have made it half so sure,
As by the unblest kisses which upbraid
The full-waked sense; or failing that, degrade!
'Tis morning; but no morning can restore
What we have forfeited. I see no sin:
The wrong is mixed. In tragic life, God wot,
No villain need be! Passions spin the plot:
We are betrayed by what is false within.

George Meredith, 1828–1909

Activity	1 With a partner, exchange your responses and read each other's work carefully, making notes on any comments or points that strike you about the response. When you have finished, discuss your ideas together. 2 Now compare your work with this example from a second-year A-level student.

The two poems by Michael Drayton and George Meredith initially appear to have the same central image. Both poets depict the failure of a relationship. The presentation of this image, however, is entirely different. Whilst Drayton portrays the loss of a love as something simple but not irreversible, Meredith shows the failure of a relationship as something dramatic and inevitable.

It is the similarity between the subject of these two poems, however, that immediately strikes the reader. Both poets emphasize that the central theme in their poems is lost love. They achieve this through their use of imagery. In both pieces the concept of love is personified and described as dying. Drayton refers to, 'The last gasp of love's latest breath,' Meredith describes, 'The death of Love' and 'Love's grave'.

This conventional theme is reflected in both pieces by their conventional structure. Drayton's poem adheres to the form of an English sonnet. The rhythm of his writing is dictated by this, he uses fourteen lines all with ten syllables. His rhyme scheme also follows a strict pattern. There are three sections which rhyme abab cdcd efef and it ends on a rhyming couplet. Meredith's poem is also based around a strict structure. His rhythm is regular and measured and there are ten syllables in every line. Similarly his rhyme scheme is very regular, the poem is divided into four sections which rhyme abba cddc effe ghhg.

The difference in the way that this conventional theme is presented, however, is also very striking. The reader is clearly shown that Drayton sees the loss of a love as something sad but common, whilst Meredith views the break up of a relationship as something momentous. This difference is highlighted through the opposing tones used by the poets. Drayton illustrates that to lose love is an everyday happening by using on ordinary down-to-earth tone. His language is simple almost conversational,

'Since there's no help come let us kiss and part.'

Meredith shows that he sees such and event as a traumatic occasion by using a very dramatic tone. Much of his language is greatly exaggerated, 'It's a skeleton shadow on the broad-backed wave!'

This difference in the presentation of their common theme is also reflected in the poets' use of imagery. Drayton depicts the ending of his relationship as a clean break. Much of his imagery suggest he is breaking free from some kind of restriction, 'I myself can free,' 'you get no more of me.' Drayton's use of language also illustrates that this is an amicable break. He repeats the word 'glad' giving it added impact, 'And I am glad, yea glad with all my heart'. Drayton also uses imagery of 'shaking hands' and 'kissing' which symbolizes the idea of a friendly parting.

Meredith's imagery, however, portrays the loss of love as a highly dramatic event. He uses extremely exaggerated imagery to emphasize that to lose love is very painful. Meredith constantly juxtaposes the seemingly opposing concepts of love and death, 'To dig Love's grave'. This poet also uses imagery of nature to reflect the trauma of a failed relationship. The weather, for example, is described as very tempetuous, 'The pressing wind shoots javelin like, Its skeleton shadow'. This simile comparing the wind to a javelin clearly illustrates how the wind seems to cut through the air. The sea is personified to illustrate the wild movement of the water, 'Ponderous breakers plunge and strike'. The waves are even compared to snakes which 'Dart their hissing tongues high up the sand'. These techniques highlight the difference in the way the two poets present the theme of a broken relationship. From Drayton the reader is given the impression that this is a 'normal' simple occurence; from Meredith he learns that this is a monumental and dramatic event.

The other major difference between these poems is the poets' viewpoint towards their conventional theme. Drayton clearly believes that a failed relationship can be healed, Meredith sees the loss of love as something inevitable over which man has little control. The poets' use of language conveys their respective viewpoints. Drayton personifies a failed relationship as a dying patient that can be revived, 'From death to life thou mightst him yet recover'. He uses poignant imagery to suggest that love is something worth preserving, 'faith is kneeling by his bed of death, And innocence is closing his eyes'.

Meredith's language clearly emphasizes that man's reason has little control over love. He uses the idea of original evil to suggest that it is no one's fault that love has died, 'I see no sin... No villain need be'. Meredith then suggests that it is man's emotions that dictate the course of love. He illustrates this through his personification of feelings, 'Passions spin the plot. We are betrayed by what is false within'.

These two poems, therefore, have very little similarity beyond their conventional theme. The poets attempt to show this subject in entirely different lights.

Drayton's success means that the reader leaves his poem feeling that the break up of a relationship is something sad but not irreparable.

The effectiveness of Meredith's poem means that the reader is impressed by the trauma of love but also by the fact that it is beyond the control of man's reason.

Suzanne

Here are an examiner's comments on this response.

Although this response does have some flaws, overall its strengths far outweigh its weaknesses. Suzanne addresses the question directly from the outset. She has been asked to 'compare and contrast' the poems and begins by noting that they both *appear* to have the same central image. Her use of this word indicates that she is aware from the outset that there are significant differences between them. This opening paragraph, which addresses the question directly, shows that she has read both poems carefully before beginning to write and that she is aware of an essential difference between them.

In the second paragraph, she returns to the similarities between the two and elaborates on these covering a range of points – the common theme, their use of imagery, their description of love – which she supports with appropriate textual references.

She moves on in the third paragraph to consider their similarities of structure and has recognized that Drayton's poem is, in fact, a sonnet. She then becomes a little bogged down in counting syllables per line and noting down the rhyme scheme. This is the weakest part of her answer; she is writing what she thinks (wrongly) the examiner wants to hear. She has obviously learned how to do this kind of technical analysis but unfortunately does not go on to describe what effect the features have on the poem and on the reader. Instead she proceeds to apply the same approach to Meredith's poem. This paragraph is a wasted opportunity. Suzanne is clearly aware of the 'mechanics' of how the poems are structured but she does not apply that knowledge – she merely states it.

She moves on to surer ground, though, in the fourth paragraph as she returns to theme and shows that she is sensitive to the differences in the ways in which the two poems present their themes. She explores this idea again using appropriate references to the texts.

Next she discusses how the differences between them are also reflected in the poets' uses of imagery, again with supporting references. She handles this clearly by devoting a paragraph to Drayton's use of imagery followed by a paragraph on Meredith's. Within this discussion she refers to the use of similes and personification, not only showing that she knows the terms and can recognize the features but more importantly that she understands the effects they create within the poems.

Paragraphs six and seven then move on to use the idea of theme to explore an essential difference between the viewpoints of the two poets. The ideas here are again backed up well with textual references and Suzanne makes some interesting comments on the effects of Drayton's use of personification and Meredith's use of the idea of original evil and the personification of his feelings.

In her final paragraph Suzanne draws her argument to a conclusion and restates her view that although the poems have a surface similarity in that they share a common theme, in fact they present this theme in entirely different lights.

The strengths and weaknesses in Suzanne's response can be summarized as follows:

Strengths
- Keeps a tight focus on the question throughout
- Well-structured for a timed piece, each point is given a measured response
- Shows sensitive awareness to how effects are created and their impact on the reader
- Supports her ideas with well-chosen close reference to the texts
- Gives a strong sense of her own voice and informed views about the texts

Weaknesses
- Gets bogged down in technical features of the poems without describing their contribution to the poetry as a whole
- Does not comment fully enough on the effects of the poet's use of language
- Does not weave quotations into fabric of essay very effectively
- Has not allowed time to check answer for technical accuracy – e.g. spellings of poet's names, verb agreements, other spellings (tempestuous)

Activity

> The passage below is a short story by Ray Bradbury, an American writer known chiefly for his work in science fiction. The story was published in 1977 and is set in the world of 2053 AD
>
> Read the story carefully and then write a critical analysis of it. You might consider such things as:
> - the personality and attitudes of Leonard Mead
> - the society in which Mead lives and the writer's attitude towards it

> - the atmosphere established, showing how this is created and controlled
> - the style in which the passage is written, referring as appropriate to details of the story
>
> (NEAB)

The Pedestrian

To enter out into that silence that was the city at eight o' clock of a misty evening in November, to put your feet upon that concrete walk, to step over grassy seams and make your way, hands in pockets, through the silences, that was what Mr Leonard Mead most dearly loved to do. He would stand upon the corner of an intersection and peer down moonlit avenues of sidewalk in four directions, deciding which way to go, but it really made no difference; he was alone in this world of 2053 AD, or as good as alone, and with a final decision made, a path selected, he would stride off, sending patterns of frosty air before him like the smoke of a cigar.

On this particular evening he began his journey in a westerly direction, toward the hidden sea. There was a good crystal frost in the air; it cut the nose and made the lungs blaze like a Christmas tree inside; you could feel the cold light going on and off, all the branches filled with invisible snow. He listened to the faint push of his soft shoes through autumn leaves with satisfaction, and whistled a cold quiet whistle between his teeth, occasionally picking up a leaf as he passed, examining its skeletal pattern in the infrequent lamplights as he went on, smelling its rusty smell.

'Hello, in there,' he whispered to every house on every side as he moved. 'What's up tonight on Channel four, Channel seven, Channel nine? Where are the cowboys rushing, and do I see the United States Cavalry over the next hill to the rescue?'

The street was silent and long and empty, with only his shadow moving like the shadow of a hawk in mid-country. If he closed his eyes and stood very still, frozen, he could imagine himself upon the centre of a plain, a wintry, windless Arizona desert with no house in a thousand miles, and only dry river beds, the streets for company.

'What time is it now?' he asked the houses, noticing his wrist watch. 'Eight-thirty P.M.? Time for a dozen assorted murders? A quiz? A revue? A comedian falling off the stage?'

Was that a murmur of laughter from within a moonwhite house? He hesitated, but went on when nothing more happened. He stumbled over a particularly uneven section of sidewalk. The cement was vanishing under flowers and grass. In ten years of walking by night or day, for thousands of miles, he had never met another person walking, not one in all that time.

He came to a cloverleaf intersection which stood silent where two main highways crossed the town. During the day it was a thunderous surge of cars, the gas stations open, a great insect rustling and a ceaseless jockeying for position as the scarab-beetles, a faint incense puttering from their exhausts, skimmed homeward to the far directions. But now these highways, too, were like streams in a dry season, all stone and bed and moon radiance.

He turned back on a side street, circling around toward his home. He was within a block of his destination when the lone car turned a corner quite suddenly and flashed a fierce white cone of light upon him. He stood entranced, not unlike a night moth, stunned by the illumination, and then drawn toward it.

A metallic voice called to him:

'Stand still. Stay where you are! Don't move!'

He halted.

'Put up your hands!'

'But –' he said.

'Your hands up! Or we'll shoot!'

The police, of course, but what a rare, incredible thing; in a city of three million, there was only one police car left, wasn't that correct? Ever since a year ago, 2052, the election year, the force had been cut down from three cars to one. Crime was ebbing; there was no need now for the police, save for this one lone car wandering and wandering the empty streets.

'Your name?' said the police car in a metallic whisper. He couldn't see the men in it for the bright light in his eyes.

'Leonard Mead,' he said.

'Speak up!'

'Leonard Mead!'

'Business or profession?'

'I guess you'd call me a writer.'

'No profession,' said the police car, as if talking to itself. The light held him fixed, like a museum specimen, needle thrust through chest.

'You might say that,' said Mr Mead. He hadn't written in years. Magazines and books didn't sell any more. Everything went on in the tomb-like houses at night now, he thought, continuing his fancy. The tombs, ill-lit by television light, where the people sat like the dead, the grey or multi-coloured lights touching their faces, but never really touching them.

'No profession,' said the phonograph voice, hissing. 'What are you doing out?'

'Walking,' said Leonard Mead.

'Walking!'

'Just walking,' he said simply, but his face felt cold.

'Walking, just walking, walking?'

'Yes, sir.'

'Walking where? For what?'

'Walking for air. Walking to see.'

'Your address!'

'Eleven South Saint James Street.'

'And there is air in your house, you have an air conditioner, Mr Mead?'

'Yes.'

'And you have a viewing screen in your house to see with?'

'No.'

'No?' There was a crackling quiet that in itself was an accusation.

'Are you married, Mr Mead?'

'No.'

'Not married,' said the police voice behind the fiery beam. The moon was high and clear among the stars and the houses were grey and silent.

'Nobody wanted me,' said Leonard Mead with a smile.

'Don't speak unless you're spoken to!'

Leonard Mead waited in the cold night.

'Just walking, Mr Mead?'

'Yes.'

'But you haven't explained for what purpose.'

'I explained; for air, and to see, and just to walk.'

'Have you done this often?'

'Every night for years.'

The police car sat in the centre of the street with its radio throat faintly humming.

'Well, Mr Mead,' it said.

'Is that all?' he asked politely.

'Yes,' said the voice. 'Here.' There was a sigh, a pop. The back door of the police car sprang wide. 'Get in.'

'Wait a minute, I haven't done anything!'

'Get in.'

'I protest!'

'Mr Mead.'

He walked like a man suddenly drunk. As he passed the front window of the car he looked in. As he had expected, there was no one in the front seat, no one in the car at all.

'Get in.'

He put his hand to the door and peered into the back seat, which was a little cell, a little black jail with bars. It smelled of riveted steel. It smelled of harsh antiseptic; it smelled too clean and hard and metallic. There was nothing soft there.

'Now if you had a wife to give you an alibi,' said the iron voice. 'But –'

'Where are you taking me?'

The car hesitated, or rather gave a faint whirring click, as if information, somewhere, was dropping card by punch-slotted card under electric eyes. 'To the Psychiatric Centre for Research on Regressive Tendencies.'

He got in. The door shut with a soft thud. The police car rolled through the night avenues, flashing its dim lights ahead.

They passed one house on one street a moment later, one house in the entire city of houses that were dark, but this one particular house had all of its electric lights brightly lit, every window a loud yellow illumination, square and warm in the cool darkness.

'That's my house,' said Leonard Mead.

No one answered him.

The car moved down the empty river-bed streets and off away, leaving the empty streets with the side-walks, and no sound and no motion all the rest of the chill November night.

Ray Bradbury

Activity

With a partner, exchange your responses and read each other's work carefully. Make a note of your comments on the response. When you have finished, discuss your ideas together.

Summary

Here are some final reminders about the unseen.

- Read all the material including the questions very carefully several times.
- If it is suggested that you discuss areas, such as theme, mood, tone, imagery, diction, rhythm etc., make sure you do address each point given.
- Do not give a line-by-line paraphrase of the poem or passage.
- Do not rush in to answering before you have absorbed the material.
- Make a range of well-thought-out points and support them with appropriate textual references.
- Avoid discussing technique without reference to the effect(s) that it creates.

16 Revising Set Texts

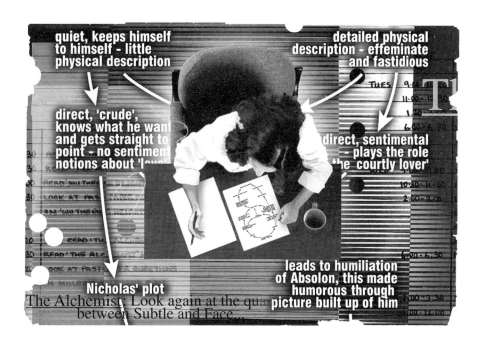

quiet, keeps himself to himself - little physical description

detailed physical description - effeminate and fastidious

direct, 'crude', knows what he want and gets straight to point - no sentimen notions about 'love'

direct, sentimental - plays the role the courtly lover'

Nicholas' plot

leads to humiliation of Absolon, this made humorous through picture built up of him

The Alchemist: Look again at the qua between Subtle and Face.

Objectives

- To plan the revision of your set texts
- To consider approaches to essay planning and working under timed conditions

A key role

Set texts obviously play a key role in your final assessment for the A-level course and it is essential that you revise them very carefully in readiness for the exam. Exactly how many texts you have studied will depend on the particular syllabus that you are following but a total of eight is typical. Your grade will depend on the quality and effectiveness of this preparation and so it is well worth planning how you intend to revise your set texts in good time. This is not a matter that you should put off until the last minute; hasty, inadequate revision could well damage your chances of getting the grade that you want. Students who do well will show an independence of mind which reveals the ability to think for themselves and to think under the pressure of exam conditions. Revision is key to these skills.

Now let us have a look at some of the things that you can do to help revise your set texts and prepare yourself for the exam.

Reading, rereading, and rereading again

By this stage you will, no doubt, have read your texts a number of times. This reading and re-reading of the texts is essential to the development of your understanding and appreciation of them.

However, different kinds of reading are appropriate depending on what your objective in doing the reading is. You may read the text quickly before you start to study it in detail. The next time you read it you will probably read it quite slowly and carefully so as to follow the plot carefully, to examine the ways in which the characters emerge, and to get used to the style and language used. Subsequent reads will be different again. You may skim through the text to quickly refresh your memory of the whole thing or you may scan the text looking for particular references to images or ideas. These various readings are extremely important for a number of reasons:

- They help you to become very familiar with the text, not just in terms of the plot (although some books do need to be read several times just to sort out what is happening) but also in terms of picking up on the details of the text. Most texts chosen for A-level are very complex and every time you read them you notice something new, something that you had not picked up the first, second, or even third time round.
- You tend to come to an understanding of a text over a period of time. You do not just read it, understand it, and that is that, you are ready for the exam. The kinds of texts that you will have encountered in your A-level studies need thinking about. You need to allow yourself this thinking time in order to reflect on what you have read, to absorb the material, and then return to it again.

Obviously this kind of reading is part of a developmental process which enhances your knowledge and understanding of your set texts and, therefore, it needs to be planned for over a period of time.

Time management

Time is a crucial factor in your revision programme. Building time into your programme for sufficient practice on a variety of tasks is vital. To make sure that you do this, it is advisable to draw up a revision programme to cover the build-up to the final exams. This can be quite loose in the initial stages but the closer you get to the exams, the tighter it needs to be. Make sure that you cover every aspect of assessment that you need to. Here are some basic principles to think about when drawing up your revision programme.

- Be realistic – do not overestimate how much you can get through in a given time. It is far better to start your revision programme earlier than to try to cram everything in at the last minute.
- Make sure that your programme gives the necessary attention to every text. Do not rely on the 'I know that one well enough so I needn't revise

it' approach. Often, when you come to revise a text that you studied months before you remember things about it that you had forgotten or that had become hazy.

- Create a balance between revision activities which are reading based and those which involve writing tasks. For example, the various reading activities mentioned on page 234 and those involving written responses, such as practice on past papers, timed essays, essay planning etc. dealt with in the rest of this unit.
- Build in to your programme some 'time off' to relax. You will not work at your best if you spend all your time studying. Revision is best done with a fresh mind and in relatively short sessions with breaks. You can only take in so much at one sitting. One to two hours at a stretch is enough.

The form that your revision programme takes is up to you. This is part of the revision programme of a student who has already taken Paper 1 of the examination on a Monday and has one week before sitting Paper 2. Her texts for Paper 2 are *The Miller's Tale*, *Hamlet*, *The Alchemist*, and *Wuthering Heights*. This revision programme covers the week between the two papers.

DAY	TIME	TASK
TUESDAY	9.00–10.30	Re-read The Miller's Tale
	11.00–12.30	Read The Miller's Tale notes.
	1.30–3.00	Read Wuthering Heights notes.
	6.00–6.30	Look at past-paper questions on WH.
WEDNESDAY	9.00–10.00	Skim read The Alchemist.
	10.30–11.30	Read The Alchemist notes.
	2.00–3.00	Look at past-paper questions on MT and plan answers on two or three not already done.
	6.00–6.30	Look at some past-paper questions on The Alchemist
THURSDAY	2.00–3.30	Skim read Wuthering Heights.
	6.00–7.00	Read notes on character and theme in Hamlet.
FRIDAY	9.00–10.30	Read Hamlet again.
	11.00–12.00	Read remainder of notes on Hamlet.
	2.00–4.30	Watch video of Hamlet (BBC Shakespeare).
SATURDAY	DAY OFF	
SUNDAY	2.00–2.30	Look at past questions on Hamlet and plan answers
	2.30–3.30	Listen to tape of The Miller's Tale being read.
	4.00–5.00	Look over notes on The Alchemist.

You will have noticed that the student has arranged her time in manageable blocks (an hour-and-a-half at a stretch seems a reasonable maximum) and she has also worked into her programme 'time off' which is important too. She varies her activities so that her revision does not consist simply of reading but writing, listening, and watching too and she allows time to think about questions and ideas. She has given over slightly more time to the revision of *Hamlet* as this is the text she feels least secure on. It is important to keep a good balance between texts though. Even if you feel you know a text really well, do not skimp on the revision of it.

Remember, though, that a revision programme will need to be flexible in order to cater for the unexpected. Also, beware of wasting too much valuable revision time trying to create the 'perfect programme'.

Activity

> Try planning out a short revision programme for yourself lasting a week. If you are approaching your 'mock' or end-of-year examinations you could make the programme a little longer and actually use it to provide some structure to your revision.

Past-paper questions

As part of your revision programme, try to look at as many questions from past papers as you can. The value of this lies in giving you the flavour of the questions types that Chief Examiners set. Certainly, looking at past-paper questions on your texts will show you a range of topics that questions have focused on in the past and sometimes similar questions do appear again. However, do not learn 'model' answers and hope to be able to use these in the exam. If you come across specimen or model answers, regard them critically and as one possible way of answering but do not take them to be the definitive answer. Remember, in the exam you will be expected to respond using your own ideas and thoughts and examiners can spot immediately if you are parroting a 'model' answer you have learned.

Activity

> Gather as many questions as you can on the texts that you have studied. Draft out a rough essay plan for each of these questions. (Do not spend more than two or three minutes on each plan.)

As well as giving you ideas of the types of things that have been asked about before, looking at past-paper questions will also give you a clear idea of how questions can be worded and the style in which they are presented. (Refer back to Unit 13, pages 204–210 to remind yourself of some of the variations you could encounter.) The more you know in this respect, the less likely you are to be thrown by question phrasing or terminology. Looking at past papers can also show up gaps in your knowledge of a set text and allow you to remedy them.

Timed essays

As we have already mentioned, one of the main worries that students have in terms of answering on their set texts is how they are going to get all their ideas down in forty-five minutes. Certainly one of the most common problems students encounter in A-level English Literature exams is running out of time. Often this is due to too much time being spent on one question in particular (usually the first one) and so not allowing enough time to deal adequately with the rest of the questions. Sometimes the problem can be cumulative. For example, if you have three hours to answer four questions and you spend an hour on question one and fifty minutes on the next two that will leave you precisely twenty minutes to answer the final question. Running over by a few minutes on each question may not seem too bad but the cumulative effect can be disastrous.

For this reason it is extremely important that you get a good deal of practice writing under timed conditions. You will, no doubt, do some timed pieces in class but there is no reason why you should not practise them at home as well. All you need are some suitable questions, a quiet place, and some time. In one sense it does not even matter if the work is not marked (although obviously you will get even more benefit from it if it is) – what really matters with this is building up your experience of writing against the clock. One thing is certain – the more you practise, the quicker you will get. It really will help you to speed up and it will also show you how much information you can deal with in a specified time and how well you can plan your work under time pressures.

Essay planning

Practice in essay planning should form another key part in your revision process. The best essays are those where students have thought about what they want to say before they actually start to write. By planning essays you can ensure that your argument is coherent and that you are using your knowledge and evidence to best effect. Essays that are not planned can easily drift away from the main point of the question or become rambling and jumbled.

In the exam itself you will have little time to spend on planning; you will feel an in-built pressure to start writing as soon as possible. However, what you do in that first two or three minutes after reading the question can be vital to the success of your answer. Practice in the build-up to the exam will help you to develop the skills to plan quickly and effectively. There are a number of things you can do to help:

- Read the question very carefully and make sure that you understand all parts of it.
- Identify what aspect or aspects of the text the question is about – use the key words approach discussed in Unit 13, page 205.

- Analyse the question and note down the key topic areas it deals with.
- Briefly plan how you intend to deal with these areas – this may mean only three or four points each summed up in a few words. The main thing is that you will have a checklist of the points you are going to cover before you begin writing your essay.

Immediately after reading the question it is likely that ideas will whiz through your mind very quickly. If you do not get these down on paper in the form of a rough plan, there is a chance you might miss out an important point in the finished essay.

As well as doing your timed essays it will also be useful preparation if you can do essay plans for as many questions as you can. This will help to get you into the routine of planning but it will also give you the opportunity to think about a wide variety of issues related to your set texts.

There are many ways in which to create your essay plans. The following examples show the different ways in which students planned their response to this question on *The Miller's Tale*:

Compare and contrast the characters of Nicholas and Absolon and examine their contribution to the overall effect of *The Miller's Tale*.

This is the spider diagram or 'pattern note' approach.

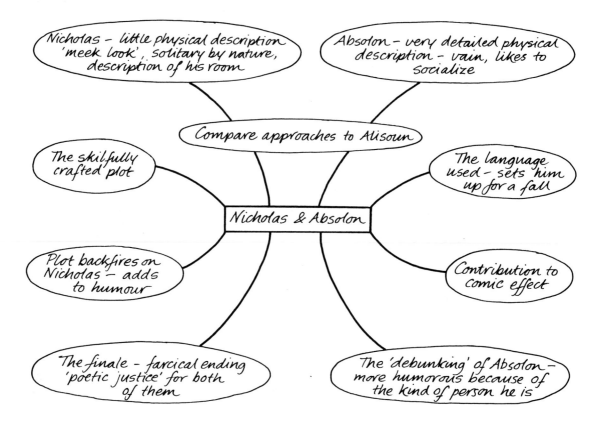

Another student preferred to use the 'flow-diagram' technique.

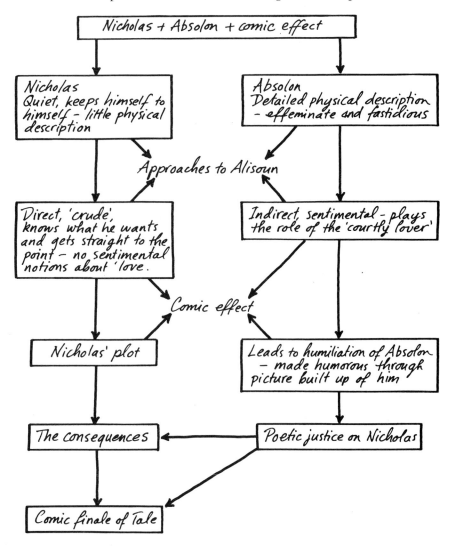

Other students find a straightforward list of points the most helpful, like this.

<u>Nicholas</u>

Quiet

Little physical description

'Described' through his possessions and interests

Direct approach

Clever

<u>Absolon</u>

Detailed physical description

Effeminate and fastidious

'Courtly lover'

Inflated opinion of himself

<u>Comic effect</u>

Through Nicholas' plot

Humiliation of Absolon

Poetic justice

'Slapstick' ending

You will need to find the method that suits your way of thinking best and which allows you to plan your work most effectively. For more methods of planning essays in detail see Unit 7, pages 140–145.

Writing your essay

Having completed your plan you are ready to write your essay. Here are some things to bear in mind.

Summary
- Always begin your essay by addressing the question directly. It can be a very useful technique to actually use some of the words of the question in your introduction. Your introduction should give a general indication of your response to the question or summarize the approach you intend to take, perhaps stating your viewpoint. The introduction might consist of your basic essay plan, expanded a little. However, keep the introduction brief and never include biographical information or plot summary.
- An alternative way to begin your essay, and one that can be very effective, is to respond to the question by starting with a strong, perhaps contentious idea that captures the reader's attention immediately. This will launch you straight into points that will support your argument.
- Develop your points clearly using evidence and references to the text to support your ideas.
- Assume that the examiner has read the text you are writing about and knows it extremely well so there is no need to explain the plot or who the characters are.
- Make sure that your essay deals with all parts of the question.
- If your answer is similar to an essay you have written before make sure that you are being relevant at all times and are not simply regurgitating a 'set' answer that is in your mind. Also, avoid rehashing your notes as an answer to a question.
- If you use quotation make sure that it is short and relevant. Do not copy out chunks of the text (see pages 215–217).
- Make sure that your essay has a conclusion in which you sum up your arguments and analysis. It is often through the conclusion that the relevance of certain points you have made is brought into focus and the essay is given a sense of unity and completeness.

Throughout your revision period bear in mind what you will be expected to show in the exam. Some factual knowledge will be required but not much. That you know the 'facts' about a text, the story-line, who the characters are, etc., will be taken as read. The emphasis will be much more on you showing judgement, analysis, sensitivity, and perception in your responses.

17 Coursework Assessment

Objectives
- To think about the requirements of written coursework
- To consider the features of coursework titles
- To think about the use of secondary sources and a bibliography

What are the benefits of coursework?

The benefits that the coursework element can bring to a course and the breadth that it can give to your studies are well acknowledged.

Summary

In particular coursework can:
- offer you freedom in terms of choice of texts and more of a say in the nature of the work you undertake
- provide you with opportunities to set your own tasks and goals and pursue particular literary interests, so developing more independence in your learning
- allow you to produce work free of the constraints of exam conditions so that you can present more carefully planned and considered responses and employ the drafting process
- develop skills which will help you perform more effectively in the exams
- help you to gain experience in undertaking research and wider reading in preparation for studying English at degree level

Coursework requirements and assessment

The specific requirements for coursework vary from syllabus to syllabus but generally the specified length of the coursework folder falls somewhere between 2500 and 5000 words. The number of assignments required and the number of texts to be studied also varies depending on your syllabus. Usually though, you would be expected to study at least two texts (three with some boards) and these normally should be selected from different genres. In some syllabuses detailed comparison of texts is important too.

Your coursework will be assessed using pre-determined criteria. The exact wording of these criteria vary slightly from exam board to exam board. Be sure to ask your teacher to show you the criteria for your board or to let you have a copy of them. Here is a typical example (this coursework folder is marked out of 20).

GOOD **Very good** 17–20	Genuine interest and first-hand, sensitive response. Close involvement. Well-organized. Coherent argument. Knowledge and full understanding. Felicitous and accurate personal style. Often concise. Evidence of critical insight. Consistent.
Good 14–16	Sound, competent, conscientious. Less sharply focused than above. Possible diffuse and unnecessarily lengthy. Argument well-organized with evidence of sound textual knowledge and understanding. Coherent, accurate style.
AVERAGE **Average** 10–13	Conscientious, solid work. Moments of sound insight but probably lacking in consistency. Capable of maintaining a clear line of argument supported by well-chosen textual illustration. Expression adequate and technically accurate.
Low average 7–9	Textual knowledge often revealed in a general or sketchy manner (e.g. plot summary). Work may contain moments of insight, but comments are not developed or explored. Basic technical accuracy in style but limited range of vocabulary and tendency to use inappropriate register.
WEAK **Weak** 3–6	Often thin in substance. Usually dull with little evidence of understanding or interest. Constant tendency simply to describe or narrate. Inconsistent. Slipshod personal style containing basic technical errors.
Very weak 0–3	Little evidence of interest or effort. Possibly some perceptive moments but not sustained. Derivative. Careless personal style, full of fundamental errors. Both content and expression inadequate.

(ULEAC)

Coursework tasks

The type of coursework task that you face will depend on a number of factors. If your whole group is studying a particular coursework text, it is likely that you will have little input into the questions that you are set. You will probably be supplied with several appropriate titles and asked to choose one as the basis of your assignment. On the other hand, if you have chosen the text you are writing on, you will probably negotiate an essay title with your teacher. If so, you will need to identify aspects of the text about which you would like to write. Your teacher will discuss these ideas with you and will help you to formulate an essay title that is both suitable and phrased in the right way.

An essential difference between an exam essay and a coursework essay is reflected in the kinds of task set. Examination questions are specifically designed to be answered in forty-five minutes under exam conditions. Whereas you might work on a coursework task for several weeks, using various research skills, reference to other writers, and critical works. For this reason, exam questions do not make the best titles for coursework assignments. For example:

How does Pip's childhood shape his adult life in *Great Expectations*?

might work well as an exam question but would be too tightly focused to allow the breadth of treatment that coursework would require you to apply to the text. On the other hand:

An examination of the characters in *Great Expectations*.

might be far too broad, lacking the necessary direction and focus to make a good coursework title. This kind of title could also become simply a catalogue of character studies. The wording and design of the question or essay title needs careful thought to allow you to show your knowledge and understanding of the text to their best effect.

Summary
Working out a suitable title is not easy. Here are some points to avoid.
- Do not mix genres unless you are quite specific in what you are aiming to achieve. For example:
  Hardy's vision of the world as expressed through his poetry and novels. This title not only mixes the genres of poetry and novel but does not present clear goals for this comparison. It is also far too broad in its scope.

A better alternative might be:
  An examination of Hardy's view of the world as expressed through three or four of his poems.

- Avoid being over-verbose in the wording of your title. For example:
  An examination of the ways in which the linguistic fluctuations interrelate with the changing socio-economic position and psychological progression of Celie in *The Colour Purple*.

Instead the title might be:
  How are Celie's changing fortunes reflected in the language of *The Colour Purple*?

- Avoid titles that only involve description or plot or character summary. For example:

  An account of the main characters in Jane Austen's *Emma*.

A title that avoids this would be:

  What techniques does Jane Austen use to bring her characters to life?

- Avoid linking texts with only superficial features in common. For example:

  Compare George Orwell's *Nineteen Eighty-four* with H. G. Wells' *The Time Machine*.

A better comparison might be:

  Compare and contrast Orwell's and Huxley's visions of the future as explored through *Nineteen Eighty-four* and *A Brave New World*.

Activity | Devise a coursework essay title for a text or texts that you have studied. Think very carefully about the wording of your title. When you have written it, add a brief description (about 50 words or so) explaining how you would tackle the essay. Include the main ideas you put forward. In a small group, look at your titles individually and discuss their strengths and weaknesses, drawing up a master list of good and bad points.

Potential weaknesses

Overall, examiners report that a high standard of work is produced by students through coursework. However, here are some points that they have highlighted as weaknesses or problem areas in some of the work they have assessed:

- inappropriately framed or worded assignments
- tasks that focus on a general discussion of themes or 'character studies'. These tend to lack interest and focus
- titles that do not require close attention to text and critical judgement
- poor handling of non-fiction work. Often this is limited to a personal response to a newspaper or magazine article. A task based on non-fiction must still generate critical analysis of its literary quality
- too much biographical or historical background is given
- too much narrative retelling of the plot or events

The use of secondary sources

In producing coursework it is important that, if you use secondary sources, you learn how to use and acknowledge them correctly. Clearly, the primary source for the essay is the text that you are studying. The secondary sources are any other materials that help you in your work, such as study aids, critical works, or articles about the text. It can also be useful to 'read around the text' – to learn about the history, the art, and the music of the time. (The Chronology on pages 261–268 provides a starting point for this.)

Certainly use secondary sources if you wish. They can help to broaden your view of the text and show you other ways of looking at it. It does not matter whether you agree or disagree with the views and interpretations you read, they will all help you to arrive at what you think. Remember that there are rarely right answers as far as literature is concerned – all texts are open to a variety of interpretations. Your view can be 'informed' by other sources but never let other views substitute your own. Have confidence in your view, develop your own voice, and avoid plagiarism (even accidental) at all costs. If you use secondary source material make sure that you acknowledge every text you have used in the bibliography at the end of your assignment.

The bibliography

In order to acknowledge appropriately the books and other materials that you have read or consulted while writing your coursework essay, it is important to understand the conventions of bibliography writing.

Even if you have only read a part of a particular book or article it should be included in your bibliography. If you have only used the text itself you should still include a bibliography simply consisting of relevant details about the edition used. This will clearly show the examiner that you have used nothing other than the text itself and it will also give information about the particular edition that you have used.

Your bibliography should be arranged in the following format.

The surname of the author (authors listed alphabetically). The initials of the author. The title of the book (underlined) or article (inverted commas) and source. The publisher's name. The date of publication (usually the date when first published).

Here is the bibliography from a student's essay on *Hamlet*:

Bibliography
Baker, S., 'Hamlet's Bloody Thoughts and the Illusion of Inwardness' in Comparative Drama (Vol. 21. No. 4) Winter, 1987–88
Bradley, A. C., Shakespearean Tragedy Macmillan, 1904
Brooks, J., Hamlet Macmillan Master Guides, 1986
Dover Wilson, J., What Happens in Hamlet Cambridge University Press, 1935
Holderness, G., Hamlet Open Guides to Literature The Open University Press, 1987
Jump, J. (ed.), Shakespeare: Hamlet Macmillan Casebook Series, 1968
Rossiter, A. C., Angel With Horns Longman, 1961

Activity | Using the library, find at least five books or articles on a particular topic, text, or author. Find the information that you would need for a bibliography, such as author, publisher, publication date, etc. and then, using the example above as a guide, order them in the way you would if you were creating a bibliography for a coursework essay.

18 The Examiner's View

Objectives
- To think about the things examiners look for in the work they mark
- To understand how examiners will mark your work

What the examiner looks for

An important person in the process of your assessment at A-level is the examiner who will mark your work. 'Examiners' are not some special breed of people who spend their lives marking examination scripts. For the most part, they are practising teachers who spend their time working with students like yourself and helping them to prepare for exams. However, they can only mark the work that you present them with and the mark that is awarded depends *solely* on its quality. It is a fallacy that one examiner might be more generous with you than another. Careful procedures are followed to ensure that the mark you receive from one examiner is just the same as the mark that you would receive if another assessed your work. Indeed, it is not simply a case of one examiner looking at your work, giving a mark and that is the end of it. Exam scripts go through a number of processes which involve responses being looked at by several people before a final mark is awarded. How well you do is up to you, not the examiner.

It is also worth dispelling another misconception that some students have concerning the role of the examiner. They picture the examiner as some kind of merciless inquisitor who takes delight in catching them out. Examiners, so the thinking goes, look only for negative aspects in responses and ruthlessly dismantle every essay that they come across. Questions are their tools, designed to catch students out.

In fact, nothing could be further from the truth. Questions (as shown in Unit 13) are designed to let you to show your knowledge to the best of your ability. Obviously examiners will not reward qualities which are not present in your responses, but they will look for the positive features in your work. Examiners take far more pleasure and satisfaction in reading good quality material that they can reward than they do in poor work that achieves poor marks. Think of the examiner as an interested and positive audience for your writing, who will award marks fairly and look positively on responses wherever there are positive qualities to be found.

Bearing in mind the large number of students who sit exams in A-level Literature each year, it is very encouraging that examiners report that very few candidates reveal lack of knowledge, skills, or preparation and very weak answers are extremely uncommon. The vast majority of students show that they have prepared themselves to the best of their abilities for the papers. Having said that, there are aspects of the exam that examiners often comment on as areas that need more careful preparation. We will now go on to consider some of these.

The questions

- Questions are rarely prescriptive. They are 'open' so as to invite you to debate the issues and encourage you to develop informed judgements on the texts and the issues they raise. It is these judgements that the examiner is interested in seeing.
- Where the question contains some kind of proposition you are never expected to simply accept it. Acceptance or rejection needs to be supported with evidence and justification. One criticism frequently made by examiners is when the student simply agrees with or rejects the proposition and then goes on to write about something else entirely. This still happens with worrying regularity.
  The key thing in all this is to read the question and do what it says.

The unseen

- One fairly universal comment from examiners is that students need to improve their practical criticism skills. The best advice is to get as much practice in as you can on this element of the paper (see Unit 10, page 159 and Unit 15, page 224 for work on this element).
- As part of this practice, examiners recommend that you actively seek out meaning from the unseen texts and pay particular attention to organizing your responses.
  (Of course, these skills can also be applied to the set texts.)

- In tackling the unseen, examiners recommend a detached perspective so that you focus solely on the text you have been given. It is better not to include biographical or other background knowledge that you might have about the authors, or the complete text, for example.
- On Chaucer and Shakespeare, in particular, examiners often complain of students giving far too much paraphrase and too little focused commentary and detailed critical appraisal based on close reading (see Special Feature on Chaucer, page 32 and Special Feature on Shakespeare, page 51).

Technical accuracy

Clearly the ideas that you express in your answers are of primary importance. However, these ideas will be not presented most effectively if your writing suffers from various technical inaccuracies. It is, therefore, crucial that your answers are as free from technical errors as you can make them.

Summary

There are several points that examiners draw attention to in this respect.
- **Punctuation**   Ensure that you use full stops, commas, quotation marks, etc. where appropriate. It is easy for these things to be forgotten in the heat of the exam but poor punctuation can mean that your ideas are communicated to the reader less effectively and this may affect your mark.
- **Sentences**   Make sure that you write in sentences and that you avoid long convoluted ones.
- **Paragraphing**   Few candidates fail to use paragraphs at all but examiners often point to the inappropriate use of paragraphs. For example, one sentence paragraphs should be avoided and so should excessively long paragraphs.
- **Vocabulary**   Try to vary your vocabulary without becoming verbose simply to make your essay sound more 'impressive'.
- **Spelling**   Obviously you should try to make your work spelling error free. However, in the heat of writing under exam conditions some errors may well creep in. You should do your best to check each answer as you complete it to keep these to a minimum. If nothing else though, make sure that you are spelling the titles of the texts, the names of the characters, and the names of the authors correctly. It does not give a good impression if, after two years' study, you are still writing about 'Shakespear's play' or 'Jayne Austin's' novel.
- **Cliché, flattery, and slang**   Avoid the use of well-worn phrases such as 'Jane Eyre is a victim of male domination' or 'Lear acts like a man possessed'. Flattery towards authors, such as 'Shakespeare's portrayal of a man in emotional turmoil is second to none' or 'It is clear that Keats is one of the giants of English poetry' are equally to be avoided; so are slang expressions, such as 'Oskar Schindler is a bit of a Del-boy character' or 'Laertes goes ballistic when he hears about his father's death'.

- **Quotation**   If you are using quotation, make sure it is accurate. If you have the book with you in the exam there is really no excuse for misquoting (although it still happens).

  If you are relying on memory, it is very easy to misquote. Perhaps all that needs to be said is that it is better not to use a quotation than to misquote or worse still 'invent' a quote based on a rough idea of how it goes.

Model and prepared answers

Examiners report that they do not see model or prepared answers anywhere near as frequently as they used to in student responses. However, they do still crop up from time to time. There is nothing wrong with reading model answers as long as you use them wisely. They can be useful in presenting you with new ideas but be aware that they present just one way of answering a question. The examiner is interested in what you have to say on a particular topic or question, not what the writer of a prepared answer has to say.

Remember that the best responses are those in which your own voice can be heard. The whole point of the course that you are studying is to develop your ability to write confidently, relevantly, and thoughtfully about your ideas on the texts you have studied. Do not be afraid to use the pronoun 'I' occasionally in your essays and do not be afraid to respond genuinely to a question. Attempts to memorize prepared answers never work.

How the examiner will mark your work

Above all, examiners marking A-level English Literature scripts are trained to be positive and flexible.

The examiners (each of your exam papers is usually marked by a separate examiner) will look for the positive qualities in your work. They will not approach your response with a preconceived idea of an 'ideal answer' but will have an open mind. They will evaluate your efforts to provide an informed personal response to the question.

You will remember the Assessment Objectives that we looked at in Unit 1, and in particular Assessment Objectives 1 and 4, which referred to the importance of being able to respond to literary texts with 'knowledge and understanding' and to 'articulate informed, independent opinions and judgements' about them. All the questions that you will encounter on A-level Literature papers have been specifically designed to give you the opportunity to do just this. Obviously your writing must be factually accurate but the opinions and ideas you explore are up to you (providing you can support them through close reference and analysis of the text).

Answering the question

Examiners are always aware of students who do not read the questions carefully enough. You should make absolutely sure that you are well trained in studying carefully the exact wording of the question (see Unit 13, page 205). Remember that the question should be the whole basis and framework of your answer.

Length

Examiners do not award marks on the basis of the length of your essay but they will look for what you have achieved in your writing. An essay may appear brief but on closer inspection it may be a succinct and well-argued response and therefore worthy of a high mark. It is true to say, though, that essays that are very short often lack sufficient depth in the development of ideas. On the other hand, over-long essays can become repetitive, rambling and lacking in a coherent structure. Do your best to create a balanced answer.

Descriptors

In addition to the question-specific guidance that examiners are given, Exam Boards also provide them with descriptors to help them to place your essay in a particular mark band. Although these descriptors vary a little in content and format from board to board (as all boards are testing the same Assessment Objectives), in essence they are very similar. Here is an example of the kind of descriptors which examiners may use to help them arrive at an assessment of student responses.

Level 1   Work of the highest standard, showing thorough knowledge, insight, and understanding. The response is conceptualized, explores a wide range of ideas, using appropriate terminology and accurate written expression, focusing on the central elements of language and style. Quotations and references to the text are effectively woven into the fabric of the essay and are used to support close analysis. The response will show a clear mastery of the text and there will be signs of real perception and independent thought.

Level 2   Work displays a clear sense of critical response based on good textual understanding. There is evidence of close reading and awareness of the ways in which the writer's choices of form, structure, and language shape meanings. Analytical skills are used effectively and the response is well-sturctured and well-expressed.

Level 3   Work reveals knowledge of the text with sound understanding and relevance. Response may be generalized in places but comment is accurate and shows some awareness of implicit meaning. Some of the response may consist of paraphrase and quotation may be over-long but some analysis is apparent. The candidate is clearly aware of the task set and its implications. The expression is adequate to convey the ideas.

Level 4 Work that shows a basic response. It contains some relevant material but consists mainly or entirely of a narrative approach and presents some misreadings. The response does not focus on the question and may contain substantial irrelevant sections, although there could also be some implicit relevance to task. Expression is weak and quotation is over-long, possibly inappropriate, or poorly chosen, and is not commented on or analysed.

Level 5 Work may show some knowledge of the text but the response is thin and there may be frequent misreadings. The work is mainly narrative or descriptive. There are marked weaknesses of expression and any comments made are entirely unsupported. Overall the response fails to engage with the demands of the task.

Activity

> 1 Study this grid and think carefully about the implications of these descriptors for your own work.
> 2 Review some of the student responses in this book and think about the marks that might be given to these in the light of this grid. You might like to use those on pages 150, 166, 174, 178, and 212, for example.

It is not possible to simply convert these descriptors to grades because examination boards do not work in that way. The marking process goes through various stages before the final grade is arrived at. However, as a rough guide work at Level 1 is likely to be of Grade A standard while work at Level 3 could be Grade C or D standard. Work towards the bottom of Level 4 is likely to be of borderline E/N standard. Level 5 would be U.

You will notice that this grid focuses clearly on three key elements of your work:

- the closeness of your reading
- your ability to convey the text and answer relevantly
- the overall quality of your writing

19 Beyond A-level Literature

| Objectives | • To contemplate the study of English Literature beyond A-level |
| | • To introduce the basic function of critical theory |

Being aware of the differences

The majority of students who study A-level English Literature will not go on to study literature beyond that point. However, it may be your intention to continue your studies, perhaps at degree level. If this is so, then it might be useful to be aware of some fundamental differences between the way you will study literature at degree level and the way that you will have studied it at A-level.

The reading

Beyond A-level you will be expected to read much more widely. Obviously, as we have already pointed out, wider reading is to be highly recommended at A-level too, but ultimately your examination focuses on a relatively small number of texts that you study in depth. In studying Literature at a higher level you will be expected to have a detailed knowledge and understanding of individual texts but you will also be expected to have a much wider breadth of knowledge across a range of writing periods, authors, and literary works. For example, for A-level you will have studied perhaps one or two

Shakespeare texts as part of your course. At degree level it is likely that you will be expected to be familiar with a much broader range of Shakespeare's works. The more widely you have read throughout the A-level course, the better you will be prepared to take your studies further.

The critics

As part of your A-level course you will have come into contact with different interpretations of literary texts and you will have formed your own opinions of these different views. It is important, however, that you do not allow the ideas of the critics or other readers to substitute or confuse your own thoughts and feelings about a text.

If you go on to study literature at a higher level, you will have more exposure to the writings of literary critics and various literary theories. The ideas and approaches that these offer can be useful in stimulating new ways of looking at texts and can often prompt ideas that might not have occurred to you had you not read them. It does not matter whether you agree or disagree with the ideas you read. Challenging the things that you read is just as important as agreeing with them when you are developing your ideas about the texts you are studying.

Literary theory

Many of the critics you will read, in studying Literature at a higher level, will approach their analysis of the text using a particular theory that they apply to all texts. There are many of these literary theories and sometimes they run counter to one another. The main thing to remember is that each one looks at a text from a particular point of view or focuses on a particular aspect of it. This is because the theory regards one particular aspect of the text as being more significant than anything else. It is important to bear this in mind when reading literary analysis based on individual literary theories. What follow are brief descriptions of the more important literary theories. You may well have already come across some of these. (Bear in mind, though, that these descriptions only give you a very simple definition of very complex theories.)

Structuralism

This is a complex theory but basically it involves the reader giving up their right to a personal response or interpretation and focusing on the text alone, describing how the text operates. The theory involves taking a much more 'scientific' approach by looking at texts with the view that all texts attempt to create a view of the world by ordering it through the structure of language. The effect of a structuralist approach can be to look closely at the language structures of a text and to place less emphasis on the ideas of what a text tells us about life, the world, and the characteristics of human nature; the latter are more common approaches at A-level.

Post-structuralism or deconstructive criticism

Post-structuralism covers a whole range of activities, so again the ideas are very much simplified here. Post-structuralism questions the structuralist idea that the reader must have knowledge of the 'literary code' of language in order to gain access to the 'meaning' of a text. It does not regard the meaning in language as being stable. It also argues that the reader's perceptions of a text are necessarily subjective so that the idea of any kind of literary objectivity is brought into question. Although post-structuralist criticism seeks to 'destabilize' the text by, amongst other means, demonstrating its contradictions and problems – and as such has sometimes been regarded as a quite destructive form of criticism – it can have more positive aspects. For example, it can encourage you to consider alternative meanings and treat the text as something that is dynamic and not as something that has finite or 'closed' meanings.

Psychoanalytical theory has made a major contribution to post-structuralist theory, taking as its starting point the ideas of Freud who sought to provide universal models and explanations for the unconscious drives and desires that motivate human behaviour. Lacan developed Freud's theories further through his view that language is the major force in shaping human identity. These theories have been applied to literature study and can provide new angles on the ways in which texts are constructed and presented.

Marxist criticism

Unlike Structuralist and Post-structuralist literary theories, which have nothing to do with history, society, and class in relation to a text, the Marxist critic brings to a text Marx's view of history in which the idea of class struggle is central. It promotes analysis of a text by creating connections between the text itself and the social and economic structure of the society in which it was written. The theory regards these connections as being fundamental to the nature of the literature produced. Necessarily, Marxist criticism challenges many of the traditional views of texts which interpret them according to the values of a bourgeois or middle-class culture. It seeks to get away from the idea that texts present universal truths about human nature, looking instead to question and reinterpret a text in the light of the period it was written and the nature of the society within which it was produced and which influenced it.

Feminist criticism

Like Marxist criticism, Feminist criticism also concerns itself with social and political issues, in this case with the presentation of women in literature. The Feminist critic is particularly interested in seeking to affirm feminine qualities within what is regarded as a male-dominated society. Most Feminist criticism takes as its starting point the idea that society is and always has been patriarchal (i.e. where men assume the dominant role) and examines texts from this perspective.

An important element within feminist criticism is that of Black, Women-of-Colour, and Lesbian critical theory. Writers and critics involved in this area are very much concerned with the interrelationship between race, sexuality, and oppression of one kind or another

An overview

This very brief look at some of the key critical theories that you might come across shows just a few examples of the varying ways in which texts can be considered through different critical theories. Your understanding of such theories can contribute to your overall understanding of literature but you should always be aware that they all approach the analysis of texts from a very particular, even partisan, point of view.

As you take your studies further, your awareness and sensitivity to the layers of meaning within literary texts will continue to grow but never forget that the fundamental element in this process is to develop your own view. Your view of a text is as valid as anyone else's, so long as it is based firmly on a study of the text itself – a view that presents those 'informed, independent opinions and judgements' is vital.

Glossary

• •

Allegory: an allegory is a story or narrative, often told at some length, which has a deeper meaning below the surface. *The Pilgrim's Progress* by John Bunyan is a well-known allegory. A more modern example is George Orwell's *Animal Farm*, which on a surface level is about a group of animals who take over their farm but on a deeper level is an allegory of the Russian Revolution and the shortcomings of Communism.

Alliteration: the repetition of the same consonant sound, especially at the beginning of words. For example, 'Five miles meandering with a mazy motion'. (*Kubla Khan* by S. T. Coleridge)

Allusion: a reference to another event, person, place, or work of literature – the allusion is usually implied rather than explicit and often provides another layer of meaning to what is being said.

Ambiguity: use of language where the meaning is unclear or has two or more possible interpretations or meanings. It could be created through a weakness in the way the writer has expressed themselves but often it is used by writers quite deliberately to create layers of meaning in the mind of the reader.

Ambivalence: this indicates more than one possible attitude is being displayed by the writer towards a character, theme, or idea, etc.

Anthropomorphism: the endowment of human characteristics to something that is not human.

Anachronism: something that is historically inaccurate, for example the reference to a clock chiming in Shakespeare's *Julius Caesar*.

Antithesis: contrasting ideas or words that are balanced against each other.

Apostrophe: an interruption in a poem or narrative so that the speaker or writer can address a dead or absent person or particular audience directly.

Archaic: language that is old-fashioned – not completely obsolete but no longer in current modern use.

Assonance: the repetition of similar vowel sounds. For example: 'There must be Gods thrown down and trumpets blown' (*Hyperion* by John Keats). This shows the paired assonance of 'must', 'trum', 'thrown', 'blown'.

Atmosphere: the prevailing mood created by a piece of writing.

Ballad: a narrative poem that tells a story (traditional ballads were songs) usually in a straightforward way. The theme is often tragic or containing a whimsical, supernatural, or fantastical element.

Bathos: an anti-climax or sudden descent from the serious to the ridiculous – sometimes deliberate, sometimes unintentional on the part of the writer.

Blank verse: unrhymed poetry that adheres to a strict pattern in that each line is an iambic pentameter (a ten-syllable line with five stresses). It is close to the rhythm of speech or prose and is used a great deal by many writers including Shakespeare and Milton.

Caesura: a conscious break in a line of poetry (see Unit 2, page 20)

Caricature: a character often described through the exaggeration of a small number of features that they possess.

Catharsis: a purging of the emotions which takes place at the end of a tragedy.

Cliché: a phrase, idea, or image that has been used so much that is has lost much of its original meaning, impact, and freshness.

Colloquial: ordinary, everyday speech and language.

Comedy: originally simply a play or other work which ended happily. Now we use this term to describe something that is funny and which makes us laugh. In literature the comedy is not a necessarily a lightweight form. A play like *Measure for Measure*, for example, is, for the most part a serious and dark play but as it ends happily, it is described as a comedy.

Conceit: an elaborate, extended, and sometimes surprising comparison between things that, at first sight, do not have much in common.

Connotation: an implication or association attached to a word or phrase. A connotation is suggested or felt rather than being explicit.

Consonance: the repetition of the same consonant sounds in two or more words in which the vowel sounds are different. For example: 'And by his smile, I knew that sullen hall, By his dead smile I knew we stood in Hell' (*Strange Meeting* by Wilfred Owen). Where consonance replaces the rhyme, as here, it is called half-rhyme.

Couplet: two consecutive lines of verse that rhyme.

Dénouement: the ending of a play, novel, or drama where 'all is revealed' and the plot is unravelled.

Diction: the choice of words that a writer makes. Another term for 'vocabulary'.

Didactic: a work that is intended to preach or teach, often containing a particular moral or political point.

Dramatic monologue: a poem or prose piece in which a character addresses an audience. Often the monologue is complete in itself as in Alan Bennett's *Talking Heads*.

Elegy: a meditative poem, usually sad and reflective in nature. Sometimes, though not always, it is concerned with the theme of death.

Empathy: a feeling on the part of the reader of sharing the particular experience being described by the character or writer.

End stopping: a verse line with a pause or a stop at the end of it.

Enjambement: a line of verse that flows on into the next line without a pause.

Epic: a long narrative poem, written in an elevated style and usually dealing with a heroic theme or story. Homer's *The Iliad* and Milton's *Paradise Lost* are examples of this.

Euphemism: expressing an unpleasant or unsavoury idea in a less blunt and more pleasant way.

Euphony: use of pleasant or melodious sounds.

Exemplum: a story that contains or illustrates a moral point put forward as an 'example'.

Fable: a short story that presents a clear moral lesson.

Fabilau: a short comic tale with a bawdy element, akin to the 'dirty story'. Chaucer's *The Miller's Tale* contains strong elements of the fabilau.

Farce: a play that aims to entertain the audience through absurd and ridiculous characters and action.

Feminine ending: an extra unstressed syllable at the end of a line of poetry. (See **Masculine ending**.)

Figurative language: language that is symbolic or metaphorical and not meant to be taken literally.

Foot:	a group of syllables forming a unit of verse – the basic unit of 'metre'. (See Unit 2, pages 19–20.)
Free verse:	verse written without any fixed structure (either in metre or rhyme).
Genre:	a particular type of writing, e.g. prose, poetry, drama.
Heptameter:	a verse line containing seven feet.
Hexameter:	a verse line containing six feet.
Hyperbole:	deliberate and extravagant exaggeration.
Iamb:	the most common metrical foot in English poetry, consisting of an unstressed syllable followed by a stressed syllable.
Idyll:	a story, often written in verse, usually concerning innocent and rustic characters in rural, idealized surroundings. This form can also deal with more heroic subjects, as in Tennyson's *Idylls of the King*. (See **Pastoral**.)
Imagery:	the use of words to create a picture or 'image' in the mind of the reader. Images can relate to any of the senses, not just sight, but also hearing, taste, touch, and smell. It is often used to refer to the use of descriptive language, particularly to the use of metaphors and similes.
Internal rhyme:	rhyming words within a line rather than at the end of lines.
Inter-textual:	having clear links with other texts through the themes, ideas, or issues which are explored.
Irony:	at its simplest level it means saying one thing while meaning another. It occurs where a word or phrase has one surface meaning but another contradictory, possibly opposite meaning is implied. Irony is frequently confused with sarcasm. Sarcasm is spoken, often relying on tone of voice and is much more blunt than irony.
Lament:	a poem expressing intense grief.
Lyric:	was originally a song performed to the accompaniment of a lyre (an early harp-like instrument) but now it can mean a song-like poem or a short poem expressing personal feeling.
Metaphor:	a comparison of one thing to another in order to make description more vivid. The metaphor actually states that one thing is the other. For example, the simile would be: 'The huge knight stood like an impregnable tower in the ranks of the enemy', whereas the metaphor would be: 'The huge knight was an impregnable tower in the ranks of the enemy'. (See **Simile** and **Personification**.)
Metre:	the regular use of stressed and unstressed syllables in poetry. (See **Feet** and Unit 2, pages 19–20.)
Mock heroic:	a poem that treats trivial subject matter in the grand and elevated style of epic poetry. The effect produced is often satirical, as in Pope's *The Rape of the Lock*.
Monometer:	a verse line consisting of only one metrical foot.
Motif:	a dominant theme, subject or idea which runs through a piece of literature. Often a 'motif' can assume a symbolic importance.
Narrative:	a piece of writing that tells a story.
Octameter:	a verse line consisting of eight feet.
Octave:	the first eight lines of a sonnet.
Ode:	a verse form similar to a lyric but often more lengthy and containing more serious and elevated thoughts.

Onomatopoeia:	the use of words whose sound copies the sound of the thing or process that they describe. On a simple level, words like 'bang', 'hiss', and 'splash' are onomatopoeic but it also has more subtle uses.
Oxymoron:	a figure of speech which joins together words of opposite meanings, e.g. 'the living dead', 'bitter sweet', etc.
Paradox:	a statement that appears contradictory, but when considered more closely is seen to contain a good deal of truth.
Parody:	a work that is written in imitation of another work, very often with the intention of making fun of the original.
Pastoral:	generally literature concerning rural life with idealized settings and rustic characters. Often pastorals are concerned with the lives of shepherds and shepherdesses presented in idyllic and unrealistic ways. (See **Idyll**.)
Pathos:	the effect in literature which makes the reader feel sadness or pity.
Pentameter:	a line of verse containing five feet.
Periphrasis:	a round-about or long-winded way of expressing something.
Personification:	the attribution of human feelings, emotions, or sensations to an inanimate object. Personification is a kind of metaphor where human qualities are given to things or abstract ideas.
Plot:	the sequence of events in a poem, play, novel, or short story that make up the main storyline.
Prose:	any kind of writing which is not verse – usually divided into fiction and non-fiction.
Protagonist:	the main character or speaker in a poem, monologue, play, or story.
Pun:	a play on words that have similar sound but quite different meanings.
Quatrain:	a stanza of four lines which can have various rhyme schemes.
Refrain:	repetition throughout a poem of a phrase, line, or series of lines as in the 'chorus' of a song.
Rhetoric:	originally the art of speaking and writing in such a way as to persuade an audience to a particular point of view. Now it is often used to imply grand words that have no substance to them. There are a variety of rhetorical devices such as the rhetorical question – a question which does not require an answer as the answer is either obvious or implied in the question itself. (See **Apostrophe**, **Exemplum**.)
Rhyme:	corresponding sounds in words, usually at the end of each line but not always. (See **Internal Rhyme**.)
Rhyme scheme:	the pattern of the rhymes in a poem.
Rhythm:	the 'movement' of the poem as created through the metre and the way that language is stressed within the poem.
Satire:	the highlighting or exposing of human failings or foolishness within a society through ridiculing them. Satire can range from being gentle and light to being extremely biting and bitter in tone, e.g. Swift's *Gulliver's Travels* or *A Modest Proposal* and George Orwell's *Animal Farm*.
Scansion:	the analysis of metrical patterns in poetry. (See Unit 2, page 20.)
Septet:	a seven line stanza.
Sestet:	the last six lines of a sonnet.
Simile:	a comparison of one thing to another in order to make description more vivid. Similes use the words 'like' or 'as' in this comparison. (See **Metaphor**.)

Soliloquy: a speech in which a character, alone on stage, expresses their thoughts and feelings aloud for the benefit of the audience, often in a revealing way.

Sonnet: a fourteen-line poem, usually with ten syllables in each line. There are several ways in which the lines can be organized, but often they consist of an octave and a sestet.

Stanza: the blocks of lines into which a poem is divided. (Sometimes, these are less precisely, referred to as verses which can lead to confusion as poetry is sometimes called 'verse'.)

Stream of consciousness: a technique in which the writer writes down thoughts and emotions in a 'stream' as they come to mind, without bothering about order or structure.

Structure: the way that a poem or play or other piece of writing has been put together. This can include the metre pattern, stanza arrangement, and the way the ideas are developed, etc.

Style: the individual way in which a writer has used language to express their ideas.

Sub-plot: a secondary storyline in a story or play. Often, as in some Shakespeare plays, the sub-plot can provide some comic relief from the main action but sub-plots can also relate in quite complex ways to the main plot of a text.

Sub-text: ideas, themes, or issues that are not dealt with overtly by a text but which exist below the surface meaning of it.

Symbol: like the use of images, symbols present things which represent something else. In very simple terms a red rose is often used to symbolize love; distant thunder is often symbolic of approaching trouble. Symbols can be very subtle and multi-layered in their significance.

Syntax: the way in which sentences are structured. Sentences can be structured in different ways to achieve different effects.

Tetrameter: a verse line of four feet.

Theme: the central idea or ideas that the writer explores through a text.

Tone: the tone of a text is created through the combined effects of a number of features, such as diction, syntax, rhythm, etc. The tone is a major factor in establishing the overall impression of the piece of writing.

Trimeter: a verse line consisting of three feet.

Zeugma: a device which joins together two apparently incongruous things by applying a verb or adjective to them which only really applies to one of them, 'Kill the boys and the luggage' (Shakespeare's *Henry V*).